DONALD J. LOFLAND, Ph.D.

*P*OWERLEARNING

MEMORY

AND

LEARNING

TECHNIQUES

FOR

PERSONAL

POWER

LONGMEADOW PRESS

Excerpts from *The Techniques of Reading*, Third Edition, by Horace Judson, © 1972 by The Reading Laboratory Inc. Reprinted with permission by Harcourt Brace Jovanovich, Inc.

Powerlearning is a registered trademark of Powerlearning® Systems, P.O. Box 496, Santa Cruz, CA 95060

Illustrations by Melani Gendron-Lofland and Donald Lofland
Cover design by Frank Stinga
Interior design by Fritz Metsch

LIBRARY OF CONGRESS CATALOGING-IN-PUBLICATION DATA
Lofland, Donald J.
    Powerlearning : states for learning, memory, personal power :
innovative learning methods to gain your personal power / by Donald
J. Lofland.
        p.   cm.
    Includes index.
    ISBN: 0-681-00460-6
    1. Success—Psychological aspects.   2. Neurolinguistic
programming.   3. Learning, Psychology of.   4. Mnemonics.   1. Title.
BF637.S8L574   1992
153.1—dc20   92-9733
                                                                       CIP

PRINTED IN THE UNITED STATES OF AMERICA

0 9 8 7 6 5 4 3 2 1

DEDICATION

This work is dedicated to Clyde A. Lofland,
my dad, who introduced me to physics, a
curiosity for how things work, and a role
model of how to live life with fullness . . .

&

in memory of Dana Butterfield,
who knew the secret,
of living wholly,
here and now,
one's uniqueness.

ACKNOWLEDGMENTS

I'd like to express my gratitude to the many people who have helped make this work possible . . .

- Frank Weimann, my agent, who never lost faith in Powerlearning;
- My dedicated editors Diane Frank and Pamela Altschul;
- Melanie Gendron-Lofland, my illustrator
- Dr. Donald Schuster who introduced this country and me personally to accelerated learning methods;
- Doris Richardson, whose unwavering faith in my work and help with mechanical details got me through the final days of completion.

CONTENTS

PART ONE

POWERLEARNING
AND STATES

CHAPTER ONE

*L*EARNING: TO GET WHAT YOU WANT IN LIFE

Educational therapists are beginning to realize that almost anyone can potentially learn anything . . . it's just a matter of establishing a *learning state* that works for each person. This book or any other cannot actually teach you *how* to learn. You are a superb learner already. Just getting up this morning, doing your daily activities, moving your body, etc., you have automatically learned thousands of impressions and bits of information. Having the motivation to read this book means you probably already have what it will take to succeed.

The secret is in how to set up states—for learning, memory, and personal power. Then it is easy to get the results we want and deserve.

What, then, is learning? When we think about learning, we usually think of a classroom or training seminar. Learning is actually much broader than that. Do you encounter new learning in any of the following?

- hobbies
- relationships
- staying healthy
- getting ahead in your career
- sports and recreation

Learning is probably the fabric of being alive. Consider, then, some of the *advantages* of improving your learning skills:[1]

- clearer thinking
- more money and a better job
- improvement with hobbies
- improved relationships
- better health
- higher self-esteem
- learning more in less time
- having fun learning new things

Consider the disadvantages of not improving your learning skills:

- foggy thinking
- less knowledge
- frustrating relationships
- poor self-esteem
- making less money
- fewer hobbies
- worse health
- shorter life

Finally, consider the "benefits" of not improving your learning skills; You:

- keep psychiatrists and counselors in business
- leave high-paying jobs for others
- don't have to risk the possibility of failure
- avoid the demands of increased responsibility
- won't threaten others by appearing brilliant

THOSE SPECIAL DAYS
- -

Men stumble over truth from time to time, but most pick themselves up and continue off as if nothing had happened.
—*Sir Winston Churchill*

One great truth is that all days are not created equal. Why is it that every once in a while we have one of those special days where everything seems to go our way? We do just the right thing at the right time . . . the tennis game is exceptional . . . or we come up with all the right answers in an important meeting. Sometimes it seems that we couldn't have planned the day better. Of course, another question might be, "Why don't we have special days more often?"

EXERCISE 1

Take a piece of paper and list all the qualities you can think of that make those special days unique. How do you feel physically? What emotions do you feel? How does the world look? Do you notice any special sounds? Take a minute or two and write down as many characteristics as quickly as you can.

Here are some of the most frequently listed qualities. Check them against your list:

- I feel relaxed.
- Everything falls into place.
- I feel spontaneous.
- I am happy and energetic.
- The day looks brighter.
- Things really click for me.
- Other people pick up on my mood.
- These days are too rare!

How do these qualities compare with your experience?

What sets these days apart is the neurological *state* we are in. Psychologists might say we are in an empowering state or a resourceful state. This state of being allows us to feel inner strength, confidence, joy, or peak performance. At other times we may experience paralyzing states that leave us fearful, depressed, confused, and unable to act. Our performance in life and our ability to learn are direct results of the state we are in.

Would you be interested in having those special days more often? We will discuss two powerful keys to create states for getting the results we want, in both learning and daily living.

WHAT ARE STATES?

- -

Pat could hardly wait for her first date with John, the new marketing director. She was in a *state* of anticipation. When she arrived and *saw* the flowers he had brought, she experienced a *state* of gratitude. When she *heard* him compliment her dress, she experienced another state, and when she *felt* indigestion from his cooking, she experienced yet another state. A state is the sum of millions of neurological processes happening within us at any point in time. The states we experience may be empowering or limiting, but mostly they are unconscious reactions to what we see, hear, feel, smell, or taste. We need to learn to choose the states we desire.

Each state we experience results in the brain producing certain chemical substances—neuropeptides and neurotransmitters. As an example, when we feel powerful and invincible, our brains produce a substance similar to interleukin 2, one of the most powerful substances known to destroy cancer cells. When we feel calm and settled, we produce a natural tranquilizer similar to Valium. When the brain produces these substances, we experience none of the undesirable side effects we would if we had injected or ingested these or similar drugs. The brain and body in their inherent wisdom know just how much of each substance to produce and how and where to distribute them.

A fascinating characteristic of states is that not only the brain experiences the state, but also the whole body experiences it. Each cell in the body has neuroreceptors for receiving the chemical "signals" (neuropeptides and neurotransmitters) put out by the brain. Thus, as Dr. Deepak Chopra points out in *Quantum Healing*, when people feel jittery, the brain produces high levels of epinephrine and norepinephrine. However, blood platelets also have neuroreceptors for these substances, so the platelets as well as the brain experience the jitteriness. When we are sad, neuroreceptors in the kidneys, stomach, and skin pick up the transmitters corresponding to sadness, so our kidneys, stomach, and skin are also sad. When we are happy, our whole body is exposed to substances that fight viruses and bacteria. We wind up with happy eyes and a happy heart.

There is further evidence that other cells outside the brain produce the same neuropeptides and neurotransmitters. Dr. Chopra postulates that each cell in the body may produce all of these substances, so in a sense each cell has its own mind to produce and experience states.

What most of us want in life—happiness, love, comfort, power, success, etc.—are simply states.

EXERCISE 2

Quickly write down five of your most important goals in life. Next to each write why you would like to achieve that goal.

Is one of your goals related to having more money? If so, why do you want more money? You might respond that you could buy certain things. I would ask further why you want to buy those things. Perhaps you would reply that it makes you feel powerful to be able to buy what you want. *Feeling powerful*, then, is the state you are after, and having money is one means to achieve that state. If your goal is to be in a relationship, again, that is not likely the core goal. Why do you want to be in a relationship? Maybe you love the feeling of being in love, or maybe you feel more secure in a relationship, or maybe you feel more connected with a sense of companionship. Again, these states are the real goals. Having a new car might provide you with a state of freedom. Having a spiritual path might provide you with more meaning in life.

CHANGING STATES

Most of us assume that states just happen to us, and they depend on external circumstances: "If only I had this job . . ."; "If only I had this home . . ."; "If only this person would marry me . . ."; "If only that person would divorce me." Goals as a means to achieve states are certainly fine, but we don't have to wait for external circumstances to change to enjoy the states we want. In fact, being in a resourceful state is a prerequisite to accelerating learning, learning is a means to achieve our goals, and achieving the goals provides states we desire.

Can we learn to change our states without having to ingest drugs or wait for the right set of external circumstances? Evidence that we have the potential to direct these seemingly involuntary states comes from research on one of the most intriguing mental disorders: multiple personality syndrome.

Researchers have studied MPS patients such as Eve, with dozens of different personalities. Each one produced states totally inconsistent with the other personalities. For example, one of Eve's personalities was allergic to bee stings—so much so that a sting could produce a life-threatening reaction. When another of her personalities kicked in, however, the reaction disappeared. One personality required glasses, while another had 20/20 vision.

Most of us change our state as an unconscious reaction to people or events around us. The first keys to direct our states *consciously* are:

1. *Physiology.* How do we feel physically? Are we rested? Are we tired? Are we energetic? Often when we have special days, it's after a good night's sleep, or a dynamic exercise session, or any situation in which we feel physically alive and vibrant.

2. *Internal representations.* How does our brain represent or model the world around us? As human beings we are totally fascinated with creating models. The hour hand on a clock models the apparent movement of the sun across the sky. Physics equations represent the way nature works. A map is a model of the layout of the land.

   Our senses also create a model. When light hits the retina of the eye, an electrochemical impulse travels to the brain. The brain doesn't directly perceive the light, but rather the electrochemical signal. The same is true of hearing. The brain doesn't directly perceive the sound, but instead the electrochemical signal generated by nerve endings within the ear. And so it is with each of the senses.

   Our conclusion has to be that we do not directly perceive reality at all, but rather a neurological *model* created by our senses. This, our internal model of the universe, together with out attitudes, belief systems, and learning strategies, constitute our *internal representations*, which I will abbreviate IR's.

Understand that our IR's do not precisely represent what is happening around or within us. Consciously, we focus on one or several things at a time, so that most perception is filtered out unconsciously. Our attitudes and belief systems can also cause distortions, generalizations, and deletions in our perceptions.

Do we see the color blue in the same way . . . or hear the same sounds at a concert? I doubt it. More likely we each have completely unique internal representations of these and other experiences. Certainly our attitudes, belief systems, and strategies for dealing with life are unique. Our IR's are probably as individual as snowflakes. Why, then, does our educational system treat us as if we all learned in the same way?

Going back to those special days, we can say that our behavior and performance are determined by our state, and our state is determined by our physiology and IR's.

STATES AND LEARNING

Think of just one area (a hobby, a type of reading, a sport, or an academic subject) in which you have found it easy and fun to learn. Simply, you were "in state" for this type of learning. Suppose, on the other hand, you find math, foreign languages, relationships, or advancing your career particularly difficult. Evidently you haven't learned how to put yourself into a resourceful state for that type of learning.

You must then learn how to change your state. This requires that you change your physiology, or change your internal representations, or both.

EXERCISE 3

Following is a list of twenty terms. Look them over for thirty seconds. Then take a piece of paper and write out the twenty terms from memory, preferably in the same order. Write as many as you can. Stop reading until you have completed this.

1. book
2. key
3. camera
4. bowl
5. cereal
6. three
7. compass
8. orange
9. tree
10. bird
11. fork
12. grasshopper
13. road
14. cough drop
15. teakettle
16. cloud
17. balloon
18. New York City
19. box
20. surprise

Once you have written the twenty words from memory, go back and check out your results against the list.

EXERCISE 4

Now let's approach the previous exercise in a different way. Stand up and stretch for a couple of minutes. If it is not convenient to stand, stretch while sitting. Take a deep breath, close your eyes, and let your whole body go limp for about thirty seconds. With each breath you exhale, let your body become more relaxed.

Next, get yourself into a comfortable position and imagine a friend of yours giving you a *book*. Attached to the book is a large golden *key*. You take the key, unlock the book, and discover a *camera* inside. You pick up the camera and take a picture of a large *bowl*. You are hungry and so delighted to see the bowl filled with your favorite *cereal*. As you eat your way down to the bottom, you notice a large number *three*. After looking more closely, you notice the three is the number on a large *compass*. You see the compass needle pointing outside, toward a nice, juicy *orange*. The orange is hanging from a *tree*. Sitting on one of the branches is a *bird*, and you are quite surprised to see the bird feeding its young ones with a *fork*. As you look closer, you are disgusted to see that on the fork is a *grasshopper*, but the grasshopper jumps down onto the *road*. Suddenly rolling down the road comes a large *cough drop*, which rolls into a nearby *teakettle*. The teakettle begins to boil up into a *cloud*, which now shapes itself into a large passenger *balloon*. You decide to go for a ride, so after a while you are way up in the sky looking down on *New York City*. As you look carefully, on the ground there is a very large *box*. Suddenly from out of the box jumps a *surprise*. The surprise is a part of you who wants you to know that you have a better memory than you think! Now take another deep breath and write the twenty terms, or as many as you remember.

Why was the exercise easier the second time? Most people better their scores because they have changed their state to one in which it is easier to remember the words. We first changed our physiology with stretching, a deep breath, and relaxation. Then we changed our internal representation by putting the words into the context of a story and using *visual imagery*. If your score significantly improved, you were more in state for this type of learning.

What does it mean if your score didn't improve that much? It may simply imply that this story, which uses *visual* imagery, did not work for you. You may do much better with the auditory and kinesthetic techniques, which will be discussed later.

But what is important is that you can discover the learning strategies that will put you in a state to facilitate both learning and having more of those special days. And that is what Powerlearning® is all about.

GETTING TO KNOW YOUR INTERNAL REPRESENTATIONS

Our internal representations or IR's allow us to "make sense" of reality. Four qualities of IR's are particularly important to accelerate learning. These are:

1. *Thinking styles—visual, auditory, or kinesthetic (VAK).*

   "You aren't *listening* to what I've *told* you. I've *explained* a hundred times that you have to keep your room clean," snapped Mrs. Schmidt at her teenage son.

   "But I just don't *see* why", he replied. "It's not *clear*. You don't have to live in here, and it *looks* just fine to me."

   "Maybe we should share our *feelings* and get a *handle* on this," interjected Mr. Schmidt. You can imagine why the Schmidts aren't communicating. They think differently!

   How do *you* learn most easily? By seeing—*visual (V)*? By hearing—*auditory (A)?* Or by feeling or doing—*kinesthetic (K)*? Our unconscious takes in data from all the senses all the time, but within our IR's we generally prefer one or two modes.

   About 60 percent of all people are primarily visual learners and thinkers. They need to *see* a picture or *visualize* what is going on. When this mode is most developed, the person is said to have a *photographic memory*: "Oh, I remember the answer to that question! It was on page thirty-seven, second paragraph, third line." Visuals are usually the fastest learners. They quickly see the picture and are ready to move on.

About 25 percent of people are primarily auditory, learning and thinking through hearing. Remember back to a class you took. Do you recall that one person who would just sit there and listen, who didn't take notes, and yet got it? Auditory learners can often pick up foreign languages very quickly by simply listening. Trivia champions are often auditory.

The other 15 percent of people are primarily kinesthetic, learning by feelings, touch, and movement. A kinesthetic learner has to get a feel for how it works. A kinesthetic learner usually learns best by doing. Einstein was primarily kinesthetic. Champion athletes are also superb kinesthetic learners.

LEARNING STYLES

Even though we consciously prefer one or two of the visual, auditory, or kinesthetic modes (V, A, or K), all of us use a combination of all three. Our individual combination is unique. In a group of fifty people I doubt that any two would have exactly the same combination.

Most teachers and study guides assume that we all learn in the same way. This is most unfortunate. In Chapter Three, you will test yourself to discover your thinking and learning style. Psychologists and counselors will often do more extended testing to give you a personal profile, but they don't tell you how to change your style. We will learn techniques to change your IR's. Then, you can change your mode to V, A, or K to match the specific learning task at hand.

---

2. *Brain functioning style.* The human brain has two sides—the right side, or right cerebral hemisphere, and the left side, or left cerebral hemisphere. Each side has its own specialized way of thinking and remembering. Most people tend to function more from one side than the other. For example, accountants and technicians will often function more from the left side, while artists and dancers will function more from the right.

We actually use both halves of our brain all the time, but most of us prefer to function more from one side or the other. More and more books are talking about how the right and left sides of the brain tie in with thinking and learning. However, very few tell you how to change your IR's by shifting toward functioning more from either the right or the left side. Later you will learn some simple brain "shifters" to match your brain functioning to the task at hand—whether it is learning, improving a relationship, or dealing with your boss or a client.

3. *Magic keys.* Related to visual, auditory, and kinesthetic learning are *keys*, sometimes called *magic keys*—the order in which we take external data and process them internally. On a crucial point in a tennis match, you might see your second serve sailing long. That is external visual input. You scold yourself mentally (internal auditory) and then feel depressed (internal kinesthetic). The key is the sequence: external visual—>internal auditory—>internal kinesthetic, which leads to a state called *depression*.

We all have distinct combinations of visual, auditory, and kinesthetic experience—both external and internal—that result in a variety of states. We each have one key to convince us to buy something, another key to become motivated, and still another for falling in love. A key is the mental combination or recipe for producing a particular state.

Once we discover our own unconscious key for motivation, we can consciously use that key whenever we want to be motivated. If we learn the unconscious key all good spellers use to be successful with spelling, we can model their key to become a good speller.

Neurolinguistic programming, abbreviated *NLP*, is a branch of psychology that in part analyzes unconscious keys we as individuals use to produce various states. NLP researchers also seek to discover unconscious keys used by the most successful achievers in sports, sales, politics, and various branches of learning. They study people who have rewarding relationships, people who can get themselves highly motivated, people who can overcome allergies, people who learn effectively, and generally people who are happy and successful. The results of using NLP for personal growth and therapy are both profound and quick.

4. *Models.* These are personal heroes, actors, friends, and famous people we use as images to help mold our behavior and growth. Just decide what you want—wealth, a relationship, better memory, technical knowledge, or a better tennis game. Find someone who produces the results you want. If you can learn to use your mind and body in the same way they do, you can duplicate their results.

Have you ever noticed yourself putting your hand on your hip when talking with a friend who has his hand on his hip . . . or folding your arms if she has her arms folded . . . or the husband and wife who laugh in the same way? These are examples of an unconscious process called *mirroring*, one way of modeling someone's behavior. We tend to imitate people we like.

A basic premise in NLP is that by modeling the states of people who are successful in doing something we would like to do, we can get the same results. For physiology we observe how they hold themselves, physical gestures, and mannerisms. For IR's we can study the values, belief systems, and specific mental *keys* they use to get the results they want.

Modeling also shows why it is important to choose friends carefully. If we are around people who consistently complain and indulge in negativity, we are likely to pick up these traits. If we are around happy, successful, and positive people, we are more likely to model these qualities.

Appropriate models provide a clear image of what success really is. The more concrete the image, the more ways our unconscious can program us to achieve the results we want. Being around successful people, watching them on TV, listening to their words, or reading their books provide conscious as well as unconscious strategies to model their success.

LEARNING TO LEARN: THE ADVANTAGE
- -

Our brain functioning style (right brain/left brain) and thinking style (VAK) determine how we think and thus represent the world internally (IR's). Magic keys are the sequence of VAK steps that

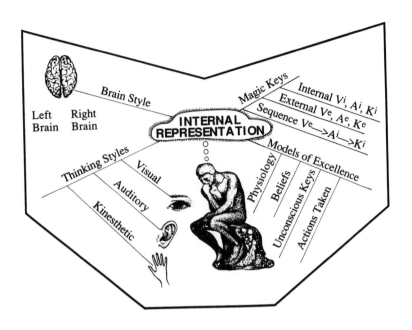

FIGURE 1.1

together with physiology lead to the states we desire. Models provide a shortcut in the process.

My purpose, then, is to provide you with new alternatives to set up states for powerful thinking, for personal power, and especially for learning . . . because achieving your goals or dreams in life will involve learning. As you learn more effectively, you gain *personal power* to achieve your goals, experience the states you like, and have more of those special days.

CHAPTER TWO

Magic Keys:

TO DIRECT YOUR

STATES

Everything should be made as simple as possible, but not simpler.

—ALBERT EINSTEIN

A famous Native American chief in the nineteenth century was asked to comment on the white people and the ingenuity of their emerging technology. His response was that these people were very smart but not wise. Wisdom comes from clarity and simplicity of thought.

Learning to produce desirable states is as simple as understanding how we think—the structure of thought. Two powerful techniques, *pattern discovery maps* and *magic keys*, provide a clear path to navigate from a present state to the more empowering states you desire.

PATTERN DISCOVERY MAPS

In the section following this one we will learn how to direct our states. The strategy to produce a desired state involves steps to change the physiology and steps to change the IR's. The key to changing the IR's is literally that—a *key*, a *magic key*.

Step by step, such a key resembles a recipe or the steps in the laboratory process to produce a certain chemical formula. A useful way to display a particular key is a tool called the pattern discovery map.

17

EXERCISE 5

Close your eyes for just a few seconds and imagine a car. See the car as clearly as you can, but if you don't see it clearly, that is okay. If you hear it or just sense it, that is also fine. Stop reading until you have completed this.

When you open your eyes, recall where in your field of view the car was located. Was it in the center of your internal field of view? Was it over to one side? Was it above you or below you?"

Most people in my seminars report seeing, hearing, or sensing the car somewhere near the center of the field. That is why a pattern discovery map begins in the center.

Figure 2.1 is an example of a pattern discovery map that summarizes Chapter One. Notice that the main idea is in the center. The most closely related ideas are closest in. From there ideas branch out on lines or curves connected with other lines or curves. This structure parallels the functioning of the right side of the brain in allowing you to see the overall picture of how parts fit together to form the whole.

A pattern discovery map also forms a nonlinear outline. The central topic is in the center. The main headings are closest in. Subheadings branch farther out, and so on.[1]

DIRECTING YOUR STATES

A state such as feeling motivated, focused, in love, or in an appropriate mind-set for learning is a desired outcome, just as a loaf of freshly baked bread is for the baker. Of course, the state may itself be a means toward further outcomes, just as the bread provides nourishment for the day's activities.

A recipe for bread has a sequence of steps we must follow in the proper order. Change the order and we do not get bread.

Achieving a desired state also involves a specific sequence of steps. We begin with physiology, then move through a mental key to direct the IR's.

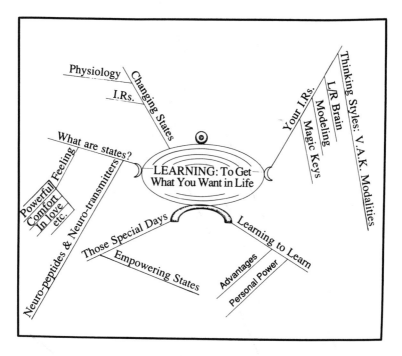

FIGURE 2.1

Adjusting physiology may involve the following:

- a few minutes of physical stretching
- having appropriate lighting, temperature, and back support;
- dietary considerations
- mimicking gestures and mannerisms of someone you would like to model
- just imagining how you would be sitting or standing right now if you were already in the state you desire

We will cover specifics of physiology throughout this book.

The heart of the recipe, though, is the magic key—the sequence of visual, auditory, and kinesthetic, internal and external experiences that lead to the desired state. A notation for *external* stimuli is V^e, A^e, and K^e, where e means external. *Internal* experiences—what we "see," "hear," and "feel" inside our heads—are designated V^i, A^i, and K^i, where i means internal. Thus if your key for getting started in the morning is to *see* the clock, *hear* a voice inside telling you why you need to get up now and what you have to do, and finally *feeling* inside that you are ready to get up, we can write the sequence as $V^e \rightarrow A^i \rightarrow K^i$. A pattern discovery map makes the key more graphic:

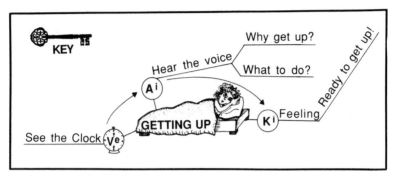

FIGURE 2.2

Visual, auditory, and kinesthetic ways of experiencing are called *modalities* in NLP. These are the ingredients of the recipe, the building blocks of a key. However, a recipe also has directions for how much of each ingredient as well as the type needed. These qualifiers of visual, auditory, and kinesthetic experience are called *submodalities*.

EXERCISE 6

Take a few seconds to think about a close friend or relative. Pick someone you can easily picture, someone with a pleasant voice, and someone you feel especially good about. When you picture this person, is he or she

- close up or far away?
- moving or still frame?
- black and white or color?
- large or small?

EXERCISE 6 (continued)

These qualities are examples of *visual submodalities*. Next, when you think about that person's voice, is it

- loud or soft?
- fast-paced, slow-paced, or in between?
- inflected or more monotone?

These are examples of *auditory submodalities*. Finally, when you think of feelings you associate with this person, which if any of these adjectives feels appropriate?

- warm or cool?
- smooth or coarse?
- firm or soft?
- light or heavy?

These are a few examples of *kinesthetic submodalities*. Submodalities provide power and precision to visual, auditory, or kinesthetic steps in a magic key.

The clock you see in the morning might seem fuzzy, dim, and far away. The voice inside your head telling you to get up might sound fast-paced, high-pitched, and perhaps have a scolding, abrasive, tonal quality. The feeling that you finally have to get up may seem heavy and rough. The completed key then looks like this:

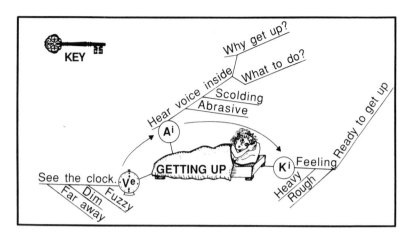

FIGURE 2.3

VISUAL SUBMODALITIES

The following are possible qualities of images you see inside (V^i):

- distance—close up or far away
- color or black and white
- moving or still frame
- bright or dim
- location of image in your field of vision
- associated/disassociated; are you in the scene or an "outside" viewer?
- size—large or small
- sharp focus or fuzzy
- panorama or narrow view
- moving quickly or slowly

AUDITORY SUBMODALITIES

Here are some possible qualities of internal self-talk—voices you might hear inside (A^i):

- high pitch or low pitch
- loud or soft
- tone of voice
- rhythm of speech
- uniqueness of sound (gravelly, smooth, raspy, breathy, etc.)
- your voice or someone else's
- pace of voice
- inflected, resonant, or more monotonous
- length of pauses
- location of sound

In addition to these qualities of what you hear, notice specifically what the voice is saying and if it is critical and demanding or helpful and supportive.

KINESTHETIC SUBMODALITIES

Here are some possible qualities of feelings you experience inside (K^i):

- softness/hardness
- rough or smooth
- a sense of pressure
- tingly
- sharp or dull
- warmness or coolness
- heavy or light

```
┌──────────────────────────────────────────────────────────────┐
│                                                                │
│         KINESTHETIC  SUBMODALITIES  (continued)                │
│                      ───────                                   │
│                                                                │
│                                                                │
│     • location of feelings in your body                        │
│     • a sense of movement                                      │
│     • a sense of tension or melting relaxation                 │
│                                                                │
└──────────────────────────────────────────────────────────────┘
```

STATE 1: MOTIVATION

Diane had always procrastinated when it came to studying French. She felt overwhelmed at the thought of learning all the details of this language. Her parents had moved from Quebec to New England when she was a baby. They had tried to teach her to be bilingual, but Diane was drawn to her English-speaking friends and TV. Recently, however, her best friend offered to pay her way to France, so they could spend a month bicycling through the countryside in the summer—now six months away. Diane was fascinated at how the same language she had labored through in high school and college was now coming so easily. Anticipation of a vacation she had long desired provided the motivation she needed to excel.

We all have times when we are totally motivated to complete a project, prepare for a vacation, or buy a gift to surprise that special someone we've just fallen in love with. At other times it's all we can do just to get out of bed in the morning. The state we call *motivation* is the springboard to the action it takes to achieve our dreams. Does it have to be by chance that sometimes we are motivated and sometimes we aren't?

According to NLP, achieving a state of motivation is something we inherently know how to do. If our own unconscious processes work well, we simply need to discover consciously what it is, and learn to use it when we want. Or we can model strategies employed by highly motivated people.

EXERCISE 7

To discover your own strategy, begin with physiology. When you are totally motivated, how does your body feel? Are you rested? Have you been exercising? What sensations do you feel in your body? How would you be sitting or standing right now if you were totally motivated and excited about what you are about to do?

For the IR's you need to discover the sequence of steps—the magic key—you unconsciously use to motivate yourself. You can do this by thinking of a specific time when you were totally motivated and consequently completely effective in what you were doing. Be in touch with all the feelings, sights, and sounds from that particular experience. It is crucial to be in touch with that experience as if it were happening *now*. Here is a seven-step process to construct your key.

1. Once you feel yourself back in the experience of being totally motivated, notice the very first thing that must happen for you to be motivated. Is it something you see (visual external—V^e), something you hear (auditory external—A^e), or something you touch (kinesthetic external—K^e)? Write down this very first step.
2. Next, notice what happens on the *inside* once you have seen, heard, or touched what started your motivation. Do you now visualize something inside, hear some words or self-talk inside, or have some internal feelings (V^i, A^i, or K^i)? Once you are aware of this step, write it down.
3. Once you have seen, heard, or felt something inside, does something else internally or externally need to happen for you to be motivated completely? Write down that step. Continue the process until it feels complete. A typical key may involve two to five steps.
4. After you have listed each step, you might conjure up another time when you were totally motivated. Put yourself back in that situation as if it were happening now, and see if that

---

EXERCISE 7 (continued)

experience involves the same sequence of steps. This may lead to some refinement in your key.

5. Often the first step in your key will be in your dominant modality. If you are primarily visual, the first step is likely to be something you see, something you hear, etc. The last step in your magic key is likely a kinesthetic internal feeling of knowing you are motivated—perhaps feeling it in your body.

6. Once you are convinced you have the correct sequence of steps, set them up in a pattern discovery map, such as shown in Figure 2.4.

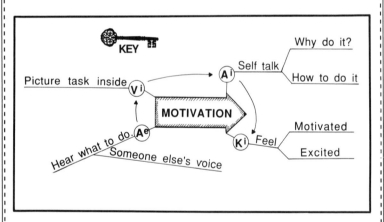

FIGURE 2.4

EXERCISE 7 (continued)

7. Finally, go back over the map and notice one to three of the most important submodalities for each step, especially internal steps. For example, if you hear a voice inside, is the voice stern, monotonous, and quick-paced, or soothing, inflected, and slow? Add submodality qualities to your map as branches from each step. The completed key might then appear as shown in Figure 2.5.

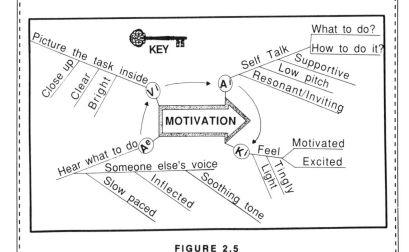

FIGURE 2.5

Exercise 7 is a powerful way to discover how you naturally motivate yourself. Yet another question you might consider is: How effective is your key? Can you easily get yourself motivated when you decide it is important, even if the task is unpleasant? Or do you often procrastinate and feel overwhelmed when thinking about what you need to do?

NLP researchers[2] have studied people who easily motivate themselves as well as people who have much difficulty getting motivated. They find people with motivation problems often taking a negative approach. Such a person might start out *seeing* that marketing presentation she needs to prepare. This may be followed by *hearing* an internal voice scolding in an unpleasant tone, telling why she *has to* do it or what she *should* do. Next, she might feel rebellion: "No, I don't want to do that!" Finally, she visualizes failing and feels terrible at that prospect. Motivation for these people is an attempt to rebel against an inner voice of authority, yet avoid the negative consequences of what would happen if they don't succeed. Since we are rarely attracted to negativity and potential failure, such a strategy leads to internal conflict and procrastination.

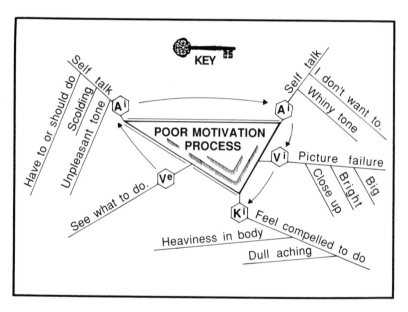

FIGURE 2.6

People who are effective self-motivators generally have positive steps in their keys. They might see what needs to be done, hear supportive and encouraging self-talk on how they can achieve their goal, visualize themselves being successful, and feel how good it will be to complete what they want.

EXERCISE 8

To see how your own self-talk affects you, try the following. Think of a project you really need to do. Imagine a voice inside telling you that you *have to* or *should* do it. How do you feel? Now change the tone to a soft, soothing, and sexy voice inviting you to start. How do you feel now?

If you don't already have one, you can acquire a powerful motivation strategy simply by changing from a negative to a positive viewpoint (see, hear, and feel success) and by changing the submodalities of each step. So instead of a fast-paced, scolding, authoritative voice telling you what you *have to do*, imagine a soft, sexy, soothing voice inviting you to start a rewarding project. Instead of visualizing a scene of failure in black and white, somewhat out of focus, and at a distance, you might picture a scene of success in color, close up, and in clear focus. Instead of feeling the painful sensations of failure, you might imagine the most important submodalities associated with achieving what you want, perhaps feeling warm, tingly, and light.

Thus positive modalities and compelling submodalities provide the magic of keys and precision of thinking.

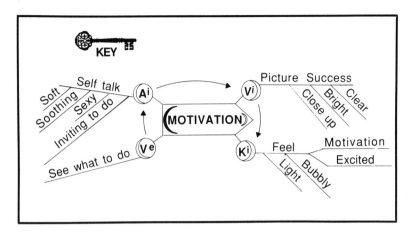

FIGURE 2.7

CHAPTER THREE

*B*RAIN STATES:

HOW YOUR BRAIN

WORKS

When we look into the animal kingdom, we might think of a centipede as a leg specialist . . . an elephant as a nose specialist . . . a giraffe as a neck specialist. But what about us as human beings? We are *brain* specialists, with a highly overdeveloped cerebral cortex.

One way to accelerate learning is to restructure the learning process to parallel the way our brain functions, instead of trying to force our brains to work the way someone else has structured education. There is a big difference here. By knowing how our brain works, it is easier to change our IR's to create a resourceful state for learning.

THE BRAIN'S POTENTIAL

The human brain weighs about three and a half pounds and contains about ten billion cells. Each of these brain cells or neurons may have thousands of fibers or dendrites branching away. The dendrites provide a network of communication pathways among the brain cells. If your brain cells were connected end to end to form a chain, the chain would be a thousand miles long. However, if the dendrites were connected end to end, that chain would be a hundred thousand miles long.

The communication capacity among brain cells is awesome. It is

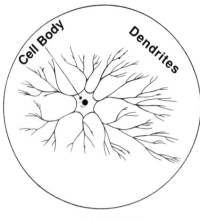

FIGURE 3.1

estimated that a chunk of brain material the size of a pea has the communication capacity of the entire world's telephone systems.[1] The interconnections possible within one human brain are calculated to be greater than the total number of atoms in the universe.[2] In fact, the brain is the most complex creation we are aware of in the universe.

The brain processes a thousand bits of information per second and interfaces with an amazing sensory system. We can perceive as few as a couple of photons of light, or enjoy a sunset, which is ten million times brighter. We can enjoy a live concert or hear corn growing on a quiet day in Kansas (about a billionth as loud as the concert).

With all this potential, you might wonder why people have trouble spelling "onomatopoeia," or working with computers, or having successful relationships. You would think we should all be supergeniuses.

WHAT'S HOLDING US BACK?

There are five major blocks to making full use of our mental potential:

1. *Learning blocks.* For most of us, our internal representations include stress-related barriers to learning. A "learning block" is a stress-related belief: for example, thinking that I can easily spell, but can't do math; or maybe I can be financially successful, but fail at relationships. These limitations are generally based on stressful learning experiences growing up—experiences with parents, teachers, and friends. In certain areas we just don't expect to excel.

EXERCISE 9

Take a minute or two to write a list of the types of learning you find most difficult, frustrating, or blocked for you. These can include sports, manual dexterity, social skills, etc., as well as academic learning. Stop reading until you have completed this.

Once you have this list written down, go back over the items and ask yourself which of these you like to change and which you have no interest in changing.

---

2. *Left-and right-brain learning.* Most education and training is directed primarily to only half of our brain: the left half. That doesn't mean the right half is not working; it certainly is. However, in most learning situations we have an imbalance between the left and right sides of the brain. A better balance would facilitate both learning and memory.

3. *Linking the conscious and the unconscious.* Many researchers believe that we have a supermemory already. Everything that happens during our lifetime is recorded somewhere. The problem is not one of remembering but rather *recalling* what is already there. We can do this by setting up consistent, reliable links with our unconscious.

4. *Development of brain cells.* You've probably heard psychologists say that we use only 5 to 10 percent of our mental potential. Only 5 to 10 percent of our brain cells are fully developed[3] in terms of the interconnections a brain cell, or neuron, can make with other neurons. The average neuron has five to ten dendrites, yet some develop thousands of these communication lines.

The number of brain cells is fixed, but the number of interconnectors increases as we learn more and make better use of our brain. The complexity of the brain and our corresponding intelligence seem to be functions of these interconnectors.

If only 5 to 10 percent of our neurons are fully developed, that means 90 to 95 percent of our brain cells are virtually undeveloped. Many of these virtually undeveloped cells will die off before they can mature. In fact, if you are over thirty and if it has taken you forty minutes to read this book so far, you may have lost 125 brain cells during this time. But don't be alarmed! It's not the book's fault; this is a natural process. You've got another 10 billion cells to go, so you won't run out soon.

If you think of the complexity among 5 to 10 percent of our brain cells vs. what might be possible among all the cells, we're not actually using 5 to 10 percent of our potential. We're probably not using a hundredth of our potential. We may not even be using a thousandth of what might be possible. Certain activities, such as learning and mental exercise, actually speed up the development of neurons, so this is another advantage of improving our learning skills.

5. *No reliable means to direct our states.* As we discussed in Chapter One, learning is a means to experience empowering states, and empowering states are means to accelerate learning.

RIGHT AND LEFT SIDES OF THE BRAIN

The human brain is shaped like a large walnut. The left half of the brain controls the right side of the body (more or less from the neck down), and the right half controls the left side. There is also connecting tissue in between called the *corpus collosum*, which allows information to go back and forth.

We have known for a long time that in most people (not everyone) the left brain is primarily responsible for language. What the right brain does—besides controlling the left side of the body—was a mystery for many years. In fact, some people began wondering whether the right brain was even necessary for higher mental functioning.

During the 1960s Dr. Roger W. Sperry conducted a series of classic experiments at Cal Tech at Pasadena to shed light on the mystery; they earned him a Nobel prize in 1981. In cases of severe epilepsy, surgeons sometimes sever the corpus collosum of the patient. This prevents seizures from spreading from one half of the brain to the other. However, in these "split brain" patients, information can no longer go back and forth between left and right, so it becomes easier to isolate what each side does.

On the surface, a split-brain person appears quite normal. Dr. Sperry discovered that while the left brain in most people is primarily

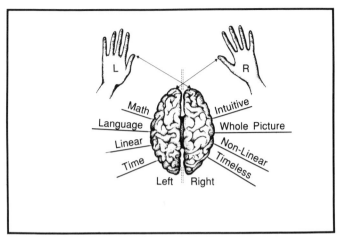

FIGURE 3.2

responsible for language, the right brain deals with feelings and emotions. You might say the left handles what we say, and the right handles the inflections and feelings of how we say it.

The right brain deals with pictures, dreams, and images, while the left has the ability to put those images into words. The left deals with logic, computers, and mathematics, while the right brain deals with math anxiety and computer anxiety—the emotional side of learning blocks. The left brain deals with *linear* thought—putting things into sequence and lists, handling one step at a time. The right brain is nonlinear and works more with parallel processing. It can handle many details simultaneously, such as recognizing a person's face or pulling together the details of a puzzling problem, as when we have a flash of intuitive insight and "see the whole picture." The left brain is aware of the passage of time and helps to keep life organized, sensible, and on schedule. The right brain is more spontaneous and timeless.

We can clearly see the specialization of the left and right hemispheres in accounts of what happens when one side is damaged. A thirty-nine-year-old school teacher with right-brain damage from a stroke found her voice flat and monotonous. Without the emotional content in her voice, she could not maintain classroom discipline. At home when she "meant business" with her children, she had to say in a mechanical tone, "God dammit, I mean it!"

In contrast, a nun sustained left-brain damage from a robber. She was not allowed to testify in her attacker's trial because of her loss of judgment and memory for left-brain sequential detail. She might have identified the attacker in court by walking over and hugging him.[5]

The left-brain/right-brain model also ties in with visual, auditory, and kinesthetic learning styles. The left brain (in most people) deals with words and auditory information. The right brain handles internal visual imagery and kinesthetic feelings.

EXERCISE 10[6]

Sit comfortably and clasp your hands together with the fingers interlocked. Notice which thumb is on top. If the left thumb is on top, this may indicate a left-brain dominance, even though the right brain controls the left side of the body. If the right thumb is on top, this could indicate a right-brain dominance.

In administering right-brain/left-brain testing to over ten thousand seminar participants, I have found a slight statistical tendency for the thumb on top to correlate with brain dominance, although the testing is certainly more accurate than the thumb method.

Stage hypnotists in the past would often have people clasp their hands together like this before inviting someone to come onto the stage. They made sure to invite someone who had the right thumb on top. Those people were more suggestible.

LIMITATIONS OF THE MODEL

Nineteenth-century researchers noted that left-brain damage seems to have more detrimental effects than right-brain damage, probably because we as a society prefer left-brain functioning. Nevertheless, this led to the opinion that the left brain is dominant and the right brain less evolved or advanced. Certainly this is not the case.

At this point you might have the feeling that some activities involve only the left brain and others only the right. This is not so. No matter what you do, both sides participate to some extent. For example, you might be working a crossword puzzle or balancing your checkbook—primarily left-brain activities, but the right brain is still involved. I don't know if you ever notice having emotions when you balance your checkbook. If you are drawing or doing a dramatic performance (primarily right-brain activities), the left brain is still involved.

The specializations of left and right are a *preference*, and when necessary either side can do functions normally associated with the other (to some extent). In fact, in a small minority of people the roles of right and left are entirely reversed (possibly if you are left-handed and your mother was also left-handed). In any case, we need to avoid too-rigid distinctions between left and right.

MEMORY, THINKING, AND LEARNING STATES

When we learn new material, memory of *words* is stored in the left brain, while memory of pictures and images is stored in the right brain.* Thus, when you meet a person, hear the name (left-brain memory), and see the face (right-brain memory), what stays with you longer, the name or the face? Most everyone says the face.

Throughout history, philosophers and writers have speculated about a dual nature of being human. The right brain/left brain model certainly support this view because there are, in fact, two distinct ways of thinking: rational, logical, reasoning states (left brain) and creative, intuitive, emotional thinking (right brain).

Often, however, the highest level of genius involves an appropriate balance between left and right. Many people would think of Einstein as being a classic left-brain scientist, yet he described his discoveries more in terms of right-brain intuitive states.

While riding a trolley to work at the patent office in Switzerland, he would observe the town clock and daydream, "How would the world appear to a beam of light leaving that clock?" Such *Gedanken* or thought experiments led to his theories of relativity.

---

*This can be reversed. A good storyteller uses words (left brain) to create images that you remember more from the right brain. You may see a picture of a car (right brain) and think the word "Chevrolet," which is remembered in your left brain.

THE HUMAN BRAIN VS. COMPUTERS

Computers for the most part simulate left brain thinking: logical, linear, step-by-step, serial. Their usefulness, of course, is in processing large amounts of left-brain data much more quickly and painlessly than we can.

In its way of thinking, the right brain is far beyond computers. It can process thousands of different functions simultaneously with continual cross-referencing and integration of new material. The right brain's ability to do a simple task such as recognizing a face from virtually any angle in less than one second would be an awesome feat for a computer.

Computers also seem unable to handle metaphors or leaps of intuition so commonplace for the right brain. In one experiment,[7] computers translated English to Russian and back to English. When given the phrase "The spirit is willing, but the flesh is weak," what came back was, "The wine is agreeable, but the meat has spoiled." And when given "Out of sight, out of mind," the computer came back with "Blind and crazy."

Learners who prefer to function more from left-brain states tend to master specific details before moving to general relationships. Most formal education favors the linear step-by-step approach and the structure a left-brain learner craves.

Right-brain learners prefer to grasp broad general relationships before proceeding to finer details and specifics. They do well learning in parallel—learning a number of ideas and concepts at once if it isn't necessary to master one topic before proceeding to the next. Also, right-brain learners often do well with unstructured, independent study.

FOUR INFAMOUS FABLES
ABOUT LEARNING[8]

At five years old, Janet could hardly wait to start school. She had so many questions her friends and parents couldn't answer. She loved to learn new skills and ideas. Her brother and sisters got to meet with people called *teachers*. She thought surely these people must have magical powers and adventurous stories to tell.

At age twenty-one, Janet could hardly wait for her last college courses to be over. Learning was drudgery. She had long ago stopped asking most of her questions except "How many units do I need to graduate?" and "Where should I look for a job?" Through her sixteen years of schooling, she had picked up a large body of knowledge, but at a high price. She had also picked up some beliefs that could cripple her learning ability for life. See if any of these "fables" tie in with your experiences.

Fable 1: "My memory is poor." The truth is that each of us already has a perfect memory, and as we discussed earlier, the problem is recalling information from our unconscious.

Hypnotists and some psychologists have believed this for many years. However, it was only demonstrated scientifically during the 1960s, at the Montreal Neurological Institute, through Dr. Wilder Penfield's brain surgery experiments. You may be aware that during brain surgery, the patient is often kept awake. Dr. Penfield found that when he stimulated one small spot on the cortex with an electric probe, the patient might suddenly remember a long-"forgotten" scene from elementary school . . . see the children's faces . . . hear the voices . . . and experience the emotions. Stimulating another spot might take the person back a few weeks ago to details of a bridge party.

When Dr. Robert True[9] of the University of Vermont College of Medicine used techniques of hypnotic age regression with adults, he found that 93% of his subjects could correctly identify the day of the week of their 10th birthday. Sixty nine percent remembered the day of the week of their fourth birthday.

FIGURE 3.3

Fable 2: "I'm not very smart. I just wasn't born that way." This is an unfortunate negative belief that shifts responsibility for poor performance from our belief system to our genetic code. Intelligence is much more related to practice and experience than to heredity. Our brains are somewhat like muscles—the more we use them, the better they get. With mental exercise our speed, accuracy, and confidence get better.

The tragedy of believing we are stupid is that the brain is such a superb learning machine, it can learn to act dumb. We can limit our perception to whatever supports our self-defeating beliefs. By believing we are stupid, we not only find lots of evidence to support us, but we also limit ourselves to a life of inadequacy.

It is absolutely essential, then, to have faith and trust in our brain and internal workings. Eric Jensen, author of *Student Success Secrets*, points out that unconsciously our brain knows how to operate over five hundred muscles and two hundred bones. Our heart beats nearly a hundred thousand times per day, pumping sixteen hundred gallons of blood through 60 miles of veins and arteries to each of the billions of cells in our body. The brain itself is the most complex creation we know of in the universe and is more complex than our solar system. The brain is nature's most superb creation—and yours is no less so than anyone else's.

Fable 3: "I just don't have *time* for new learning." Thomas Edison, when asked the secret to his success, responded that he did only one thing at a time. That is probably an oversimplification. More likely he put *full concentration* on one task at a time, while still handling all the other details of his life.

Psychologists tell us that we can keep track of about seven things at once—seven numbers, seven introductions at a party, seven items on a grocery list—without breaking the list down to smaller units. Yet how many of us have only seven things happening in our lives? For most of us life becomes a juggling game. We juggle our seven items, and the other pieces fall on the floor. Then we pick up those pieces, and still others fall. How can we possibly keep on top of all the activities, commitments, and interests in our sphere of influence?

Later we will learn some simple and powerful time-management principles to keep our movement through life balanced. These allow us to "see the whole picture" (right brain) easily and yet focus totally on the details at hand (left brain), the way Edison advised.

If you don't have enough time for new learning, you may literally run out of time sooner than you hope. There is an increasing body of research suggesting that better use of your mind promotes longevity.

Fable 4: "The older you get, the harder it is to learn new ideas and

FIGURE 3.4

skills." This is a most harmful belief, with little basis in fact. The more an aging person believes this, the more evidence they find to support their belief. This vicious circle leads many elderly people to unstimulating lives with few creative or intellectual challenges. It is likely that memory loss is more connected with stress and worry about memory loss than physiological causes.

A number of studies have demonstrated the potential that senior citizens can learn as well as or even better than high school or college students. In one study done by Else Harwood and Geoffrey Naylor[10] at the University of Queensland in Australia, a group of students sixty years or older studied German. In just six months of class (two hours per week plus one hour of homework), most achieved a level comparable to two years of daily classes in high school.

Age, then, is no barrier to better use of our brains. And by understanding the brain's true potential, the right-brain/left-brain specializations, and limiting beliefs holding us back, we are more likely to live up to our role as the brain specialists we are.

PART TWO

STATES OF THOUGHT

CHAPTER FOUR

DISCOVERING HOW YOU THINK

Brain: brān n: an apparatus with which we think we think.

—*Ambrose Bierce*

How do you think? Do you think more in pictures or internal self-talk, or feelings? Are you more intuitive and emotional, or logical and reasoning? Knowing the way you think affects how you can learn most effectively and how you can go about fulfilling your dreams.

This chapter has two tests for determining how you think, together with explanations and interpretations of your styles.

TESTING FOR YOUR BRAIN FUNCTIONING STYLE

This first test is designed to give you information on your internal representations. Do you prefer to function more from the right or the left side of the brain? What is your particular style of functioning? For each question there are four answers.

- number your *best* choice "4"
- number your next-best choice "3"

• number your third choice "2"
• number your last choice "1"

For example if you rated responses to question #1 like this:

1. _____

   _3_ a.
   _4_ b.
   _2_ c.
   _1_ d.

your top choice would be "b" and your last choice "d." Work quickly, and go with the first feelings of your preference.

BRAIN PREFERENCE AND STYLE INVENTORY[1]

1. New ideas are true for me if
   ____ a. they reflect my values and ideals.
   ____ b. they are scientific and logical.
   ____ c. I can personally verify them with observable facts.
   ____ d. they are in line with my own experience and opinions.

2. My memory is best for
   ____ a. mainly general ideas with some specific details.
   ____ b. mainly specific details.
   ____ c. mainly specific details with some general ideas.
   ____ d. mainly general ideas.

3. Rate your preference for the following *types* of activities:
   ____ a. camping, dancing, or tennis.
   ____ b. writing, collecting, or chess.
   ____ c. reading, playing a musical instrument, or home improvement.
   ____ d. swimming, doing nothing, or a leisurely walk.

4. My planning for the day usually involves
   ___ a. imagining the people I want to see and things I want to do.
   ___ b. listing out things to do.
   ___ c. making a schedule of activities with priorities and perhaps a time frame for each.
   ___ d. just letting the day unfold as it will.

5. To solve a difficult problem, I prefer to
   ___ a. go for a walk to think about it and then talk with others.
   ___ b. think it over and analyze the options on paper.
   ___ c. tackle the problem with approaches that worked for similar past problems.
   ___ d. do nothing and see if the problem will solve itself.

6. Rate how the following pairs of statements relate to you:
   ___ a. I am very much in touch with my feelings, *and* I like to let someone else take charge in group or team activities.
   ___ b. I control my feelings well, *and* I would rather let someone else take charge in group or team activities.
   ___ c. I control my feelings well, *and* I like to take charge in group or team activities.
   ___ d. I am very much in touch with my feelings, *and* I like to take charge in group or team activities.

7. I can estimate pretty accurately the amount of time that has passed without checking a clock
   ___ a. rarely.
   ___ b. often.
   ___ c. sometimes.
   ___ d. hardly ever.

8. In my spare time I would rather read about
   ___ a. how someone solved a social or personal problem.
   ___ b. historical or scientific research.
   ___ c. a true-life adventure or experience.
   ___ d. an interesting or humorous story.

9. With regard to intuition or hunches
   ___ a. I have strong hunches and sometimes follow them.
   ___ b. I don't go on hunches when it comes to important decisions.
   ___ c. I sometimes have hunches but usually don't trust them.
   ___ d. I often have strong hunches that I act on.

10. My mood goes through frequent swings
    ___ a. sometimes.
    ___ b. not true.
    ___ c. rarely.
    ___ d. often.

11. Which activities best describe you? I
    ___ a. am good at reading diagrams or listening to another's feelings.
    ___ b. am good at reading contracts or taking detailed notes.
    ___ c. enjoy chatting or can have difficulty operating mechanical devices under stress.
    ___ d. strongly visualize the setting and characters in stories I read or am good at creating innovative ideas.

12. Which best describes you? I am
    ___ a. caring.
    ___ b. orderly.
    ___ c. practical.
    ___ d. intuitive.

13. When speaking with others I
    ___ a. sometimes make up metaphors or stories.
    ___ b. use a clear, precise choice of words.
    ___ c. sometimes make up puns.
    ___ d. sometimes make up new words.

14. When it comes to adhering to rules or policy, my attitude is
    ___ a. Question authority.
    ___ b. Follow the rules.
    ___ c. Rules and policies usually allow for the best results.
    ___ d. I would just as soon break the rules as follow them.

15. For the following, rate yourself on a scale from 1 to 4. Circle the number that best fits you.

1 —————— 2 —————— 3 —————— 4

I prefer to master	I would rather know
one of two areas of	a little bit about
learning rather than	many different
spread myself thin.	subjects.

- If you circled 1, record: 4 for b, 3 for c, 2 for a, 1 for d.
- If you circled 2, record: 4 for c, 3 for b, 2 for a, 1 for d.
- If you circled 3, record: 4 for a, 3 for d, 2 for c, 1 for b.
- If you circled 4, record: 4 for d, 3 for a, 2 for c, 1 for b.

———— a.
———— b.
———— c.
———— d.

16. My attitude about daydreaming is that it
———— a. can be useful in solving problems.
———— b. is a bad habit.
———— c. is amusing but not very practical.
———— d. is a valuable technique for planning.

17. When learning new material I would rather
———— a. be spontaneous and flexible in my approach to learning and study with some specific planning or directions.
———— b. follow closely a specific schedule or action plan for learning.
———— c. follow a specific plan with flexibility and leeway.
———— d. not be tied down to any particular plan for learning.

18. When getting together socially with others I
———— a. occasionally like to be spontaneous.
———— b. definitely prefer activities that are planned in advance.
———— c. usually prefer activities that are planned in advance.
———— d. prefer to be spontaneous.

19. The following are most true for me:
    ____ a. I remember directions and facts by visualizing, and I prefer security to risk-taking.
    ____ b. I remember directions and facts best by writing them down, and I prefer more certainty to risk-taking.
    ____ c. I remember directions and facts best by writing them down, and I am willing to take risks.
    ____ d. I remember directions and facts by visualizing, and I enjoy taking risks.

20. When people argue over some point, I favor the one who
    ____ a. reflects my ideals and values.
    ____ b. is most logical and orderly.
    ____ c. delivers the arguments in a practical, forceful manner.
    ____ d. agrees with my personal opinions.

When you are finished, add up the numbers for each of the "b" choices. For example, if this were your test:

1. _____
   _2_ a.
   _4_ b.
   _1_ c.
   _3_ d.

2. _____
   _4_ a.
   _2_ b.
   _1_ c.
   _3_ d.

3. _____
   _1_ a.
   _3_ b.
   _4_ c.
   _2_ d.

Add the *4* from the b on question #1
with the *2* from the b on question #2
with the *3* from the b on question #3, etc.

Once you have completed this, add the "c" scores (e.g., 1 from question 1 plus the 1 for question 2, etc.). Do the same for the "a's" and the "d's":

Total of numbers next to "b" responses _____
Total of numbers next to "c" responses _____
Total of numbers next to "a" responses _____
Total of numbers next to "d" responses _____

The sum of these four numbers should be 200.

Next, record your results in Figure 4.2 (or in a copy of Figure 4.2 if you wish). Where it says "sum of 'b' scores," put a dot *on that line* opposite the scale. Where it says "sum of 'c' scores," again put a dot on that line across from the scale, and so forth for the "a" and "d" scores.

Finally, if you connect the dots with lines, you will create your profile. Here is one reader's profile as an example.

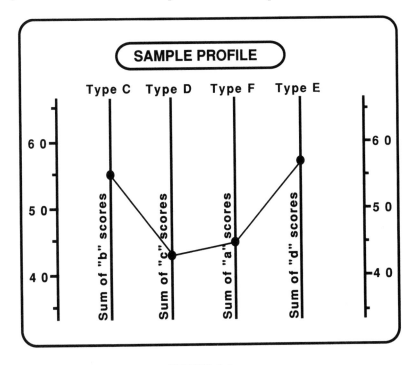

FIGURE 4.1

Stop reading until you have added your scores and recorded them.

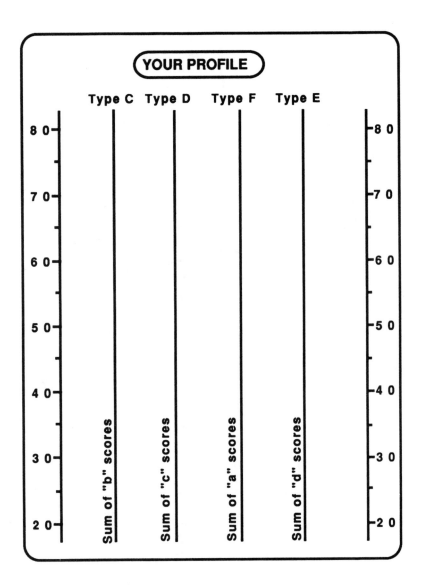

FIGURE 4.2

INTERPRETING YOUR PROFILE[2]

Notice that if your highest score is on the first line (sum of b's), you will be a *type C* individual (see the top of the chart). If your highest score is on the second line (sum of c's), you are a *type D*. If your highest score is on the third line, you are a *type F*, and on the fourth, a *type E*. What do these types mean?

Type C = cerebral. The cerebral person prefers to function very much from the left side of the brain. Cerebral people tend to be quite articulate, but sometimes more flat and unexpressive than other types. They are generally very meticulous and good with detail.

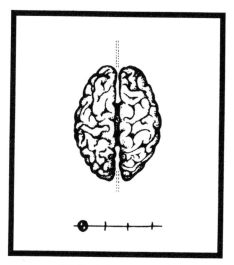

FIGURE 4.3: Cerebral

Dr. Sharon Crane points out in her professional presentation seminars that a cerebral person doing a wallpapering project would probably start in the closet to perfect the skills. Then, when he or she did the walls, the seams would line up perfectly. A past president who was probably a cerebral type was President Richard M. Nixon, an outstanding debater.

Cerebral people are sometimes more formal and reserved than other types. They may not do well with criticism because they want to be perfect. Their strength lies in the high standards they set for themselves and their attention to detail.

Type D = doer. The doer prefers to function moderately to the left side of the brain. The doer type tends to be articulate like the cerebral but more expressive. They are often "bottom line" and results-oriented.

They are good at getting things started and moving—hence the term "doer"—although they may not always complete things.

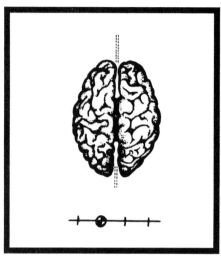

FIGURE 4.4: Doer

Doers have a high ego strength and are decisive, competitive people. In contrast with the cerebral, who will often listen a great deal to take in data, doers may not listen well. They usually have their own ways of doing things.

Again, Dr. Crane points out that a doer working with wallpaper would probably start at one end of the room and work straight across. If a seam didn't line up, he or she might cover it with a picture. President Lyndon Johnson, who was strongly results-oriented, was most likely a doer. President Ronald Reagan was probably also in this category, although he was likely a combination of types.

The doer's strength lies in his or her ability to get things moving—which is often the hardest step in an activity.

Type F = facilitator. The facilitator tends to function moderately from the right side of the brain. They generally are more people-oriented and sensitive to feelings than the left-brain types. They often listen more than they speak and thus make good counselors. A facilitator doing a wallpaper project would probably do it in such a way as to please other people—that is, ask others how they wanted it done. A past president who was very much a facilitator, as I'm sure you can imagine, was President Jimmy Carter, a people-pleaser.

Facilitators often crave security. Their strength lies in their ability to be holistic thinkers (seeing the whole picture), and they often work well in groups.

Type E = expressive. The expressive type tends to function far from the right side of the brain. They are often very humorous, colorful, spontaneous, and outgoing with people. Their talking and ways of

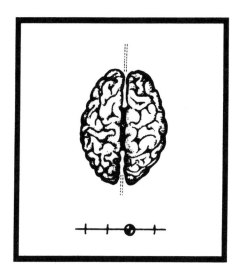

FIGURE 4.5: Facilitator

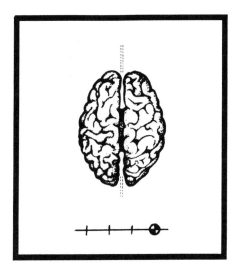

FIGURE 4.6: Expressive

doing things may seem disorganized to others, but they have their own means of order. They are sometimes drawn to flashy clothes and cars.

An expressive doing a wallpaper project might choose bold color combinations and patterns. President John F. Kennedy was most likely an expressive. President Reagan was probably a combination of doer and expressive.

If your top two scores were within three or four points of each other, you might be one of the following combinations:

Doer and facilitator. This is what Wonder and Donovan in *Whole Brain Thinking* refer to as a *mixed dominant*—a little left and a little right. This is an ideal pattern for a manager, who needs to be "bottom line"- and results-oriented but also good with people and feelings. The mixed dominant can *simultaneously* attend to left-brain detail *while* maintaining the whole picture. This is also useful in new learning.

A problem can occur with this type if one side of the brain does not clearly dominate.[3] Then you might feel like you have two competing voices within, pulling you in different directions. The result can be dyslexia or stuttering. However, this problem is rare, and the mixed dominant type is generally a good learning combination.

Cerebral and expressive. This combination is called high lateral—you can function very much from the left brain *or* very much from the right brain, but not both at the same time. This type is more common with men. The classic example is the accountant during the day who comes home and spends the evening swimming or dancing . . . or Einstein, who spent his spare time daydreaming or playing the violin.

Cerebral and doer. This basic left-brain combination is described by Dr. Crane as being potentially one of the most dynamic productive combinations. The doer gets things moving, and the cerebral handles fine details. She also describes this as potentially one of the most stress-producing combinations. The doer wants to get things done quickly, while the cerebral demands a perfectionist slowness. The key here is an appropriate balance between these two tendencies.

Facilitator and expressive. This is a fairly frequent right-brain combination. When you read characteristics of the facilitator and the expressive types, you will probably find some of each that apply to you.

Cerebral and facilitator or doer and expressive. These combinations are a bit more unusual. Frequently, a person who prefers right-brain functioning takes on left-brain skills to get a job. When it comes to employment, our society strongly favors left-brain skills. When you look in the want ads, how many times do you see an ad for a poet . . . or a philosopher . . . or a fine artist? Instead, the ads are usually for engineers, accountants, technicians, and clerical workers, whose work demands primarily left-brain skills.

Another possibility for these combinations is a person who prefers left-brain functioning but has added right-brain skills to deal with people and feelings or right-brain problem-solving strategies. A classic example is the engineer who is promoted to management.

LIMITATIONS OF THIS TESTING

You will notice that you didn't score 0 on any of the types. We are each a combination of all four, and you may have noticed characteristics in you from each category. In most situations, however, we tend to function primarily in one or two modes.

When I do this testing in my seminars, most people feel that the description of their type pretty closely matches their own self-image. That's not to say that the test is foolproof. Clinical psychology testing to determine your brain preference style can go into much more detail.

Also, our mode of functioning can change with time. The results on your test a year from now might be quite different from what they are today. Even with these limitations, however, this test is a fairly reliable quick indicator of your style of thinking.

TESTING YOUR MEMORY AND THINKING STYLE

Following are some questions to determine how you think and remember. The questions are structured similarly to those in the first test you just took.

For each question there are three answers:

> 3 = your best choice
> 2 = your second-best choice
> 1 = your last choice

For example, if you rated responses to question 1 like this:

1. _____
   _2_ a.
   _3_ b.
   _1_ c.

your best choice would be "b," and your last choice "c."

INTERNAL REPRESENTATIONS ASSESSMENT

For each question rate each of the three answers:

> 3 = your first choice
> 2 = your second choice
> 1 = your last choice

Work quickly and go with whatever seems right for you.

1. I most effectively communicate what is happening inside of me
   ____ a. through my tone of voice and choice of words.
   ____ b. through my eyes.
   ____ c. through my posture and the emotions I convey.

2. When I don't quite understand or remember something
   ____ a. it doesn't ring a bell or resonate.
   ____ b. it seems hazy or unclear.
   ____ c. I can't get a handle on it or a feel for it.

3. I most easily notice
   ____ a. the quality of music from a stereo.
   ____ b. if colors or shapes clash.
   ____ c. if clothes feel uncomfortable.

4. When I am fully involved, I am _____ what I am doing.
   ____ a. tuned in with
   ____ b. focused on
   ____ c. in touch with or connected with

5. I express myself best by
   ____ a. speaking my ideas.
   ____ b. describing my picture or vision.
   ____ c. writing my thoughts or expressing my feelings.

6. In a discussion, a person will most quickly get my attention by
   ____ a. their tone of voice and choice of words.
   ____ b. their point of view.
   ____ c. their emotional expressiveness.

7. When I have leisure time I prefer to:
   ____ a. listen to music.
   ____ b. sightsee.
   ____ c. go dancing.

8. An effective way for me to make decisions is to rely on
   ____ a. what resonates or sounds best to me.
   ____ b. what looks clearest to me.
   ____ c. gut-level feelings.

9. Learning academic or technical material is easiest for me when
   ___ a. someone explains the ideas to me.
   ___ b. I visualize the concepts and see the whole picture.
   ___ c. I can learn by doing or get a feel for the ideas.

10. At a party, I am most attracted to people who
    ___ a. are interesting, articulate speakers.
    ___ b. radiate visual beauty.
    ___ c. convey a warm, relaxed feeling.

11. The most important thing to help me remember directions is to
    ___ a. repeat them to myself as I hear them.
    ___ b. visualize them.
    ___ c. write them down or intuitively sense how to get there.

12. Once I completely understand a new idea or concept
    ___ a. I have it loud and clear.
    ___ b. I can envision it.
    ___ c. it is now concrete or I have a feel for it.

13. In my environment I am mostly to notice
    ___ a. sounds and quietness.
    ___ b. visual coordination and beauty.
    ___ c. feelings of warmth and/or comfortable furniture.

Once you have finished, add up your scores as you did in the previous test:

- Add up the numbers next to each "b" response. Put the total below.
- Next, add up the numbers next to each "a" response and again put the total below.
- Finally, add the numbers next to each "c" response and record the total.

Sum of numbers next to "b" responses ___
Sum of numbers next to "a" responses ___
Sum of numbers next to "c" responses ___

Now you can plot your results in Figure 4.8 (or in a copy of Figure 4.8 if you wish).

To either side of the page you will see a scale. The first line over to the right of the leftmost scale is the sum of your "b" scores. Put a dot on that line opposite the appropriate position on the scale for the sum of your b's. The next line over is the sum of your "a" scores. Put a dot on that line representing the sum of your "a" scores. The last line is the sum of your "c" scores.

For example, if the sums of your scores were

Sum of numbers next to "b" responses <u>21</u>
Sum of numbers next to "a" responses <u>31</u>
Sum of numbers next to "c" responses <u>26</u>

Your profile would look like this:

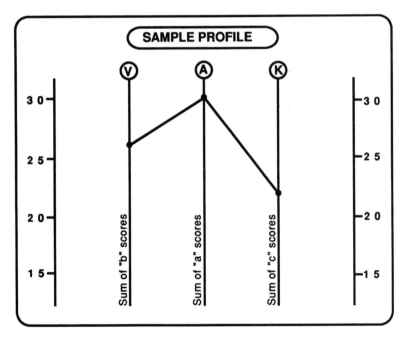

FIGURE 4.7

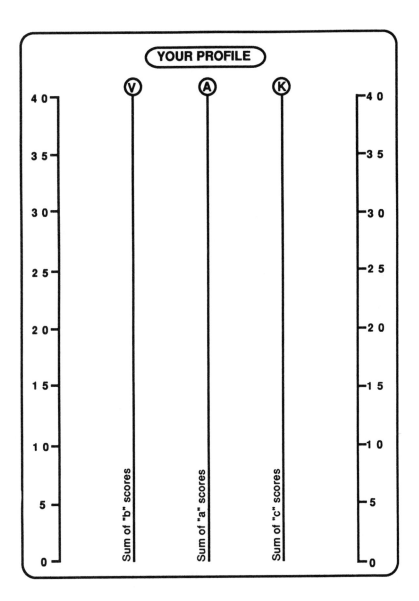

FIGURE 4.8

I N T E R P R E T I N G   Y O U R   M E M O R Y   A N D T H I N K I N G   S T Y L E

Once you've charted your results, you'll notice three additional letters, at the top of the chart: "V," "A," and "K." If your highest score is on the first line over, your thinking and memory style is primarily *V*, for visual. If your highest score is on the second line, you are primarily *A*, for auditory. The highest score on the third line over is *K*, for kinesthetic. Here are some general characteristics for each type.

Visuals. Visual people prefer to think, imagine, and remember in terms of pictures or images. They like to look at visual presentations, visualize what they are learning, or see the whole picture. To recall images, most visuals will look up to their left. Some will look up to their right, and a few straight ahead with a glazed appearance as they look inside.

In my seminars I illustrate part of how their strategy works with spelling. I have good spellers come up to the front of the room and give them a difficult word to spell. Inevitably they will look up to the left or more rarely up to the right to remember how the word looks. Such people have evolved an unconscious strategy to "see" the word. English is not always spelled the way it sounds. Looking up is part of accessing that visual image.

E X E R C I S E   1 1

To find your direction of visual recall, read each of the following questions and notice which way you naturally look to answer them.

- How many windows are in your house?
- What was the first thing you saw when you woke up this morning?
- Do you remember what your first-grade teacher looked like?
- Which of your friends has the longest hair?

Visual people tend to have an erect posture and breathe from high and shallow in the chest. Their speech is filled with visual references:

- "I see what you mean."
- "Things are looking up."
- "I can picture what you're saying."
- "Today is so bright and clear."

Visuals frequently talk in a high pitch at a fast rate. They see the pictures so quickly, their words can hardly keep pace.

FIGURE 4.9

Auditories. Auditory people think and remember more in terms of sound quality and words. They often learn well by listening or having someone explain something to them.

Talking on the telephone is 100 percent auditory. Think of how you most effectively listen: tilting your head slightly one way or the other and looking straight across toward one side—most likely to your left. Part of the auditory strategy for recall is to look straight across toward the left or occasionally toward the right.

Auditories generally have a more relaxed posture than visuals and breathe more in the middle of the chest. The language of auditories contains phrases like:

- "That really clicks with me."
- "That doesn't ring a bell."
- "It sounds good to me."
- "I hear what you mean."

Auditories speak more slowly than visuals, and the music of their speech is often rich with inflections and intonation. They often take pride in having a resonant voice (e.g., radio announcers and singers).

Kinesthetics. Kinesthetic people involve feelings and tactile sensations in their learning and memory. They often learn by doing or via tactile sensations in their bodies. They need to get a "feel" for the material, make it "concrete," get a "handle" on it. Professional dancers are superb kinesthetic learners.

FIGURE 4.10

To remember feelings and tactile sensations, kinesthetic people will generally look down toward the right or sometimes down toward the left. The posture of a kinesthetic is the most relaxed of the three types, and their breathing is often deep, slow, and from the diaphragm. The language of a kinesthetic often contains phrases like:

• "I'll be in touch."
• "I'm trying to get a feel for how this works."
• "I can't get a handle on it."
• "That guy is such a pain in the . . ."

The speech pattern of a kinesthetic is the slowest of these three types because it takes more time for the kinesthetic to get in touch with his feelings as he is thinking. Once he had grasped a new idea, however, the kinesthetic learner often has a deeper understanding than the other types. Einstein was probably kinesthetic.

EXERCISE 12

To discover the direction you look for kinesthetic recall answer the following questions and be in touch with the feelings described. Notice which way you naturally look to access the feelings . . . down to your left or down to your right.

• Can you imagine how it feels when you are in love?
• Can you imagine the feeling of a nice hot bath or hot tub?
• Can you imagine the feeling of grease covering your hands?
• Can you sense the feeling of movement when you dance freely or participate in your favorite sport?

The direction you look for auditory recall (information you have heard) is likely the same direction (right or left) in which you look for visual recall, except straight across to the side or slightly down. Knowing the directions you naturally look to access visual, auditory, or kinesthetic memories is an important step in learning how to direct your states.

Combinations. Most of us are combination of all three types. You'll notice you didn't score 0 in any one category. We usually have a preference to function from one or two modes, with one or two being weaker or less used. Furthermore, the healthier and more balanced we are, the easier it is to shift our modality to match the task at hand.

If you want to be a good speller or remember the locations of bones and muscles, it is useful to set up a visual state for yourself. If you want to learn music appreciation or a foreign language, an auditory state is more appropriate. For a sport, dancing, or processing emotions, a kinesthetic state works best.

LEARNING, KEYS, AND THINKING

Knowing your preferred modality or modalities connects with learning and magic keys. Most of the time you'll do best to have your first exposure in new learning be in your preferred modality. Thus, if you are studying accounting and are primarily visual, your most effective first step might be to read the material or see charts, diagrams, or pictures of how the methods work. If you are auditory, you might do better to start out hearing the instructor or a friend talk about the material, with opportunity for you to discuss it and ask questions. If you are kinesthetic, it may be important for you to write the material down or get "hands on" experience as quickly as possible.

The first step in your unconscious keys for motivation, falling in love, feeling empowered, etc., are also quite often the same as your preferred modality. Beyond the first step, our overall process or key for a particular state or for learning may ultimately involve all three modalities with both external and internal steps.

Our IR's are determined by how we think. Thoughts have structure and building blocks, just as matter is composed of atoms and molecules. Thoughts and beliefs are structured from visual, auditory, and kinesthetic impressions, based on how we are using the left and right sides of the brain. Now that we understand this structure, we are in a better position to direct our thinking.

CHAPTER FIVE

POWERTHINKING

For those who only feel, life is a tragedy.
For those who only think, life is a puzzle.
For those who think and feel,
in the freedom of NOW,
life is a romantic comedy.

—ANONYMOUS

The human brain is the most complex creation we know of in the universe. We have the gift of nature's most remarkable engineering feat, but we were not given an instruction manual!

This chapter is a collection of brain stretchers to balance thinking and feeling and thus allow us to shift our states. We contrast left brain vs. right brain thinking, and how to promote visual, auditory, and kinesthetic thinking.

RIGHT-BRAIN AND LEFT-BRAIN THINKING [1]

The ideal situation in learning is an appropriate *balance* between the left and right sides of your brain for learning the task at hand. Remember, too, that learning is not just academic, but covers life in general.

Here is a test of your knowledge of the left and right sides of the brain. We will look at five social situations where one or more people are acting from an imbalance between left and right thinking. Before you read my interpretation, you might take a separate piece of paper and identify what you think the imbalance is in each case.

PROBLEM 1

You and a close loved one are having a totally unproductive argument. You are each caught up in your own feelings. Neither is really listening to the other. What do you think the imbalance is?

My answer: The two of you are functioning too much from the right side of the brain—you are too caught up in your own emotions to deal rationally with the issues or to hear the other person.

One elegant way to shift more toward the left is for the two of you to separate and write a letter to each other. The letter should be a description of what you are feeling, not the issues or put-downs of the other person. Write a vivid description of *how you experience your feelings.* The description should be so graphic and vivid that anyone reading your words will literally be able to taste what you experience: "I feel such intense anger . . . like ropes coiled around my chest and sandpaper burning across my forehead."

By expressing your feelings in written form, what are you doing? You are shifting more toward the left brain to diffuse the feelings. You are certainly not ignoring them. In fact, you are dealing with the feelings first, but in a left-brain way.

When you get together and exchange letters, you taste what the other person experiences. After reading the letter, take a few minutes for each of you to discuss feelings you perceived in the letter and to convince the other you understand the feelings. This step is crucial. Isn't one of the most frustrating things in an argument that the other doesn't know or care about your feelings? Once you have dealt with the feelings in a left-brain way, you can handle the issues more easily.

PROBLEM 2

You are working on a detailed problem, start to feel over-whelmed by the amount of detail, and can't see how it fits together. What do you think the imbalance is?

My answer: You are too much to the left. You can't see the forest for the trees. You aren't getting the whole picture or perspective.

Here what you need to do is to shift back toward the right. Shortly we will see several techniques to promote that shift. See the "For Right-Brain Thinking" box.

PROBLEM 3

Someone lays into you with heavy criticism. What do you think the imbalance is liable to be?

My answer: Very likely you will shift too far to the right and be caught in your own emotions and defenses. The person criticizing is probably already in that state.

Again, here you need to shift left. Dr. Sharon Crane[2] describes an effective technique called "fogging" to get out of this situation. When the person criticizes you:

1. Repeat back to them the criticism as you understand it. This assures them that you are getting what they are saying.
2. Then ask them, "What *in particular* is the problem here?" Step 2 is what creates the fog. "What in particular" demands that they search out left-brain detail. They initially may not be able to answer the question because they are caught in right-brain feelings. So if they hit you with more criticism, you repeat

steps 1 and 2. If you keep hammering away at "what in particular," they will have to shift left at some point. Now you have diffused the emotions and can get on with the actual issues.

PROBLEM 4
_____

You are sitting in a class or lecture and are completely bored. What do you think the imbalance is?

My answer: Probably *both* sides of your brain are shutting down. Here you must decide if the information is important for you to get. If the material is important, you are obviously not in a resourceful state. What do you do to change your state? By changing your physiology and your IR's, we know that you can get yourself into a more productive state. For your physiology, stretch while you are sitting. Imagine how you would be sitting if you were totally fascinated with the class. Move your body in some way.

To change your IR's you can activate your left brain by taking detailed notes. Even though this might be the most boring material or speaker you can imagine, analyze it to pieces.

To activate your right brain, notice things such as voice inflections or body language. Is there any emotion behind what the speaker is saying? "What does this person really want to say?" "What would this person rather be doing?" Within a few minutes you can completely change your state and get the information you need.

PROBLEM 5
_____

You are talking on the telephone and want to listen carefully to the words and detail spoken. Which ear should you use?

My answer: Above the neck, right and left crossover does not work in exactly the same way as below the neck. However, most of the signals (not all) from the right ear goes to the left brain, and most from the left ear goes to the right brain.

To listen to verbal detail, use the right ear. To listen more to emotional content or what they really want to say, use the left ear. Most of us have a habit of using one ear or the other, so it may feel odd to switch. It's not that by using the left ear you won't get the words or detail, or by using the right ear you won't get the feelings. Information goes back and forth across the corpus callosum in a fraction of a second. It's just that by using your right ear, the first impulse or impression goes to the left brain, and visa versa. As a test, you might listen with one ear, then ask them to repeat the material and listen with the other ear.

STATES OF RIGHT-BRAIN THINKING

This section and the next present some techniques[3] to allow you to shift easily between right-brain and left-brain thinking.

You will want to shift right if you are overwhelmed by details of a problem and want to step back to see the whole picture. If your job and daily activities are primarily left-brain, you can create more balance in your life by spending more time with right-brain activities. As you will see shortly, this also enhances left-brain functioning.

Unlike other states, such as motivation, feeling in love, etc., with a specific set of steps for your physiology and a magic key, right-brain thinking and left-brain thinking are a bit more elusive to establish. Nevertheless, here are some suggestions to promote right-brain thinking.

FOR RIGHT-BRAIN THINKING

- Look for general relationships in material.
- Go for a leisurely walk.
- Spend time drawing or even doodling.
- Allow time for daydreaming, humming, whistling.
- Allow time to be light, playful, and joking.
- Use pattern discovery maps.

STATES OF LEFT-BRAIN THINKING

You will want to shift left when you are caught up in feelings, such as an argument, criticism, or depression. Or perhaps your daily activities and work are primarily right-brain, but you would like to create more balance in your life.

FOR LEFT-BRAIN THINKING

- Ask detailed questions (e.g., What in particular?).
- Take detailed notes.
- Do outlining and structured writing like the love-letter technique or keeping a personal journal.
- Do crossword puzzles.
- Do math problems.
- Make up puns.
- Break problems up into separate parts.
- Stick closely to a time schedule.*
- Use pattern discovery maps.

---

*Right-brain people can be very unaware of time.

You'll notice pattern discovery maps in the last two boxes. As we have discussed, this way of organizing material simulates right-brain functioning. The pattern discovery map is also a beautiful device for balancing right-brain/left-brain thinking. The left brain deals with the words, ideas, and details of the map, while the right brain deals more with the overall pattern—how everything links together and interconnects. This way of organizing material has some big advantages over traditional note-taking or outlining.

HOW TO ENHANCE LEARNING

If you are primarily a doer or cerebral, you will probably learn material best in a left-brain way. You are most effective in a highly structured learning situation and do best one piece at a time. You have the advantage that most formal education favors your learning style.

Your strength is in handling fine detail, and your weakness is in discovering broad, general relationships. When setting up a study plan, you would do well to construct a detailed schedule and action plan for learning and covering the material. Your natural style is to learn specifics first and then put them together in broad, general relationships.

Since left-brain learners often have difficulty discovering broad, general relationships and seeing the whole picture, your study plan includes a good portion of time putting things together. A very useful tool toward this end is to structure the material into a pattern discovery map.

If you are a facilitator or an expressive, you will learn material better in a right-brain way. You have an advantage over left-brain learners in being able to do better in less structured, independent study. Your natural learning style is to discover broad general concepts first and then focus on the details. Where you may fall short is in getting around to all the details.

If you can find several different topics in your study that don't depend on each other, you can learn them at the same time. For example, if you are taking a tennis class, you might study the rules of tennis, execution of strokes, and strategy all at the same time. A left-brain type might prefer to take them in sequence.

In studying a text, you don't need a detailed study plan. Just get moving. Of course, this can be one of the hardest steps. You are spending less time putting things together than left-brain learners, and you need to focus more on picking up the details. It is also valuable for you to organize your notes in pattern discovery maps.

SEXUAL DIFFERENCES

Generally, girls develop language skills earlier than boys. This gives them a head start on left-brain skills. H. T. Epstein[4] has estimated that by age eleven, girls' brains are developing at about twice the rate of boys'.

By spending more early time with right-brain activities, boys usually wind up being better with spatial relationships. By age fifteen their brains are developing about twice as fast as girls'.

Women have a thicker corpus collosum than men. Presumably this provides more nerve fibers connecting left and right—which may account for women seeming more intuitive.

RIGHT-BRAIN/LEFT-BRAIN MEMORY ENHANCERS

The memory of words and verbal detail physiologically is stored more in the left brain, and memory of pictures, images, and spatial relationships is more in the right. The most superior memory however, is one that is simultaneously right brain and left brain *plus a way of connecting the two*. When you did the twenty-term exercise in Chapter One, your first exposure probably resulted primarily in left-brain memory. The second time we added right-brain visual images for the words, plus a story that connected the words with images.

If you were learning the Portuguese word *solteiro* (sohl-$\overline{\text{tay}}$-ee-roo), meaning bachelor, you could repeat the word and meaning a few times and create an unreliable left-brain memory.

You might, however, notice that this word sounds a little like "salty hero." You could imagine Popeye the Sailor, who is a salty hero and also a bachelor. Again, you have left-brain sounds and words, a right-brain picture, and a connection.

VISUAL THINKING

Improved visual thinking can sharpen your observation skills, promote photographic recall, and provide you with a clear picture of the goals and states you desire. As well, visualization may develop the corpus collosum linking the left and right hemispheres of the brain. Dreams and images are the language of the right. Interpreting and understanding these images is a job for the left. The corpus collosum allows flow of thought back and forth.

Improved visual thinking has three components: improved external visual perception (V^e), modeling the physiology and IR's of the best visual thinkers, and improved internal visualization (V^i). Here are a couple of approaches to enhance visual perception:

- Take a course in drawing. One of the best I've seen is a self-directed course presented in the book *Drawing on the Right Side of the Brain*, by Betty Edwards. Her exercises promote enhanced right-brain functioning and sharpened visual skills, and they are fun. They also provide a great metaphor, because most of us have strong learning blocks when it comes to drawing. To discover that you can draw much better than you thought may open up new possibilities to do other things you didn't think you could do. Furthermore, they promote communication between the left and right hemispheres through the corpus collosum.
- Another approach to sharpen visual perception is to *reverse a familiar scene*. Take a familiar setting, such as your bedroom, office, or front yard, and study it through a mirror. Reversing the images will bring out many mundane details you've seen many times but failed to notice.

We can best model powerful visual thinkers by modeling how they handle their physiologies. If you were such a person you would

- assume a straight, upright posture.
- look in your direction of visual recall to picture something you've seen before.
- look up and to the opposite side to picture something you've never seen before. Thus you may look up to your left to imagine your best friend smiling. However, you would probably look up and toward your right to imagine how you'll look in five years with your first million dollars or to picture yourself with that man or woman of your dreams.

We can illustrate how to model strong visual thinkers' IR's through the *key* most of them unconsciously use to be excellent spellers.

THE MAGIC KEY FOR SPELLING

1. If the word is longer than 5 or 6 letters, break it down into smaller units or chunks (e.g., onomatopoeia—> ono-ma-topoe-ia).
2. Look (V^e) at the whole word for a shorter word or just the first chunk for a longer word, and imagine your eyes and brain are a camera taking a picture of the word.
3. While you are doing this, assume a visual posture and physiology (K^e).
4. Look in your visual direction and visualize the letters (V^i). Some people visualize more clearly with their eyes open, others more clearly with their eyes closed. If you don't "see" the letters, repeat step 2.
5. Trace the letters in the air with your finger (K^e).
6. Look again in your visual direction to see the letters (V^i).
7. Read the letters out loud in *reverse* order (A^e). If you can do this, you have a clear visual image, since English is almost impossible to sound out backward.
8. Do step 2–7 for each chunk of the word, then for the word as a whole. You will experience the feeling (K^i) that you know the word, and with your mental picture, you will never forget the word, just as you are unlikely to forget someone's face.

THE MAGIC KEY FOR SPELLING (continued)

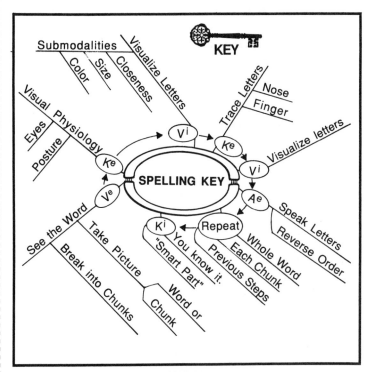

FIGURE 5.1

Most good spellers unconsciously do many of these steps to learn a difficult word. You can further refine the key using submodalities—that is, visualize the letters in your favorite color, or have them be close up or large. With practice the whole process will take only a few seconds.

Exercises to promote internal visualization often start with words (left-brain instructions) such as "imagine yourself lying on the warm sand at the beach . . . staring into a clear, blue sky . . . at a bone-white sea gull gliding in lazy circles." You then convert the words into right-brain images.

Some people get very clear and sharp images, while many people feel frustrated that their images are vague or nonexistent. People frequently ask me at my seminars if there is some way to increase the clarity of their imagery. There are three techniques I can suggest:

1. *Physiology.* Look in your visual direction when you close your eyes. As discussed, this is typically up and to the left for something you've seen before, and up to the right for something you've not seen but want to imagine. You might further imagine (with your eyes closed) that your forehead is a television screen. Look up to see the picture. You may find the imagery more vivid at certain locations.

   Experiment for yourself. You might scan the field from one temple to the other to see where it is clearer. This is what we do in the dream stage of sleep, during rapid eye movement (REM). We look up and scan the visual field—left to right to left.

2. *Sensory overlap.* Some people find it easier to imagine sounds like a running creek or wind rustling leaves in a forest. Others can more easily imagine tactile feelings—walking over the warm sand at the beach or dipping their hand into a cool, rushing creek.

   The procedure here is to start with the sense that you can most easily imagine. As you become absorbed, you may notice visual glimpses of what you are imagining. With practice, those glimpses give way to clearer pictures. In effect, images through one sense enhance production of images through the other senses.

3. *Spontaneous visualization.* This is an innovative third technique, offered by Dr. Win Wenger in *An Easy Way to Increase Your Intelligence.** Instead of trying to force or concoct imagery from the left brain, we simply allow it to occur spontaneously from

*(Gaithersburg, Md.: Psychogenics Press, 1980) pp. 4–7

the right and describe it in words using the left. You can try this out for yourself using the following steps:

- Find a comfortable spot where you can sit undisturbed for ten minutes.
- (Optional) Set up a tape recorder to record your descriptions for future reference and interpretation.
- Close your eyes, relax, take a few deep breaths, and allow any imagery just to happen.
- When imagery comes, describe it aloud in such detail that someone listening would see what you are seeing. Don't label or explain; just describe in vivid detail.
- If imagery is vague, you might look up (with eyes closed) and scan back and forth. Even if it is vague, describe vividly what is there. Often the process of describing it increases the intensity.
- If imagery doesn't come at all after relaxing for a few minutes and looking up, just start describing, aloud, details of a remembered scene or dream. Again, use vivid detail and describe in the present tense, as if it were happening now. As the detail gets finer, you will notice new details streaming in. Just flow with the new imagery, and it will become clearer.

If you practice this procedure ten minutes a day for a few weeks, you should notice a dramatic improvement in your visualization powers. If you want to experience how sharp and clear the imagery can be, do this procedure as you are lying in bed, just starting to fall asleep.*

The crucial factor here is the vivid description in words (left brain). That demands increased functioning of the corpus collosum.

Be patient. Improvement may be slow at first, but your efforts will be rewarded in increasing creativity and the ability to visualize your success.

---

*Rarely some people do not have visual imagery—even during dreaming. They will dream only in sound and feelings. If you "see" things when you dream, you can visualize.

AUDITORY THINKING

"Dammit, you idiot! Can't you get anything right?" Mark blurted to himself as he double-faulted for the second time during the weekend tennis match he plays for fun and recreation. Powerthinking in the auditory mode involves cleaning up such unsupportive self-talk (A^i) as well as refining listening skills (A^e).

Much has been written recently about the detrimental effects of negative self-talk—most of which we may not be consciously aware of. It is well and good to follow the advice of pop psychologists and consciously change the content of self-talk when we become aware we are beating ourselves up internally. The crucial missing piece, however, is taking advantage of *submodalities*. The *qualities* or your inner voice that are most important for you—the pitch, the pace, the resonance, the tone quality, etc.—can have a more profound effect on you than the content.

The external side of auditory thinking is the art of listening. As crucial as careful listening is for classes, relationships, and business transactions, many of us find it difficult to listen carefully. For this reason a purely auditory activity such as talking on the telephone can be quite stressful in long stretches.

The ear is a remarkable sensory detector. The faintest sound the average person can hear is a millionth of a millionth of the loudest sound we can tolerate. Furthermore, the brain has the remarkable ability of filtering out irrelevant sounds, as when a mother can hear the cry of her baby among many in a nursery, or as lovers hear whispered words through the noise of a party.

An important step toward powerful auditory thinking, then, is to sharpen hearing and listening skills. Five approaches are useful here:

1. *Alternate generalized and focused listening.*[4] Focused listening is having your attention on one sound. Generalized listening is allowing your attention to wander. For example, when you are out on a walk, notice what sound or sounds you are focused on—probably that little voice inside your head. Then notice what you are *not* listening to—the sounds of your footsteps, the sound of the afternoon breeze, birds in the background, etc.

You might do the same at a party. Notice the person you are listening to. Then switch to all the other sounds in the room you've been ignoring. This exercise will not only enhance your awareness of the sounds around you but will also reaffirm your confidence in your ability to focus on sounds and to ignore irrelevant sounds.

2. *Model good listeners.* Model the characteristics we discussed in Chapter Four—looking across to one side (most likely your left side), tilting your head as you do on the phone, and assuming a posture slightly more relaxed than the visual one. Of course, in our culture when someone is talking to you, it is considered polite to look at them, but that isn't the best way to hear them. You might explain that what they are saying is really important to you, and to hear them even better you look to the side.

EXERCISE 13

Your direction of auditory recall is most likely straight across on the same side as your direction of visual recall. Verify this for yourself. Listen carefully now to whatever sound is in the background.

1. Look straight ahead and listen as intently as you can.
2. Next, look straight up and listen carefully.
3. Finally, look straight across or slightly down on the same side as your direction of visual recall (probably to the left), tilt your head, and listen. Move your eyes around a little in this position to see where the sound is the clearest.

No doubt you can hear the sounds in all three positions, but which is most comfortable for you? Musicians and people who are quick to pick up foreign languages usually assume the third position.

---

3. *Listen longer.* It is said that wisdom brings us the ability to listen more than we speak. If you are too quick to respond to what

people say, you may be putting more attention on your response than on what they are saying. It is much wiser to make sure they have finished and to verify that you understand what they are saying before launching into your point of view. Even if you disagree, others will feel complimented that they were heard.

4. *Mirror unconscious mannerisms to establish rapport.* Notice a person's submodalities (the pace, inflections, pitch, etc.) and words, and expressions frequently used. Then, *without being obvious*, mimic those mannerisms. This is a very powerful strategy from NLP used in sales to gain unconscious rapport with potential clients. Being in rapport makes it much easier to listen to what they are saying. In a sense you are stepping into their shoes and making it easier for you to see their viewpoint.

5. *Use sensory overlap.* Do this especially when on the telephone or listening to an instructor or trainer who lectures with no emotion or visual aids. While listening, visualize what the person is talking about, and pay attention to feelings or tactile sensations that may be stirred up by what the person is saying.

KINESTHETIC THINKING
- -

Kinesthetic thinking is the ability to access internal tactile sensations and feelings as well as heightened sensitivity to external touch and movement. Champion athletes and professional dancers rank among the best kinesthetic learners. People who are completely in touch with their emotions and "body language" unconsciously practice kinesthetic thinking.

Powerthinking involves being in touch with movement and tactile sensations in a tennis match or with emotions when sorting through a destructive pattern in an intimate relationship. However, powerthinking can just as well involve shifting away from feelings or emotions if they are counterproductive, such as feeling panic during a test or a phobic reaction at the dentist's. Exercise 14 demonstrates some simple shifting into and out of a kinesthetic state.

EXERCISE 14

Think back to a specific time when you were sad or depressed. Be careful to pick an event you feel okay about now so you won't be depressed for the rest of this chapter. Be in touch with the feelings or events as if they were *happening now.*

Next, look down, take a deep breath, slump your shoulders, and intensify your feelings and body sensations. Immerse yourself in that state.

Now sit straight up, put a big smile on your face, look up, and try to be in touch with those sad or depressed feelings. I'll bet you will find it much more difficult to access those feelings in this visual pose. On the other hand, you probably found it easy in the kinesthetic posture.

This exercise provides one method of shifting out of the state called *panic during a test.* When taking a test, you are naturally looking down to answer the questions. If you should start to panic, looking down will perpetuate those feelings. If you simply shift to a visual posture and look up, the panic may subside.

If you watch champion athletes mentally rehearse just before a competition, you will likely see them looking up in their visual direction to see themselves competing in top form. You will probably see them looking down in the kinesthetic direction to remember how it feels to do the winning movements.

Kinesthetic thinking also involves "listening" to your body—that is, being aware of the sensations of how your body reacts to a potential decision or action. For example, if you are thinking of buying a new sports car, your body will react in subtle or sometimes not so subtle ways if you have misgivings—one way or the other. Paying attention to such feelings should not necessarily be the basis of your decision, but it can certainly bring inner conflict to your conscious awareness. Your body does not lie.

At the onset of fatigue, most of us want to run away from the feelings through coffee, diversions, or ignoring the feelings. The next time you feel fatigue, try the opposite approach. By briefly being in touch with your body and its experience of fatigue, you can actively facilitate the body's natural production of neurotransmitters to switch out of that state. On the other hand, the experience may convince you of the wisdom of taking a nap.

Allowing your attention to briefly be with all the sensations happening in your body can also enhance a pleasant perceptual experience, such as a sunset or your favorite musicians in concert. It grounds you in the experience of yourself as well as what your senses are experiencing.

The power you gain through powerthinking methods is not only the ability to recognize your mode of thinking (right brain/left brain or VAK), but also the ability to deliberately shift your mode to match the learning task, the desired state, or the social situation at hand. This is the tool to balance thinking and feeling.

PART THREE

*M*EMORY
*S*TATES

CHAPTER SIX

How to Improve

YOUR MEMORY

I'll never forget what's his name.

—Norman Pliscou

The famous memory expert Harry Loraine once memorized the first three hundred pages of the Manhattan telephone directory—over thirty thousand names and numbers.[1] He believes that developing a good memory is easy. It is like developing any other skill, such as driving a car or learning to use a computer.

Memory performs the remarkable function of connecting the past with the present. Without it we would wake up each morning not knowing our name, how to speak, how to make breakfast, or how to get dressed. When people claim to have poor memories, they are focusing on the small fraction of facts they temporarily cannot recall, as opposed to the enormous majority of life they do remember.

Memory is our constant companion[2]—our tutor, our library, the poet with whom we all travel. It allows life to become simpler from birth through adulthood as we learn from experience and are better able to act more efficiently in new situations. Furthermore, memory is the basis of analytical reasoning, decision making, and problem solving.

HOW MEMORY WORKS

Donny had just gotten up enough courage at the party to introduce himself to Carla and strike up a conversation. They hit it off well, and he asked for her phone number as she was leaving. Neither of them had anything to write with, so he decided to impress her by memorizing the number after hearing it just once.

As she left he knew he had about fifteen seconds to find a paper and pencil to write it down. He pictured the numbers, made a few associations with them, and tested himself over graduated intervals to encode the number effectively into his long-term memory. A few days later, when he phoned her, he still knew her number by heart.

This illustrates the "three r's" of memory—*reception* of the information into short-term memory, *registration* or *encoding* the material into long-term memory, and *recalling* it back out of long-term memory. The first two processes take place automatically, but recall depends on the quality of encoding. The more associations you make with the material, the easier it is to recall. The secret of memory training is to transfer the material as quickly as possible from short-term to long-term memory with encoding that makes it easy to access. Forgetful people have recall problems, not memory problems.

No one knows the exact mechanics of how memory is created and stored, but we do know some of the details. Short-term memory, which gives you enough time to get a telephone number from directory assistance and dial the number, lasts up to about fifteen seconds. Short-term memory seems to be related to electrical activity in the brain, where electrical impulses travel from neuron to neuron along axons and dendrites. Memory formation involves creation of neurotransmiters, which in turn facilitate the passage of electrical impulses. The electrical signals and neurotransmitters somehow change the neurons, leaving behind a "memory trace"—probably through the formation of certain proteins.

Long-term memory—such as remembering your name, how to tie your shoes, and your personal history—usually lasts a lifetime, although recall may become more problematic with age. Interestingly, a relatively recent study[3] shows that short-term memory seems to be more effective earlier in the day, while long-term memory seems to work better later in the day.

The brain's memory center seems to be an S-shaped ridge in the hippocampus, with some memory stored in the cerebral cortex. As discussed in Chapter Three, memory of auditory words and verbal detail is more associated with left-brain functioning, while memory of pictures, images, spatial relationships, and emotions is more associated with the right. Beyond that, we can categorize memory into seven types:[4]

1. *Unconscious processes*—remembering how to breathe, how to digest food, and instinctual memory.
2. *Sensual memory*—remembering the feeling of a warm bath or how a strawberry tastes.
3. *Skills*—remembering how to swim, how to write, how to walk.
4. *Language*—remembering the meanings of all the words and phrases you commonly use.
5. *Facts*—remembering the number of feet in a mile, how to spell, how to balance your checkbook.
6. *Past events*—remembering the first time you fell in love or last year's birthday party.
7. *Future plans*—wanting to remember to get a birthday present for your friend or to put out the garbage for tomorrow morning's pickup.

Each type of memory except item 1 can involve visual, auditory, and kinesthetic recall, and almost everybody has nearly a perfect memory for items 1 through 4. What usually concerns us is items five through 7, and even here, the problem is effective encoding and recall, as opposed to memory.

As children most of us learned basic factual material by "over-learning"—endless repetition of our address, "ABC's," multiplication tables, etc. As we become older such brute-force tactics became tedious, boring, and exhausting. The bad news is that many of us were left with a negative association or *anchor* that memorizing is not fun. The good news is that there are much easier and more effective ways to remember. In fact, mere repetition may have a dulling, hypnotic effect and may not enhance memory, as Exercise 15 illustrates.

EXERCISE 15

Right now, without looking, describe and roughly sketch the back of a dime. You probably handle dimes thousands of times per year. Speak out or jot down whatever features you can remember.

If you don't remember much detail, don't be alarmed. You are probably in the majority.

I wonder how many times you have had an experience like this: You are working on a project when you get distracted and look over at a newspaper. The article is about an increase in the price of gasoline, so you think about the Middle East. That reminds you of Africa, at which point you think of the drought in Ethiopia, and your thought turns to food. Now you start to feel hungry, when suddenly it occurs to you that you were supposed to meet your friend at a restaurant five minutes ago, so off you go. The association of one idea with another is the basic mechanics of effective encoding and recall.

Trying to recall one unconnected memory among millions of others would be like walking into a library and finding the books arranged at random with no numbering system. The more organized the numbering system, the easier it will be to find a book. In a similar way, the more visual, auditory, and kinesthetic associations we use to encode new knowledge, the easier it will be to access the memory. The overlearning we endured as children may have been necessary to some extent because we didn't have as much prior knowledge to associate with new information.

EXERCISE 16

Start with the first line, with a sequence of five shapes. Glance at it for up to four seconds and then write down the sequence on a piece of paper without looking back. After you finish, check your results.

Now go on to the next line, with a sequence of six shapes. Again glance at it for up to four seconds and write down the sequence without looking back. Once you've reconstructed it, again check your results. Continue with the longer sequences.

FIGURE 6.1

Most people find it increasingly difficult to remember the sequence as they get to seven or more shapes.

THE MAGIC NUMBER SEVEN

George Miller[5] of Harvard University discovered that the average person can retain up to about seven items in short-term memory—seven new names at a party, seven numbers, seven items on a grocery list.

Miller discovered further that each of the seven units could consist of several items, and this would expand the number of items we can remember. As an example, we commonly break telephone numbers down into groups or "chunks"—for example, 1–408–967–3359, and perhaps another 3157 as a credit card number.

The process of breaking down a larger number of items into smaller chunks is called "downchunking." As another example, most of use probably learned Mississippi as Miss-iss-ippi, and the ABC's as ABCD—EFG—HIJK . . .

A reverse process to this, called "upchunking," is seeing the larger picture. Children with reading disorders are often still sounding out words one letter at a time, as they did in the first grade, instead of seeing whole words or short phrases as a single unit.

Downchunking, or breaking the material down into smaller units, is probably more a left-brain process. Upchunking, or seeing the bigger picture, is more likely a right-brain process.

A few additional features of memory are important to understand.

EXERCISE 17

Read through the following list of words at your normal pace without going back over any of them.

1. spoon
2. and
3. bread
4. squirrel
5. napkin
6. candy
7. when
8. dog
9. plate
10. there
11. salt
12. bird
13. cup
14. of
15. coffee
16. frog
17. King Kong
18. over
19. carrot
20. knife

Now, from memory, write down as many words as you can remember.

As you compare the words you remembered, you may notice several things about them. First, you may have remembered more words from the beginning. This is called the *primacy effect*—we tend to remember more from the first part of a class, a study session, or people we meet at a party.

You may have remembered more words from the end. This is called the *regency effect*, wherein memory is enhanced toward the end of the time period. You remember more from the end of a class period, what you've just read, or the last few items on a grocery list. These two effects together give a memory curve that looks like that shown in Figure 6.2.

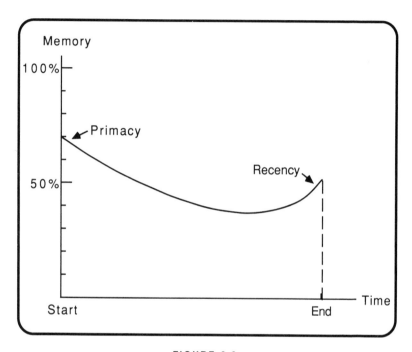

FIGURE 6.2

Another point is that you probably remembered "King Kong," because it stood out from the rest of the words. This principle, the *Von Restorff Effect*, is that unusual, colorful, or humorous items are easier to remember. What is even more interesting is that you probably remembered the words just before and just after "King Kong." Unusual words tend to "highlight" the words around them. This modifies the memory curve to look like that shown in Figure 6.3.

One last observation is that you may have grouped the words into the categories in which they fall—foodware, animals, food, and abstract words. Even though the words were not presented in groups, our unconscious looks for patterns and ways to organize things. As we'll see later, organizing by itself is a powerful memory tool.

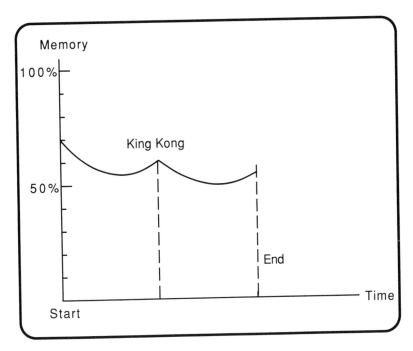

FIGURE 6.3

THE HISTORY OF MEMORY

One of the oldest systematic methods of memory began twenty-five
hundred years ago, when Simonides of Ceos delivered a poorly
received lyrical poem to an audience. Shortly after he left the room, the
roof collapsed, killing many of the guests. Simonides was asked to help
identify the guests, many of whom were no longer recognizable. By
recalling where each guest was sitting, he was able to identify them.

From this tragedy Cicero developed one of the first systems of
mnemonics (pronounced neh-mon-iks)—associating items to be remembered with places in a room. This system was useful in the ancient
world, where not all knowledge was written. Roman orators later
adapted this system to deliver speeches by the system of loci—
associating each part of a speech with a place in their home. To deliver
a speech they would mentally take a walk around their home, and each

location would remind them of that part of the speech. This practice is still reflected in our language by the phrases "in the first place," "in the second place," etc.

St. Thomas Aquinas in the thirteenth century revived some of Aristotle's ideas on memory and formulated laws of remembering, a few of which connect with the modern neurolinguistic programming concept of *memory anchors*. St. Thomas observed that one memory evokes another if they are similar, if they are opposite, or if they occur simultaneously. Also, the more vivid the association, the easier it is to remember.

The father of modern experimental memory research was Hermann Ebbinghaus, who conducted experiments in Germany from 1879 to 1885. He knew the strong effects of association and meaning on memory, so he eliminated these factors in his research by trying to remember long lists of nonsense syllables like wux, zop, trefth, etc.

He soon discovered a law of forgetting—that after learning these lists, forgetting was highest just after learning the words, and gradually decreased with time. On average, 50 percent of the words were forgotten within one hour, 60 percent within nine hours, and 80 percent within a month.[6] Recall of the words can be graphed as shown in Figure 6.4.

Research since Ebbinghaus has confirmed the shape of his forgetting curve, with two qualifications: (1) The greater the meaning and the interest level, the slower the rate of forgetting, and (2) the reminiscent effect: For a few minutes to ten minutes after a class or study session, recall increases as we unconsciously integrate the material. These two qualifications modify the curve shown in Figure 6.5.

By taking the opposite approach as Ebbinghaus and including association, organization, meaning, and interest, we can greatly reduce the rate of forgetting.

WHY WE FORGET

Have you ever begun to introduce two friends and forgotten one of their names? Or maybe you left your keys in a "safe" place, only to find they've disappeared when you go to find them. Memory lapses, a common annoyance for many of us when we are younger, can become terrifying as we get older.

On the other hand, remembering small, seemingly insignificant

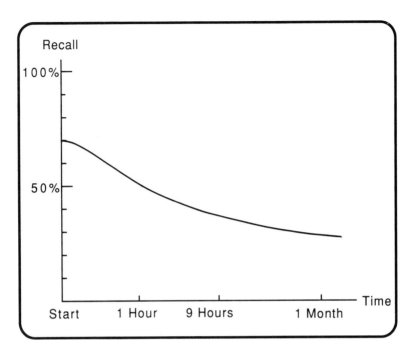

FIGURE 6.4

details about someone can be regarded as flattery. I remember walking into Ronnie's Shoe Store in San Jose, California, to buy a new pair of shoes. The owner struck up a conversation and seemed genuinely interested in learning about me. A year later, when I walked into the same store, the owner immediately said, "Oh, aren't you the physics professor over at West Valley College?" As you can imagine, I've bought all my shoes from him ever since.

Forgetfulness can happen in four ways:

1. We draw a complete blank.
2. The information is "on the tip of our tongue," and we feel frustrated with not being able to access it.
3. Recall is incomplete.
4. Wires get crossed, and we "remember" what's not so.

Again, it's doubtful that we actually forget, but why we have difficulty recalling is not completely known. Seven factors may contribute:

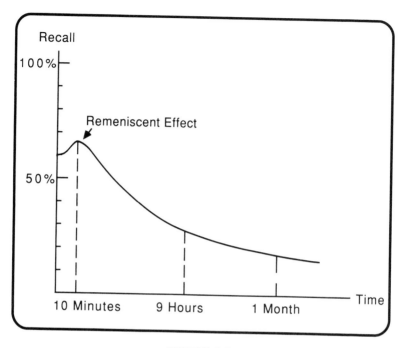

Recall

100%

Remeniscent Effect

50%

10 Minutes   9 Hours   1 Month   Time

FIGURE 6.5

1. *Memory "traces"* may fade with time. Perhaps the cellular protein changes that took place to store memory revert back to their original state, like house paint eventually fading with exposure to sunlight. This once-popular theory has been widely replaced with the "interference theory."

2. *Interference*—as we accumulate more memories, the brain has increasing difficulty distinguishing among them, especially memories with similar associations or meaning. The problem is not so much one of overcrowding as of not having a specific enough retrieval system.

3. *Negative thinking* based on self-talk such as "I have such poor memory," "I can never remember anything," or "I must be getting old because my memory's shot" can help program the brain to bring about these self-fulfilling prophesies.

4. *Absentmindedness* happens when we don't think about what we're doing and function on "automatic pilot." Poor encoding results by not paying attention, thinking the information is not important, or not understanding it in the first place.

5. *Freud's repressive forgetting* occurs when certain memories are painful, threatening to the individual, or conflict with a person's values or beliefs.
6. *Smoking* decreases blood oxygen and adds significant amounts of carbon monoxide to the circulatory system, with adverse effects on the heart, lungs, psychomotor functioning, and memory. In one study,[7] smokers experienced a 24 percent reduction in memory after just one cigarette.
7. *Alcohol* and other drugs measurably impair memory.[8]

A pertinent question related to forgetting is: How much do we really want to remember? One estimate[9] is that we can recall about one of every hundred bits of information we encounter in daily life. The famous Spanish writer Jorge Luis Borges tells the story[10] of a boy who fell off of a horse and suddenly could remember literally everything that happened to him—the shape of each leaf on every tree he passed, each word in every conversation with each person he encountered. Life became like viewing a color print too close and seeing the individual dots instead of the whole picture; he became an idiot.

Perhaps some memory loss with age is more a matter of unconscious wisdom in choosing to remember only what's important. This may be valuable as long as we have the *choice* to forget what we want and can just as easily remember.

SIX TIPS FOR A SHARPER MEMORY

Since most of us have cultivated the ability to forget, how can we better develop the choice to remember? For especially difficult memory material such as Japanese vocabulary words or the names of bones and muscles, the supermemory techniques presented in Chapter Eight constitute the most effective approach. In this section we will explore six powerful strategies to improve memory in general. In Chapter Seven we will focus specifically on techniques to improve visual, auditory, and kinesthetic recall.

1. *Set up a state conducive to memory.* A restful, relaxed state with your physiology is useful to improve memory. For your IR's, motivation and interest are the strongest driving forces to

improve memory. If you are not motivated or interested in what you want to remember, imagine what it would be like if you were. How would you feel? How would things sound? How would they look?

2. *Make memory sensory.* Were you to learn the rare English word *mackel*, meaning "a blurred print," you could tie in the information with your senses in one of three ways.

- *Visual imagery.* You might notice that mackel sounds a bit like mackerel, so you might imagine (V^i) a mackerel jumping up and down on a piece of paper, blurring the print. Thus you could remember "mackel—a blurred print" using that internal visual image.

- *Auditory imagery.* You might speak the word and its definition aloud (A^e) and then imagine yourself speaking it aloud (A^i). You might speak it, whisper it, and subvocalize it a couple of times. Either approach establishes an auditory recall.

- *Kinesthetic Imagery.* You might write the word and its definition (K^e), and then imagine yourself writing it (K^i). Get one of those four-colored pens and print the definition in capital letters, switch colors and print it in small letters, switch again and write it in script. Writing something in upper case, lower case, and script a few times produces imagery that is both kinesthetic and visual. If you speak as you write the definition, you add the auditory and thus cover the senses.

From my personal experience, kinesthetic imagery is most useful in technical fields such as mathematics, computer programming, and accounting. As a graduate student in physics, I had long equations with complicated derivations to memorize. I was not familiar with sensory memory techniques, but I discovered that if I simply wrote out the material a few times, I had it memorized. I find that most people attending my seminars instinctively do the same.

Another approach to make memory more kinesthetic is to connect it with feelings and emotions. People who remember the day John F. Kennedy was assassinated have never forgotten the fine details of what they were doing that day. If you think of a day that was especially traumatic—the death of a close friend or relative—or a day that was an emotional high point for you, you probably have a similar experience with unusual recall of details. Connecting memory with emotions relates to the NLP concept of anchors we'll be discussing later.

3. *Use graduated interval recall.* This is a powerful strategy to encode memory from short-term to long-term painlessly. Although the general strategy has been known for some time, the Sybervision® Corporation has recently popularized contributions made to this method by Dr. Paul Pimsleur, who applied the method to foreign-language acquisition.[11]

   Dr. Pimsleur realized that the pure-repetition method of most foreign-language courses has a dulling, hypnotic effect and is not particularly effective. A powerful alternative is to ask the learner to reproduce a word or phrase at certain time intervals. The timing is crucial. If the interval between learning and being tested is too short or too long, the encoding loses effectiveness.

   After learning new material, the learner is immediately tested. After a certain time interval, the learner is retested. Subsequent intervals become longer, allowing a smooth transition from short to stable long-term memory.

   Sybervision® and Powerlearning® Systems have each structured foreign-language courses using this principle. Sybervision® claims that nine of ten people using this method can acquire a 1 + level of fluency* practicing one-half hour per day for only thirty days. I have personally experienced this and can verify the claims are true.

   If you were learning Japanese words, technical definitions, or names at a party, you might proceed like this:

- Repeat the word or definition as you learn it.
- Test yourself on it within about eight to twelve seconds (transfer short-term to long-term memory).
- Test yourself again within thirty to fifty seconds (optional).
- Test yourself again within ninety seconds to three minutes (optional).

*Conversationally "intermediate high" as established by the FSI (U.S. government's Foreign Service Institute).

• Test yourself again within five to ten minutes.
• At this point you should have secured a good encoding for long-term memory. A few more reviews following a pattern given in Chapter Ten will further stabilize your long-term memory.

This pattern is particularly useful for auditory information such as foreign words or people's names. Of all the senses, auditory is the most difficult for most people to remember. This pattern is also an ideal structure for audio cassette tapes you can listen to while commuting. As you practice, you may require fewer repetitions than the pattern, and you can follow the timing guidelines in a general way that works for you.

EXERCISE 18

What are the two missing letters in the following sequence? J I H G F E _ _ B A. Of course, it's easy to recognize the alphabet backward and the missing "D" and "C."

See if you can identify the missing letters in Figure 6.6.

This pattern is not so obvious, so if you haven't already done so, read the letters as in Figure 6.7

You can now easily identify each missing letter as a "Y" and can memorize the exact sequence immediately. If you know the letters but not the pattern, it would take some brute-force memorizing to remember it. Even with that, you would probably forget the sequence as quickly as you memorized it.

---

1. *Look for principles and patterns of organization.* In one study at Stanford University,[12] two groups were each given 112 words to learn. One group was instructed to sort the words into four categories: occupations, animals, forms of transportation, and clothing items. The other group just learned the words at random. The sorters were able to learn two to three times more words than the random memorizers.

   In fact, other studies[13] have shown that organization by itself

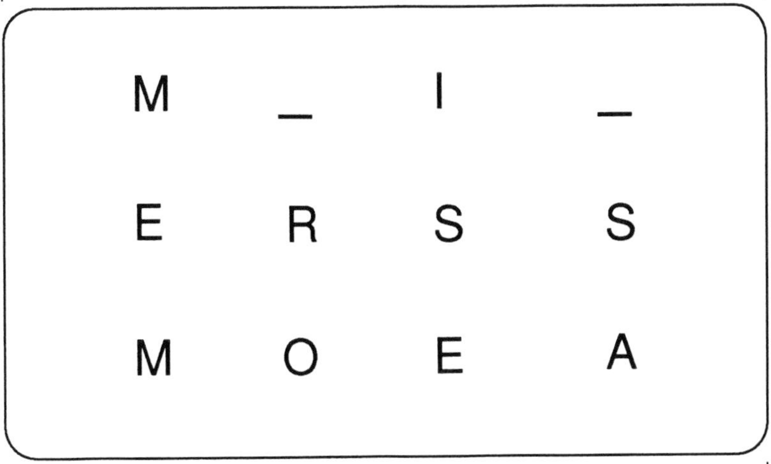

M   _   I   _

E   R   S   S

M   O   E   A

FIGURE 6.6

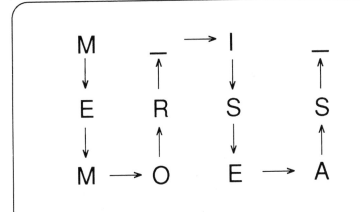

FIGURE 6.7

is just as effective as memorizing. George Korona[14] describes a study in which two groups were each given three minutes to learn a sequence of numbers. One group looked for principles while the other group just memorized. After three minutes the recall of each of the two groups was about the same. However, after three weeks none of the memorizers remembered the sequence, while 23 percent of the principle recognizers still remembered all the numbers.

Organizing material into meaningful patterns promotes active involvement and personal meaning, both of which enhance memory. This is one reason why note taking can be useful—particularly pattern discovery maps. This also explains the value of studying the grammatical structure of a foreign language.

2. *Future pace, a desired memory with a sensory stimulus.* The term *future pace*, used in NLP, is the process of projecting a desired behavior into future situations that might test that behavior. If you need to stop at the post office on the way to work, imagine the scenery you will naturally see as you approach the vicinity of the post office, and visualize yourself remembering to stop off. If the visual image of the scenery is anchored strongly enough with the feeling of remembering, seeing the scenery will automatically trigger the memory. Similarly, you might future-pace the sound of a friend's voice to remind you to ask if you can borrow her tennis racquet.

3. *Make memory a habit.* Good memory is a skill. The more you practice and trust the workings of your unconscious, along with avoiding negative self talk about your memory and having to rely on elaborate lists, the sharper your memory will become. These simple techniques should help memory become part of everyday life.

CHAPTER SEVEN

VISUAL, AUDITORY, AND KINESTHETIC MEMORY

It's not so astonishing the number of things I can't remember, as the number of things I can remember that aren't so.

—MARK TWAIN

Artists and photographers often have extraordinary recall of visual detail. Composers and expert debaters can usually remember fine nuances of sound and words most of us would find insignificant, while athletes and dancers are superb with remembering psychomotor skills and movement. In this chapter we will focus on developing specific skills to access visual, auditory, and kinesthetic memories.

ENHANCING YOUR VISUAL RECALL

Most people have a much better visual memory than they think. The ability to close the eyes and see vivid detail in sharp focus and color is quite rare. Instead, most of us see more vague images, with just enough general structure and form to allow us to act and make decisions. One study[1] on five hundred people showed that 97 percent of them had some visual imagery, even if vague; 92 percent also had auditory imagery—they could imagine words or sounds.

Ralph N. Haber[2] of the University of Rochester showed subjects twenty-five hundred pictures during seven hours spread over three days. They saw a new picture every ten seconds. After viewing all the slides, they saw three hundred pairs of pictures—one they had seen and another, similar picture they hadn't seen. At that point they were asked to identify the picture they had seen. In some cases they were given a reversed, mirror image of the one they had seen. The results were that the subjects averaged 85 to 90 percent correct. In fact, even when the study was repeated and viewing the photos was speeded up ten times, the scores were still high. The evidence in this and other studies indicates that visual recall is nearly perfect for most of us.

In another study[3] it was found that we can all improve memory by using visual imagery. People with vague, indistinct images were able to improve memory to 70 percent when given instruction to visualize what they were to remember. People with sharp, clear visual images were able to improve to 95 percent. What is fascinating is that each group had about the same *change* or *increase*. Of course, if we can learn to improve the clarity of what we visualize, our memory will improve. Here are some ways to sharpen your visual memory:

1. *Carefully observe an object.* Pick one object each day—preferably something interesting or amusing—and spend a few minutes studying it. Later in the day, recall as many details about the object as you can. Then compare your memory with the object to see how you did. With a little practice you'll be surprised how your visual recall improves.
2. *Assume visual recall training.*
   • visual posture (upright), breathing (shallow and high in the chest), and your eye position.
   • sensory overlap
   • spontaneous visualization

REMEMBERING WHAT YOU'VE HEARD
- -

"What do you mean, where is dinner? You promised to take me out tonight," snapped Don. "I didn't say that. You promised me you'd make lasagne for us," retorted Doris.

Most of our interpersonal communication and classroom learning involve the auditory mode, yet of the three types of memory—visual, auditory, and kinesthetic—most of us find auditory to be the least reliable. The problem has two parts: recalling what you heard, and listening carefully in the first place.

When listening to a conversation or a lecture, there are six ways to improve your listening skills and thus the likelihood of remembering what you heard.[4]

1. *W.I.I.F.M?* Think, "What's in it for me?" If you are clearly aware of how you might benefit from listening, you are more than halfway toward setting up an appropriate state.
2. *Notice the mode of delivery but only judge the content.* It has been estimated that only 7 percent of the message in conversation is communicated with words,[5] 38 percent of the message lies in voice inflections and perceived attitudes about the person, and 55 percent is based on nonverbal body language. That is why we are often more affected by how someone says something vs. what they actually said.
3. *Distractions.* When you become aware of being distracted from what the person is saying, easily and gently bring your attention back. Getting upset with yourself or the outside distraction only compounds the interruption.
4. *Pay attention to your physiology.* Careful listening is work. Periodic stretching, walking, and breaks help maintain long-term focus.
5. *For boring or hard-to-follow speakers.* Take the viewpoint of a strongly opposed critic. Expert debaters have learned to listen carefully for holes in the opponent's argument and points to refute. You might also imagine that you were going to write a critique of the talk. How would you be listening to write a convincing article taking the opposite viewpoint of the speaker?
6. *Assume auditory recall training.*
   • eyes in your direction (toward one side)
   • listening longer
   • generalized and focused listening
   • mirroring unconscious mannerisms
   • sensory overlap in purely auditory situations (e.g., the telephone)

To recall what you've heard after listening, use pattern discovery maps during a lecture or after a conversation to construct a picture of what was said and to engage a more whole-brain approach to memory. By incorporating these methods to improve your listening and hearing skills, you will find your sensory experience of life richer. Also, it will be less likely that information will go "in one ear and out the other."

KINESTHETIC RECALL AND MEMORY ANCHORS

Kinesthetic memory, like visual memory, is nearly perfect for most people. If you haven't ridden a bicycle or gone swimming for five years, you probably won't have to start over to relearn these skills. Of course, remembering the subtleties of finely tuned psychomotor skills, such as controlling your ace serve in tennis, is the subject of peak-performance research in athletics and dance.

You can enhance kinesthetic recall in a couple of ways:

1. *Assume kinesthetic recall training.*

   • a relaxed posture
   • deep diaphragm breathing
   • looking down

2. *Use memory anchors.* This is a nice way to take advantage of the kinesthetic component of memory. A *memory anchor* occurs when we have an intense emotional or tactile kinesthetic experience and something else happens coincidentally. The unconscious then links them together in the future.

   Have you ever walked into a department store and smelled a perfume you haven't smelled in ten years? You feel yourself pulled back in time. Or maybe you are driving down the highway listening to the radio. A song comes on that was popular when you were in high school, and suddenly you are back on a date in your junior year. The stimulus of the smell or the music was enough to "fire" the anchor—to elicit feelings, sights, or sounds connected or anchored to the stimulus.

   A bizarre example of a memory anchor was illustrated with scuba divers[5] in a study done by Drs. Alan D. Baddeley and

Duncan R. Godden. The divers were given forty unrelated words to remember while they were under water. Half of the group was tested on the words out of the water, while the other half was tested under water. The ones tested under water remembered twice as many words as the dry testers.

This and many other studies suggest that our mood and the environment become anchored to what we are learning. Thus, re-creating the mood and the environment can help facilitate recall. Certainly happy occurrences evoke happy memories, and a depressed state evokes depressing memories. Likewise, if you can study and succeed answering questions in the same room you will be tested in, this can facilitate recall when you are tested.

Memory anchors have influenced pioneers in accelerated learning methods like Dr. Donald Schuster of Iowa State University in Ames to beautify their learning environment with plants, posters, subliminal messages, stately music, and color—partly to engage the right brain in the learning process better and partly to anchor learning to that beauty.

Many students incur too much stress during last-minute study for a test. Then when they take the test, they experience the same tension and stress. And guess what? It works. The stimulus of the stress fires the anchor of the memory. On the other hand, people using super memory techniques in Chapter Eight learn the material in a relaxed, nurturing, playful environment. Taking the test in that same environment again fires the memory anchor. Now think about it. Which way would you rather learn?

In his research Dr. Schuster has discovered that someone who is used to stressful learning may initially not do as well when taught stress-free learning. After some practice, however, this learning becomes more effective than the old way.

DISCOVERING YOUR MAGIC KEY FOR MEMORY

One of the most powerful ways to engage your senses to improve memory is to discover your personal key or formula for remembering. This is the specific sequence of internal and external visual, auditory, and kinesthetic images you already use when you're most successful at remembering.

EXERCISE 19: YOUR MEMORY AND LEARNING KEY

1. To begin, think of a specific time in the past when you remembered something especially well. Mentally put yourself back in that situation. It is crucial you engage as much of that experience as possible as if it were *happening now*.

2. What is the first thing necessary for you to have a strong memory? Did you need to *see* what you wanted to remember (visual external: V^e), or *hear* someone tell you about it (auditory external: A^e), or move with it, get a *feeling* for it, or write it down (kinesthetic external: K^e)? Again, focus on that very *first* thing that had to happen. Chances are it will be the same as your primary modality discovered in the internal representation assessment test.

3. Once you have seen, heard, or felt what you want to remember, what happens inside? Do you picture or visualize it (visual internal: V^i), or hear an internal voice repeating it inside (auditory internal: A^i), or perhaps get a sense or feeling of what you want to remember, or feel it in your body (kinesthetic internal: K^i)?

4. What happens next? Do you need to see it again, hear more about, explain it to someone, or do it (V^e, A^e, or K^e)? Or do you further process it internally with pictures, sounds, or feelings (V^i, A^i, or K^i)?

5. There may be additional steps involving internal or external processing, although the whole sequence typically involves only two to four steps.

6. The last step is when you *know* that you remember it correctly. How do you *know* that you know it? Quite often this is an internal sense or feeling (K^i), although it could also be an internal auditory or visual comparison (A^i or V^i).

7. Once you have listed the steps, you might construct a pattern discovery map with the information. To complete and refine your key, add submodalities that enhance various steps.

The exact sequence of steps in this key is like a recipe. If you do the steps in the proper order, you get the results. If you reverse any of the steps, it doesn't work.

As an example, my key to understand and remember physics is first to read it V^e and try to sense how it works K^i. I then write and problem-solve with it K^e. I try to see the whole picture V^i, and finally know that I understand it K^i. Sometimes I add a step just before the last of explaining it to someone else (A^e), since my formula doesn't otherwise have an auditory component. Thus my key is as in Figure 7.1.

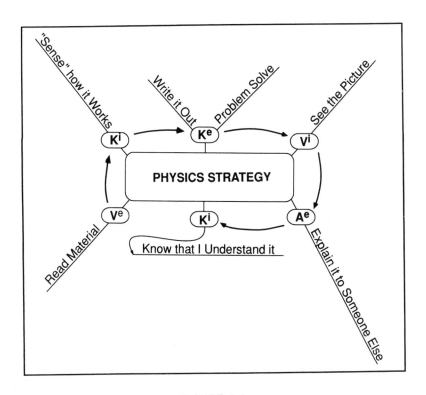

FIGURE 7.1

A NEW APPROACH TO MNEMONICS

When we read books on memory, we find instructions to create associations, visualizations, and other *mnemonic* devices to aid memory. The word *mnemonic* means an associative device designed to aid memory. Examples of mnemonics may include:

- You meet a lady, Dana Crosby. To remember her name, you imagine a Great *Dane* with her face getting stung by a *cross bee*.
- You want to remember the rare English word *kidcote*, meaning jail. You might imagine Billy the *Kid* wearing a *coat* in jail.
- You're trying to remember the Portuguese word *noz* (pronounced nawsh), meaning walnut. You might imagine a walnut feeling nauseous.

Books on memory are consistent in telling us we should create associations for memory, but no one provides a systematic way to create these mnemonic connections. Some people who read memory books can naturally think of associations, but many of us find the process time-consuming, tedious, and not applicable to most of what we need to remember.

I ask my seminar participants, "If you had a systematic process to create mentally the kinds of images and associations we've talked about, how could you use that personally? Would it even be useful to you personally?" Participants respond that if they did have such a system, they could use it to remember

- names and faces
- historical dates
- vocabulary words
- foreign words
- shopping lists

A method I've developed strongly facilitates creation of these associations and uses pattern discovery maps. To illustrate how you might use a map to create a visual picture or mnemonic device, imagine you were studying technical terms or vocabulary words and you come across the rare English word *basiate*, which means "to kiss." Split the word into syllables, with each syllable being the center of a pattern discovery map. The entire meaning can also be a map center. The centers would then look as in Figure 7.2.

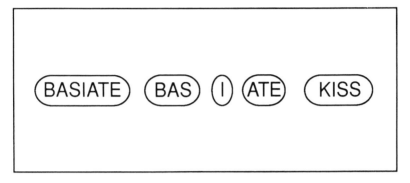

FIGURE 7.2

Now create three or four connections or associations from each syllable and the meaning. A connection can be

- a similar-sounding word
- a word you are reminded of
- another word that contains the syllable
- a rhymed word

For "bas" you might think of words such as fish, basket, bass, and shoes. For "I" you might think of me, eye, and aye. For "ate" you might be reminded of eat, food, the number 8, and the rhymed word mate. For the meaning "kiss" perhaps pucker, love, candy, and the rock band named Kiss. Adding these connections creates something like that shown in Figure 7.3.

It takes about a minute or two to do this process. But once you've gone through it, it is unlikely you'll forget the meaning. Instead of having just the words, you've now created a picture. Pictures are always easier to remember than words. However, something else may happen in the process. You might think of a story connecting basiate with kiss—connecting a few but not all of the associations.

For example, you might imagine a largemouth *bass* giving you a *kiss* just before you *ate* it. Or maybe I got a *bass* for *me* at *8*:00 P.M. so I could

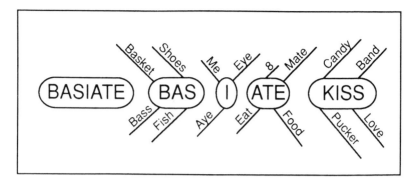

FIGURE 7.3

play with the *Kiss* band. Perhaps *I* took a candy *kiss* out of the *bas*ket and gave it to my m*ate*.

Look at all the possibilities for creating a story from the map, as opposed to just looking at the definition. The picture is sufficient and the story is not necessary, but creating the story makes the process more fun.

EXERCISE 20

Try this process out for yourself with the rare English word *kidcote*, meaning jail.

Sometimes when people first see this process, it seems like too much work just to connect the word with its meaning. In my seminars, I usually ask how many participants have ever taken tennis lessons. To those who respond, I ask if they remember the first day on the court: Ready position . . . pivot sideways on the balls of your feet . . . all right, racket head back, perpendicular to the ground . . . now swing low to high . . . remember to follow through . . . on and on. By the time you tried to do all that, the ball was likely back at the fence. It probably seemed awkward and mechanical. With practice, however, you began to flow properly through the movement without thinking about it. It's like that with this process.

Probably the only difference between you and a memory expert who can get onstage and name a hundred names and addresses of people in the audience is that the memory expert does something similar to the mapping process unconsciously and automatically. For you it is initially a mechanical process, but with time it gets easier, quicker, and more automatic.

In my experience studying foreign languages, I find that many Spanish, French, and German words are so similar to English that I don't have to do anything special to learn them. With other words, however, I couldn't begin to imagine how they connect with English. By using the mapping technique, I can always create a picture and often a story for each word. For a list of words I use a stack of 3″ by 5″ cards, with one map on each card.

This technique to create mnemonics systematically is the last of the memory secrets used unconsciously by the best visual, auditory, and kinesthetic learners. With practice we can begin to develop the seemingly elusive perceptual and memory skills of the artists, composers, athletes, and dancers we all admire.

CHAPTER EIGHT

SUPERMEMORY

Man's mind, stretched to a new idea, never goes back to its original dimension.

—OLIVER WENDELL HOLMES

Is it really possible to learn a foreign language in one month or to speed up learning three to ten times? This is what the authors of the popular book *Superlearning* claim. Can learning and memory be accelerated yet be stress-free? This chapter presents a practical introduction to super-memory techniques based on Superlearning®,* my training in these methods, and my years of experience training others to use them in my Powerlearning® seminars given throughout the United States.

BACKGROUND OF SUPERMEMORY METHODS

Six thousand years ago, before the advent of written language, techniques related to Superlearning® probably flourished. Supermemory may have been a tool of necessity—the only way to pass down

---

*Superlearning® is the registered trademark and service mark of Superlearning® Inc., 450 Seventh Avenue, New York, N.Y. 10123

folklore, legend, and practical knowledge for survival. The techniques were most likely rooted in music, chants, drama, rhythm, and emotion. Even today some cultures, such as the Maoris in New Zealand,[1] display remarkable feats of memory. One leader, Chief Kau Matana, could reportedly recite the entire history of their tribe in three days without notes, and their history covers forty-five generations extending over a thousand years. In India, pundits routinely memorize their religious scriptures in case a catastrophe destroys all the books.

In the 1950s Dr. Georgi Lozanov,[2] a Bulgarian physician and psychologist, began a systematic study of those few people left today with the gift of extraordinary memory, concentration, and learning ability. His Ph.D. thesis was a study on the application of suggestion to medicine and education. Of special interest to him were people having hypermnesia or "photographic memory," as well as Indian yogis and pundits with remarkable mental skills.

He wondered if there were any patterns in how they learn and concentrate, or any systematic methods. In his research, he discovered certain patterns of rhythm, relaxation, music, and breathing that convinced him that we all can develop supermemory skills. Lozanov then combined his observations with his own ideas from psychotherapy to develop a system called *Suggestopedia*.

Two American adaptations of Suggestopedia are now popularly called SALT (Suggestive Accelerative Learning and Teaching) and Superlearning®. My approach to supermemory incorporates methods from these adaptations together with principles from NLP, pattern discovery maps, and keys.

In any case, Lozanov tested his new system with foreign languages and other types of education and training. The results were phenomenal. Reports began circulating of people learning a thousand foreign words in one day, becoming fluent in a foreign language within one month, and speeding up learning ten to fifty times.

Word of these techniques first reached the West through *Psychic Discoveries Behind the Iron Curtain** by Sheila Ostrander and Lynn Schroeder in 1970. Dr. Jane Bancroft, a professor at Scarborough College of the University of Toronto, was one of the first North American scholars to contact Lozanov and actually see firsthand what he was doing. Dr. Donald Schuster, a psychology professor at Iowa State University in Ames, read the initial account in *Psychic Discoveries*.

*(Englewood Cliffs: Prentice Hall, 1970)

With very little knowledge of the specifics of the methodology, Dr. Schuster, Ray Benitez Borden, and colleagues began experimenting with the principles and got encouraging results right from the start. This initial work eventually led to the formation of a professional society of educators and researchers using accelerated learning methods, The Society for Suggestive Accelerative Leaning and Teaching or SALT.* This group now has members throughout the world and publishes a quarterly research journal, as well as conducting annual conferences and teacher training courses.

In 1979 Ostrander and Schroeder published the book *Superlearning®*, an interpretation of Suggestopedia shared by the authors, Dr. Bancroft, and the SALT Society. Since its publication, *Superlearning®* has been a milestone in popularizing accelerated learning concepts.

HOW DO SUPERMEMORY METHODS WORK?

The system I present in my seminars uses a unique combination of music, relaxation, suggestion, imagery, and play to promote accelerated, stress-free learning. This is accomplished by five key elements.

1. *A global approach to learning.* In various fields of study, including foreign languages, the strategy is a right-brain one of picking up broad general relationships before proceeding to finer detail. Pattern discovery maps can be useful toward this end.
2. *Rhythm.* With SALT and Superlearning®, you structure the material you want to commit to memory in a certain rhythm. You also accompany this with music of specific rhythm. You can even breathe in a similar rhythm. As yogis in India have known for centuries, certain rhythms make it easier to learn. This may correspond with natural internal biological rhythms.
3. *Suggestion.* Because Lozanov felt that suggestion is such a key component, he named his system "Suggestopedia." Suggestion is an integral part of how we communicate with others, and more importantly, how we communicate with ourselves through

*SALT Society, 3028 Emerson Avenue South, Minneapolis, MN 55408.

internal self-talk. We can inwardly reaffirm our confidence in ourselves as learners or call ourselves stupid and incapable. Positive inward suggestion can develop powerful links between the conscious and the unconscious, and allow for quick permanent changes in our skills and behavior.

Internally, you can tell yourself your tennis serves will be fast and accurate today, but it is more powerful to combine this message with the auditory submodalities that work best for you. This, together with *visualizing* the correct form and imagining how it *feels*, give power to your internal suggestions.

4. *Restful awareness.* Stress and anxiety often block memory. In contrast, a sufficiently deep state of relaxation can have the opposite effect of enhancing unconscious recall. Researchers have used instruments to monitor yogis when they perform remarkable physical and mental feats.[3] They found that the yogis' bodies are physically relaxed while their minds are intensely focused with a production of alpha waves. We call this state *restful awareness.*

Lozanov discovered that the Indian yogis with phenomenal memory can maintain restful awareness. They can stay in this state for extended periods of time. Supermemory methods take full advantage of this ancient knowledge and use a unique combination of rhythm, music, and breathing to maintain that state.

5. *Making work play.* Due to lack of confidence in our ability to learn and remember, many of us experience tension when we try to do these things. As a result, we strain our muscles, and then the physical and mental stresses actually reduce our memory and learning ability. A tired and frustrated learner may conclude that the material is beyond his or her ability— but often this isn't true.

Supermemory methods solve these problems through an approach called *infantilization.* We establish a childlike state for learning. As young children we were spontaneous, full of curiosity and questions, totally open to learning, and free of most of the learning blocks we have now. Even as adults we sometimes experience a childlike joy when we become so absorbed in work that it seems more like play. These times excite us, stretch us, challenge us, and make life richer.

Work is love made visible.
—*Anonymous*

Your six-step supermemory master key is shown in Figure 8.1.

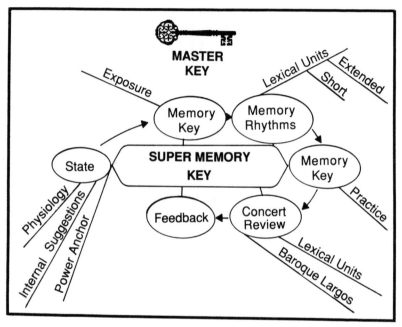

FIGURE 8.1

STEP ONE: STATE

This is a five- to six-minute phase designed to put you into an empowering state for learning, so as you can imagine we start with:

1. *Physiology.* In my seminars we begin with a minute or two of stretching. I select four or five from the group of simple exercises shown in Figures 8.2a and 8.2b. Hold each for seven to ten seconds.

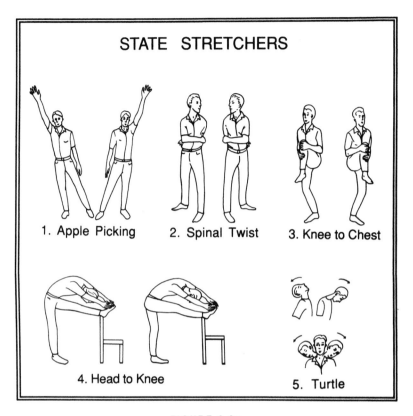

STATE STRETCHERS

1. Apple Picking   2. Spinal Twist   3. Knee to Chest

4. Head to Knee   5. Turtle

FIGURE 8.2a

To relax your physiology further you can spend a couple of minutes with *progressive relaxation*. Relax one muscle group at a time until your whole body feels relaxed and limp. Start from your head and work downward toward your feet. As an alternative, you can tense each muscle group and then relax it. After completing, slowly take five deep breaths, and as you exhale, feel your body going limp and melting into your chair.

An alternative for a relaxed state is called *Zen breathing*. Just observe your breathing for a few minutes without trying to control it. Whenever you breathe in, silently think "in" to yourself. When you breathe out, think "out." When you find your attention wandering, easily bring it back. Again, just observe your breathing for a few minutes without controlling.

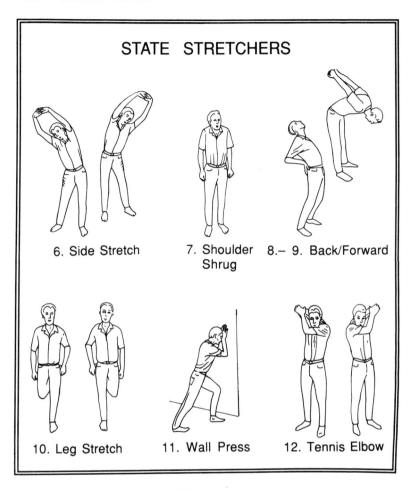

STATE STRETCHERS

6. Side Stretch

7. Shoulder Shrug

8.– 9. Back/Forward

10. Leg Stretch

11. Wall Press

12. Tennis Elbow

FIGURE 8.2b

Beyond this, just imagine how your body would feel if you were really excited about what you want to learn and remember. How would you be sitting? What posture would you assume? Would you be smiling with confidence? If you are not particularly excited about what you have to learn and remember, just imagine what it would be like if you were.

2. *Internal suggestions* provide a way to improve your IR's, that is, the quality of how you represent the learning task internally. Mentally project yourself into the activity. For example, if you

are going to take a test, imagine yourself feeling confident and energetic. The adrenaline is starting to flow, and this leads you to peak performance. You are answering the questions, remembering everything, and working quickly.

When test-taking is this easy, notice what emotions you feel. What do you feel in your body? How do things look? How do they sound? Be sure to cover the modalities (VAK) and submodalities (close up or far away; bright or dim; soothing, inflected, or resonant voice; warm, light, or tingly feelings, etc.) that are most important for you. You might also thank yourself internally, as if you had already succeeded.

The other possibility for internal suggestions is to go back in time to a pleasant learning experience from the past. Maybe you had a hobby you were very good with. Or maybe there was a book that absorbed your interest so much you could hardly put it down. Think of some situation where you learned well and had fun learning. What emotions did you feel? How did your body feel? How did things look? How did they sound?

Consider the possibility of whatever you experienced in the past being available in the present for what you want to learn now. For example, if I could learn computer assembly language and have as much fun as I did learning how to ski, it would still be a lot of work. But if I'm having fun while I'm learning, it won't seem like work. Also, I will be much more effective at learning and remembering the material. Finally, thank your unconscious for allowing those feelings from the past to come into what you are doing now.

An easy way to get started with relaxation and internal suggestions is to purchase a prerecorded audiocassette tape. Powerlearning® Systems* offers a tape called *Learning Power.* Side 2 has five selections—each is a combination of relaxation and internal suggestions, and each lasts four to five minutes. Of course, once you get used to the process, you will probably want to put the exercises into your own words. That establishes more direct communication between you and your unconscious self.

3. *Power Anchor.* This optional third step is one of the quickest

---

*Powerlearning® Systems, P.O. Box 496, Santa Cruz, CA 95061.

ways to establish an empowering state of motivation and high energy. Specifics of how to set up and fire a power anchor are discussed in Chapter Twelve. Once you have read that chapter and established a power anchor for yourself, it will only take a few seconds to engage that anchor.

STATE (FIVE TO SIX MINUTES)

1. Take a minute or two to stretch, using four or five of the exercises shown.
2. Relax yourself with a couple of minutes of

   • Progressive relaxation of one muscle group at a time; or
   • Zen breathing—just observing your breathing.

3. Imagine your posture and physical sensations if you were excited about what you want to learn and remember.
4. Do a few minutes of internal suggestions. You can mentally project successful learning with the sights, sounds, and feelings you will experience paying attention to important submodalities. The other alternative is going back to a past successful learning experience and bringing sights, sounds, and feelings from the past to the present learning task.
5. As an optional last step, employ a power anchor described in Chapter Twelve.

STEP TWO: MEMORY KEY FOR EXPOSURE AND UNDERSTANDING

Approach what you want to learn and remember through the first part of your memory and learning key from Chapter Seven. Proceed just far enough to gain exposure and understanding of what you want to remember. Obviously it does no good trying to memorize something you don't understand.

For example, the first three steps in my physics key are read the material (V^e), sense how it works (K^i), and write it out (K^e). At this point if I still don't understand it, I might reread it or have someone explain it to me (A^e).

Knowing your memory and learning key is crucial. Knowledge of your personal key allows you to customize supermemory to the way that works best for you.

STEP 3: MEMORY RHYTHMS [4]

After going through the first several steps of your memory key for initial exposure and understanding, notice which items or concepts you find most difficult to remember. This next step will greatly facilitate memorizing those most difficult items by structuring them in a certain rhythm. You can do this with a friend, a prerecorded audiocassette tape, or perhaps make a tape as part of this process.

Memory Rhythms with a Friend—Short Lexical Units

An easy approach is to work with a friend. Suppose you want to memorize a list of short ideas such as foreign words, short foreign phrases, technical definitions, spelling words, bones, muscles, equations, computer commands, or historical dates. The friend speaks for four seconds, pauses four seconds, speaks four seconds, and pauses four seconds alternately. Each four seconds of material, called a *short lexical unit*, consists of one complete idea, such as:

- a foreign word, the English translation, and the foreign word again
- the English version of the short phrase (not more than four or five words) and the foreign version
- a technical term or vocabulary word with its definition
- a word and its spelling (not more than eight or nine letters long)
- a bone or muscle, what it connects to, and what it does
- an equation
- a computer command and what it does
- a historical date and what happened on that date

As long as you can speak the information in seven to nine words or less, it will normally fit comfortably into four seconds. For example, a list of Portuguese words might be structured like this:

Speak four seconds	*Pause four seconds*
"*noz*, walnut, *noz*"	. . . .
"*pai*, father, *pai*"	. . . .

A list of bones in the big toe might be set up like this:

Speak four seconds	*Pause four seconds*
"At the end of the toe is the distal phalanx."	. . . .
"The second bone in is the proximal phalanx."	. . . .
"The base of the toe is the metatarsal."	. . . .

Lines of a poem can be set up in the same way:

Speak four seconds	*Pause four seconds*
"Shall I compare thee to a summer's day?	. . . .
Thou art more lovely and more temperate:	. . . .
Rough wings do shake the darling buds of May,	. . . .
And summer's lease hath all too short a date:"*	. . . .

Memory Rhythms with a Friend—Extended Lexical Units

Suppose, on the other hand, you are memorizing more extended ideas that don't fit into four seconds. Maybe you are memorizing principles from accounting or chemistry, or perhaps the spelling words or foreign phrases are too long for four seconds. In this case use *extended lexical units*. Speak the point in a complete sentence for however long it takes, and then pause about four seconds. If the point is more than one sentence long, each sentence is a separate lexical unit. For example, to solve $ax + b = c$ for x:

*William Shakespeare, Sonnet 18.

Speak	*Pause four seconds*
"Subtract the quantity 'b' from both sides of the equation"	. . . .
"This gives ax = c−b"	. . . .
"Now divide both sides of the equation by the quantity 'a'"	. . . .
"This gives x equals the quantity (b−c) divided by a"	. . . .

If you were memorizing lines in a play, each sentence could be an extended lexical unit:

Speak	*Pause four seconds*
PRINCE: "Why, what a pox have I to do with my hostess of the tavern?"	. . . .
FAL: "Well, thou hast called her to a reckoning many a time and oft."	. . . .
PRINCE: "Did I ever call thee to pay thy part?"	. . . .
FAL: "No, I'll give thee thy due, thou hast paid all there."*	. . . .

If you were reviewing Chapters 4, 5, and 6 for a test, you could list the main points in sentences. Of course, list only the points you find most difficult to remember. You can get the easier points with the simpler reading and study techniques presented later.

Now have your friend speak short or extended lexical units with a four-second pause between units. While he or she does this, you have a photocopy of the list in front of you. While your friend reads aloud, you read silently.

If your list has short lexical units, you can also breathe a certain way to enhance the process. As your friend speaks, hold your breath in. When he or she stops, breathe out and in. Then, just as your friend starts to speak again, hold your breath in, etc. It's very simple. When they are speaking, you hold your breath in. When they are not speaking, you breathe—first out and then back in. The breathing is

*William Shakespeare, *Henry IV*; Act I.

synchronized so you are taking in a new breath of air each time you hear a new lexical unit. It is also part of the overall memory rhythm.

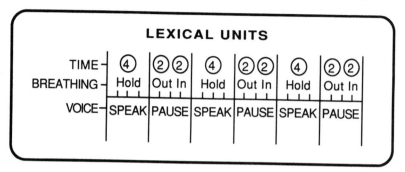

FIGURE 8.3

In my seminars some of the participants wonder why you have to do active organizing with a friend. Why couldn't you just speak the material yourself? The answer is that for short lexical units, you can't hold your breath and talk at the same time. If you have extended lexical units, you will not do this breathing pattern, but you may need the friend anyway for a later step.

Memory Rhythms on Your Own

Another approach if you want to use supermemory methods without a friend is to record an audiocassette tape. Once you have your list, speak the lexical unit into the tape recorder, pause four seconds, speak the next, pause four seconds again, etc. Once you've recorded on the tape, play it back, read along silently from your list, and do the breathing (for short units only). For extended units, just read along.

Of course, by the time you have (1) picked out the main points, (2) decided which of these are most difficult to remember, (3) set up your lexical units, and (4) recorded on your tape, you probably half-know the material already. You may want to stop after recording on the tape. If the material is not too difficult to remember, just recording on the tape is enough. If it is especially difficult, play back the tape, read silently, and do the breathing pattern if appropriate.

Appendix Four goes into detail on the mechanics of recording on your own tape with the appropriate timing.

STEP FOUR: MEMORY KEY FOR PRACTICE

The supermemory strategy in this next step is to incorporate the rest of your memory key not covered in the second step. In most cases this requires some type of practice. For example, two of the remaining steps in my Physics key—problem-solving (K^e), and possibly explaining it to someone else (A^e)—are practice.

The practice could include the visual, auditory, and kinesthetic memory techniques or the mnemonic strategy. It might also involve creating pattern discovery maps to see broad general relationships.

SALT also encourages making such practice creative and innovative—making work into play. Thus if you are studying history, you might imagine yourself to be a magazine reporter. Suppose you could step into a time machine and travel back to that historical period. What questions would you ask those people? How do you think they would respond? How would you feel? How would you write your article?

Again, the idea here is that since you have to do some kind of practice to get the material down, why not make the practice creative, fun, and enjoyable? This not only makes the material easier to remember and the learning more effective but also reinforces the notion that learning can be fun.

STEP FIVE: THE CONCERT REVIEW

The concert review is probably what SALT and Superlearning® are best known for—the unique combination of music, breathing, and rhythm that promotes a relaxed state of restful awareness. In this stage you are committing the material you have set up in lexical units to a deeper level of memory.

At this point you need a friend or a prerecorded tape. The voice speaks a lexical until, pauses four seconds, speaks another unit, and pauses as before. Set up a comfortable and pleasant environment for yourself. Perhaps take your shoes off, sit in a comfortable, overstuffed chair, prop your feet up, close your eyes, and relax.

For extended lexical units, breathe normally. For short units, do the breathing pattern we discussed earlier. When the voice is speaking, hold your breath in. When the voice stops, breathe out and back in. When the voice speaks again, hold your breath in again, etc.

The procedure here is the same as in the memory rhythms step, but instead of reading along with the material, close your eyes and relax completely. In addition, the concert review uses music.

The use of music to accelerate learning dates back to antiquity. Oral tradition was often passed down in songs, chants, or verse. Even today the melody of a song enhances memorization of lyrics. In ancient Greece[5] people attended performances of the *Iliad* accompanied by the lute. Many reportedly walked away with the verses memorized.

For best results Lozanov recommended baroque largos at about sixty beats per minute. Baroque dates from the late Renaissance to about 1750, the year Bach died. Some of the composers are Bach, Telemann, Vivaldi, Handel, and Pachelbel. The term "largo" refers to the tempo. Largos typically range from forty to sixty-five beats per minute.

Use of baroque largos is not arbitrary or a matter of personal taste. Research by Lozanov, the SALT organization, and individual accelerated-learning specialists has verified that this music is the most effective. Sheila Ostrander and Lynn Schroeder, authors of *Superlearning*, also recommend primarily string instruments for the music.

You can put together a music tape by going to a music library, picking out baroque record albums, and using those selections clearly labeled "largo." The only tricky thing is the tempo. Most largos are not exactly sixty beats per minute, so you need to time the music and pick out selections close to this tempo.

If you don't want to record on your own tape, the Learning Power tape available from Powerlearning® Systems has twenty-five minutes of baroque largos performed at exactly sixty beats per minute on side one. The last five minutes of this tape have baroque music that is a little faster. You can rerecord this faster music for a minute or two at the end of your memory tape. This serves as transition from the concert review back into activity.

The concert review requires two tape recorders if you are doing it by yourself. One plays the material you have set up in lexical units. The second plays the baroque largos at sixty beats per minute. You set the two at about the same volume; sit in a nice, comfortable chair; close your eyes; and do the breathing pattern if you have short lexical units, or just relax for extended units. If you have one to two minutes blank at the beginning of your study tape, the music from your second recorder will provide a soothing introduction by itself. The whole process is designed to settle you into a state of restful awareness. When the list ends, shut off the baroque largo tape, and your memory tape will end with a minute or two of the faster baroque music you have recorded.

When people first experience this process, they usually find it easy and relaxing, but the breathing may seem awkward. Be aware that this breathing pattern is unusual and that you should not breathe too deeply while doing it.

Learning the breathing technique recommended here is somewhat like learning to play a new musical instrument, or perhaps learning a new tennis stroke that feels awkward at first and simply requires practice. If you learned to drive with a stick shift, think back to your first time out. Do you remember trying to work the gas pedal here, the clutch over there, and the brake in another place while shifting gears with your hand? It was probably awkward, and you may even have wondered how you could possibly look through the windshield while doing all that. Pretty soon, though, you were driving down the road, working the pedals, shifting the gears, listening to the radio, talking with the friend next to you, watching the highway, and maybe even thinking about something else. The whole process became unconscious. The breathing process is something like that—it's just a matter of practice.

You can do the concert review without doing the breathing pattern; however, it seems to facilitate learning short lexical units. In fact, research suggests that the breathing pattern by itself may improve memory by 78 percent.[6] However, it doesn't seem to help with extended lexical units.

Research[7] at London University using brain-scanning tomography shows clearly that listening to words stimulates more activity in the left side of the brain, where as listening to music stimulates more activity in the right brain. The orchestrated combination in the concert review promotes balanced functioning of the two sides.

When you first experience a concert review, you may notice that the whole process centers on rhythm: You have the material in a rhythm . . . the music supports that rhythm . . . and you may even breathe in rhythm. The continual monotonous rhythm is what lulls you into a relaxed state of restful awareness.

The concert review typically lasts about ten to fifteen minutes. If you figure it out mathematically, in ten minutes you will cover sixty-seven lexical units. That means sixty-seven foreign words or phrases, sixty-seven bones and muscles, sixty-seven technical terms, sixty-seven equations, or sixty-seven of the most difficult-to-remember main points from your review session. That is a lot of material to commit to memory all at once, so I think you can begin to sense the power of this technology.

THE CONCERT REVIEW

- Play the tape with your lexical units, or have a friend read the units aloud.
- Play the baroque largos on a second recorder (your better-quality recorder). Set the two at about the same volume.
- As soon as you start the recorders playing, take your shoes off, put your feet up, and relax in that comfortable chair.
- The two minutes of silence at the start of the memory tape allow for a musical introduction on the other recorder. A friend reading the material should also allow the music to play for two minutes before starting to read.

THE CONCERT REVIEW (continued)

- Close your eyes and listen to the material. For short lexical units you can also incorporate the breathing pattern.
- When the material has finished, shut off the largo tape. If you have ended the material with a minute or two of faster baroque music, this will complete your concert session.

STEP SIX: FEEDBACK

This last step in the cycle is a self-quiz to verify how much of the material you have mastered and that the system really works. You may also discover some material you need to review. As your success grows, this will reinforce the internal suggestion portion of state, the first step. You won't be taking the system on faith because you will have the experience of how effectively it works.

HOW BEST TO USE SUPERMEMORY METHODS

The whole six-step cycle takes one to two hours to complete, depending on how much material you want to absorb at once. Intensive foreign-language courses set up in the Lozanov format are often structured to meet four hours a day. Using these methods, students are able to learn and retain at two to five times the rate of traditional courses.

You might wonder about the best way to use supermemory. I suggest using this technology only for your most difficult *memory* material. If you can simply read through a chapter a few times and have it down, why do all the work of making tapes and doing the six steps? It's not going to save you time.

The whole idea of these methods is to save time and make things easier. If you wanted to learn 150 or 200 German words in one day, you can easily do that using this method. Even with the time it will take you to organize the list, set up your lexical units, record on the tape, and complete the six steps, you can still learn two to five times faster than with any other method of learning.

In my seminars I demonstrate supermemory by having students learn Portuguese vocabulary words at a rate of 80 to 100 words per hour. Afterward, students remember an average of 85 to 90 percent of the words. Sometimes students will come back two or three months after the class and tell me they still remember most of the words.

In the summer of 1975, Ray Benitez-Borden,[8] one of the founders of the SALT Society, conducted several one-year Spanish courses. Each class met four hours a day for ten days—a seven-to-one speedup over traditional techniques and probably the best speedup we've experienced in this country.

Dr. Lin Doherty[9] taught German at the University of Massachusetts for a number of years using Lozanov's Suggestopedia. He taught two years of German in one quarter and had the students put on a dramatic production at the end of the course. That is something a normal language major could not do at the end of four years.

PART FOUR

*L*EARNING

*S*TATES

CHAPTER NINE

POWERREADING

Every problem offers a gift.
Am I willing to accept it?
—ANONYMOUS

Most speed-reading courses don't work. As a typical example, Janet, a physical therapist, knew she should keep up with reading current research in her field, but she felt bogged down with long work hours, and learning business skills to establish her practice. Also, she was not a very good reader. A local speed-reading course promised benefits that looked like they would solve her problems, so she signed up.

For a while some of her reading skills improved, especially reading light fiction. At the conclusion of the course, however, she was disappointed that the course did not live up to the claims. In fact, within a few months her reading skills had slid back to her former level.

It has been estimated that 90 percent of books and courses on reading skills and speed reading—including university courses—make claims that directly contradict the scientific evidence. This chapter is a collection of reading techniques that do work. They also require the least amount of practice to master.

READING PROBLEMS

Many people dislike reading, despite its extreme importance to business, education, and leisure activity. Generally, skilled readers enjoy reading, and poor readers don't. The problem is that most of us were taught enough basic skills to get through school, but few of us learned advanced techniques for speed, comprehension, and recall. Those of us who read slowly and ineffectively are penalized throughout life. We can't keep up with the enormous volume of reading necessary for higher education or staying on top of the latest developments in our field.

EXERCISE 21

Take sixty seconds to list all the things you don't like about reading. Work quickly and list as many as you can think of. When the sixty seconds are over, take another thirty seconds to review the list, make changes, and add new items. *Stop reading* until you have completed this.

Here are what my seminar participants generally dislike about reading; see if any of these things are on your list:

- I read too slowly.
- I am easily distracted.
- My attention wanders.
- I have too much to read and too little time.
- The material is boring!
- I lack comprehension.
- I have trouble concentrating.
- I tend to reread the text too much.

Another problem is illustrated in Figure 9.1. This reader is reading just one word at a time. When she gets to "possible," she thinks,

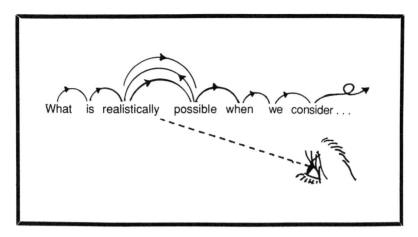

FIGURE 9.1

"Oh, what was that last word?" Her eyes jump back to "realistically." This is called backskipping. Children backskip 25 to 33 percent of the time; adults backskip on 15 percent of the words they read; and even highly efficient readers backskip 5 to 10 percent of the time. This habit, of course, slows reading speed considerably and disrupts the flow of ideas.

One final problem: have you ever noticed that after reading two or three pages, nothing seems to have registered? In northern California we have a technical term for this phenomenon: "spacing out."

When the reader in our illustration gets to "consider," she spaces out. Her eyes move away from the sentence. This may be due to external distractions, boredom, or perhaps contemplating that strawberry short-cake in the refrigerator. Finally, after twenty seconds she remembers, "Oh, I'm supposed to be reading!" But even after those twenty seconds, she back skips to find her place.

EMPOWERING READING STATES

To set up an appropriate state for better reading, you might start with your IR's. Imagine what it would be like if you could significantly improve your reading speed, comprehension, focus, and recall. Also imagine that it would not take a lot of time and energy. How would you *feel* about yourself, and what would you want to read? Can you *picture* yourself being more confident and successful? Would you be *hearing* words encouragement and congratulations?

EXERCISE 22

Now take about sixty seconds to list all the benefits you will gain from improved reading. These could tie in with your job, your personal life, or your education. Again, write down all the possible gains as quickly as you can. When the sixty seconds are up, take another thirty seconds to look over the list for additions and refinements. Stop reading until you have completed this.

Here are a few possibilities:

- I could read more in less time.
- I would have more fun reading.
- If reading were easier and more enjoyable, I would learn new things and expand my horizons.
- I would have more knowledge to share with my friends.
- I could finally keep up with the professional reading I'm supposed to do.
- Studying wouldn't take up all of my spare time.

Reading is power. We acquire most of our knowledge through reading books, magazines, newspapers, reports, and journal articles, as well as an occasional sweet escape to the land of exciting fiction. Improved reading skills is the logical starting point to gain knowledge.

EYE MOVEMENT WHILE READING

Improved reading has a lot to do with how we move our eyes as we read. My seminar participants find it fascinating to observe other readers' eye movements.

EXERCISE 23

Closely watch a friend's eyes while he or she is reading. You will observe a fine jerky motion as the friend stops on each word momentarily and then jerks to the next. In fact, if you watch carefully, you may observe occasional backskipping.

The time we spend stopping on each word is called a *fixation*. For most of us, fixations last one-quarter to one-half second. The quick jerks from one fixation point to the next are called *sacades*.

We can scientifically study patterns of eye movement by taking a narrow beam of light and bouncing it from the eye of a reader onto a piece of photographic film. As the reader's eye moves across the line of print, the light reflected from his or her eye moves across the film. If the film is also moving during the process, we can record the pattern of fixations and sacades. *Eye movement photography* research has been done for the past sixty years, and much of our present scientific understanding of reading skills is based on this research.

Figure 9.2 shows a reader who, at this moment, is fixating on the letter "l."

Only two or three letters to either side of this fixation point are entirely in focus. This is the shaded region—the area of 100 percent visual acuity. At one-half inch to either side of the fixation point, clarity is reduced to 30 percent. Beyond that the letters are out of focus and thus indecipherable.

Most people are surprised at how narrow our region of sharp vision really is. Because of this, we cannot take in an entire line of print at once. We gradually move across it, momentarily putting each part within our narrow field of sharp vision.

Another fact we have learned from eye movement photography is that the typical reader takes in an average of only 1.1 words with each stop or fixation. The best readers take in 2.5 words with each stop. Beyond 2.5 words, the print appears too distorted to recognize.

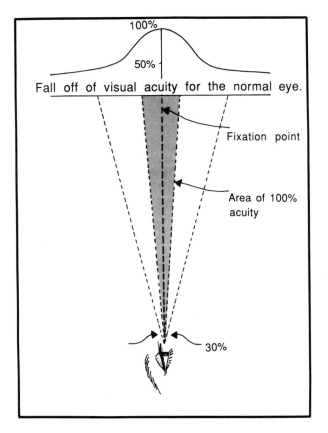

FIGURE 9.2

SPEED-READING FACT AND FICTION

How much can you improve your reading skills if you practice the exercises presented later in this chapter? What speeds are possible? What claims are realistic? Here are the most common misconceptions:

1. *Possible reading speeds.* Many of the commercial speed-reading courses claim possible reading speeds from 1,000 to 80,000 words per minute. However, if you figure it out mathemati-

cally, the best reader spends about 0.25 second with each fixation and takes in about 2.5 words. That sets a practical speed limit of 800 to 900 words per minute if you are going to see each word. And you do have to see each word to understand everything except light fiction.

No doubt there are exceptions. John F. Kennedy reportedly could read a newspaper at 2,000 words per minute. Once in a while you hear of people with photographic memories who look at a page once and have it down. However, for the average person, 800 to 900 words per minute seems to be the practical limit. On the other hand, if you can reach even 500 words per minute, that's still better than the vast majority of readers. As you will discover, these levels are not difficult to reach. Exercises in Appendix Two, "Your Sixty-Day Reading Program," will provide you with the vehicle to increase your reading speed.

2. *Phrase reading.* Almost every book on speed reading and every course on the subject will tell you not to read one word at a time. With each stop or fixation, you are advised to take in a whole phrase. This is inconsistent with eye movement photography that shows the very best readers take in no more than 2.5 words with each stop or fixation.

Commercial and university courses train students to expand their side or *peripheral* vision with a device called a *phrase flashing machine.* The student stares straight ahead at a screen, and the machine flashes a phrase or a short sentence in a short fraction of a second. With a little practice, most people can take in the whole line that quickly. The line is in fact considerably longer than 2.5 words.

The catch, however, is this: When you read, your eyes are moving and not just staring straight ahead. Once your eyes move, you have a much narrower field of visual acuity.

There are some "phrase flashing" exercises in Appendix Two. They are useful for expanding your peripheral vision. Using these exercises can enhance your skills from the usual 1.1 words per fixation to the peak performance level of 2.5 words with each stop. It is very unlikely, however, that you will take in an entire phrase at a time while reading.

3. *Eliminate backskipping.* Almost all speed-reading books and courses will tell you to *eliminate* backskipping. Generally, this is

not possible. While reading, the eyes start and stop so fast (four times per second) that it is almost involuntary where they finally stop. Periodically they will go back, whether you want them to or not. However, you can minimize backskipping simply by increasing your reading speed. The faster your speed (up to a reasonably quick pace), the less tendency there will be to backskip. The *visual aid* technique described later also helps to reduce backskipping.

4. *Speed and appreciation.* The idea here is that "those fast readers don't appreciate the material as much as we slow readers do." I think the slow readers started that rumor. It's just not true. If you're a fast reader, you have more choices. You can slow down and savor something you enjoy. You have time to reread material if you desire. And just knowing that a reading assignment will not take up your whole evening could add appreciation to the process. It's much more enjoyable to have the ability and choice to read faster.

5. *"It's more work to read fast."* This isn't so. Research has shown that faster readers, on average, backskip only about half as much as slow readers. In addition, faster readers do only half as many fixations per line.[1] Now, just think: Your eyes are starting, stopping, moving back, and jumping around four times per second. This is what wears you out as you read. This is also what causes the fatigue, the boredom, and a lack of concentration. If you are a fast reader and your eyes jump around only half as much, you are doing less work yet getting more done.

6. *"The faster the speed, the lower the concentration."* Again, this is not true. A big problem in reading is that our mind works so much faster than the rate at which we are reading. That's why some people get bored with it. It would be like listening to someone speak . . . one . . . word . . . at . . . a . . . time. When we take in information faster, it is easier to concentrate because our reading speed matches the natural rhythm of our mind. A simple analogy would be driving down a residential street at twenty-five miles per hour with your attention wandering, as opposed to driving on a German *Autobahn* at ninety miles per hour with total concentration.

MODELING EXCELLENT READERS

Just now as you are reading notice . . . is this book flat on the table
or on your lap like this,

FIGURE 9.3

or are you holding it upright like this?

FIGURE 9.4

EXERCISE 24: READING PRETEST

Before learning specific techniques of how to improve your reading skills, it is useful to know what your starting level is. To do this you will read an article in Appendix One, time your reading speed, and answer some questions to test your comprehension. Turn to Appendix One and complete this pretest *now* before continuing to the next section.

When people read at my seminars, 90 percent of them have their book flat on their desk or on their lap, as in Figure 9.3. Only 10 percent hold the book upright, as in Figure 9.4. Notice what holding the reading material does for your posture: It's more upright. This is a *visual* posture that promotes alertness. By laying the reading material flat on your table or on your lap, notice what happens: Your posture is slouched . . . a kinesthetic pose—a good way to go to sleep.

EXERCISE 25

Now try this for yourself. Go back a page or two and read for a few seconds with the book flat on your lap, desk, or table. Next, hold the book up, place it a comfortable distance from your eyes, and continue reading. See what differences you feel between the two postures.

What happened when you did this exercise? My seminar participants report that after using the more upright position:

• I feel more alert.
• It's easier to breathe.
• I can read faster.

• I feel more connected with what I'm reading.
• The print is easier to see.

Think about this last statement. It's got to be easier to see! If the book

FIGURE 9.5

is flat, look at your viewing angle to the print.

When you're holding a book this way, look what happens: The angle, perpendicular to the page, makes the print clearly more visible.

When we model the very best readers, we imitate their physiologies, IR's, and the unconscious keys they use. They generally do two things with their physiologies (K^c);[2] They:

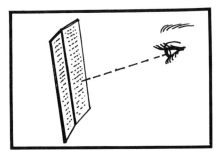

FIGURE 9.6

• hold the material with a visual posture
• use a visual aid

Of course, holding the material can be difficult with some textbooks that feel like they weigh ninety pounds. But

with a heavy book, you can get a book holder to place on your table or desk. This will give you the proper viewing angle. You can still hold on to the material for that sense of connection.

A visual aid could be your finger, a pen, or better, a pencil. Move the pencil underneath the line you are reading. Don't underline, just move the pencil. If you are not using a visual aid as you read this book, try using one right *now*.

FIGURE 9.7

Do you notice any difference?

Some of the most highly skilled readers always have a pencil in their hand as they read. Watch a proofreader. But you may be thinking, "Isn't that what I used to do in elementary school, and the teacher told me not to do it?" That's true. Small children are discouraged from pointing to words as they read. What the teacher ought to do is have them move their fingers faster. A visual aid provides a point of focus, and we are instinctively drawn to motion. Research done on the simple technique of moving a pencil under the line of print shows that within the first few hours, most people experience a 40 percent reduction in the number of stops per line. Backskipping is reduced by 50 percent, and reading speed jumps 40 to 50 percent. The reduction in backskipping is easy enough to understand. With a pencil moving forward, it is less likely that the eyes will fall back.

YOUR KEY FOR READING EXCELLENCE

One thing I learned quickly when I first started presenting Powerlearning® seminars is that most participants want to improve their reading skills, but very few have the patience or time to do extended training to get results. My motivation then was to provide this key as a collection of simple, practical techniques that require no practice and give immediate improvements. What follows is the result of my research and the experiences of my seminar participants.

1. K^e—*physiology.* This, as we discussed in the previous section, is modeling the way excellent readers hold the material (or use a book holder) for a visual posture and use a visual aid.

2. *Right brain.* Involve the right brain more through *prereading.* Many of the steps in the key will promote higher speed when you read. Equally important, however, is the ability to *focus* and *comprehend.* Prereading is an important tool toward that end.

Prereading can take a number of different forms. One simple approach is to read the first sentence of each paragraph of a book chapter the first time through. If it's a long paragraph, reading the first two sentences might be better. Exceptions would be the introduction, summaries, and conclusions. Read these thoroughly.

Within five or ten minutes you'll be all the way through the chapter and have a pretty good idea what it's about—without reading very many words. This allows you to begin *seeing the whole picture* of the material, a right-brain approach. Now when you go back and speed-read (a more left-brain activity), you'll have a mental skeleton to put things together. This makes it easier to focus and concentrate.

One exception to this prereading approach occurs when you are reading difficult or technical material. In this case, read everything the first time through. See each word, each equation, each chart or graph without being concerned about whether you understand it. That is very difficult for many of us. We refuse to move to page 2 unless we have completely understood page 1. You need to trust that you are working on it unconsciously. The material gradually makes more sense on the second or third reading.

3. V^e—*optimize the quality of visual input.* As we discussed, holding the material improves the viewing angle, and the visual aid provides a moving point of focus. Of course, proper lighting is important here. Beyond this, four strategies provide optimal visual input:

- *Use high-speed practice.* Suppose you were riding in a high-speed train at ninety miles per hour. You travel at this speed for half an hour, so you get used to it. Then the train begins slowing down for the station up ahead, and the passenger next to you estimates that you are now traveling at thirty-five miles per hour. The average person would probably estimate thirty-five miles per hour when the train is actually moving at forty-five to fifty-five miles per hour. This is because they've acclimated to the moving rate of ninety miles per hour as opposed to a highway speed of fifty-five to sixty-five miles per hour.

Reading at high speeds is a similar phenomenon. One of the exercises in Appendix Two for improving your reading speed is to spend ten to fifteen minutes a day reading considerably faster than your normal speed. Don't worry about seeing all the words or having total comprehension; just get used to reading faster. Afterward, return to your normal reading speed and watch what happens: Your speed will spontaneously begin to increase.

• *Shorten the lines by one-half inch on each side.* Take your visual aid (pencil) and put a vertical line on each side of the page about one-half inch from the margin.

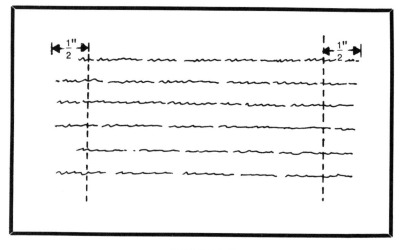

FIGURE 9.8

Draw the lines very lightly so you can erase them easily later without damaging the book. Now move under the line of print with your pencil, but stay between the two vertical lines. You won't miss the outside words; you'll pick them up with your peripheral vision.

It's much easier to read across short lines with a smooth, consistent rhythm than longer lines. Perhaps this is why newspaper lines are so short. With practice you won't have to draw in your vertical lines. You'll know to start one-half inch from one margin and end one-half inch before the next.

• *Expand fixation size.* Work to develop your peripheral side vision. Here is a way to demonstrate the quality of your peripheral vision:

Put your arm out straight in front of you. While looking

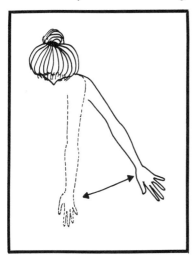

straight ahead, rotate your arm by about forty-five degrees, back toward your side. Now, at a forty-five-degree angle, raise one finger, then two, then three, etc. You will probably see the movement, but I doubt that you can count the number of fingers going up. Our peripheral vision is very poorly developed, except for movement.

With proper training, though, you can significantly improve your peripheral vision. It will never be as clear as your central vision because of the structure of the retina.

FIGURE 9.9

Your peripheral vision can, however, certainly be improved and expanded. A good step in this direction is the "phrase flashing exercises" described in Appendix Two. With practice you can expand your potential from the usual 1.1 words per fixation to the best: 2.5 words per stop.

• *Learn to vary your reading speed.* You might experience that when you read for pleasure, you go considerably faster than for technical reading. It's likely that you do vary your speed somewhat, but probably not as much as you think. The average person varies his or her reading speed by only 10 percent and should have a much larger range that that. You should be able to vary from 100 or 150 words per minute for difficult reading, up to 800 to 900 words per minute for lighter fiction.

Just be aware that your speed should naturally vary from subject to subject. Using techniques in this key, you can speed up any type of reading, but you will never read *Calculus IV* at the same rate as *Reader's Digest*.

4. A^i—*eliminate subvocalizing.* Do this for nontechnical or lighter reading. Subvocalizing is that little voice inside your head that allows you to hear the words as you see them. Some people even move their lips or whisper the words as they read.

Where did that voice come from? It probably started in your first grade of elementary school. Most of us were taught to read aloud. Then we learned to read to ourselves. Then the teacher hoped that little voice would go away. Guess what? After all these years, it's probably still there.

We usually assume we need to hear the material to understand and remember it. When people take speed-reading courses and read the words without hearing them, they initially feel they don't remember what they read. When they are tested on the material, however, it is there.

As we have discussed, visual memory is more reliable than auditory memory for most people. Recall without subvocalizing is through a visual link instead of the more familiar auditory loop. Subvocalization keeps our reading speed under about three hundred words per minute. The fact that the little voice can't talk any faster than three hundred words per minute creates a barrier to reaching higher speeds.

There are several ways to get rid of that little voice.

- One way many people find helpful is *knuckle-biting.* As you read, bite down lightly on a knuckle of the hand you do not write with—you may be moving your visual aid with the writing hand. The idea of biting down on something is to throw the muscles associated with speech off balance. This makes it easier to remind yourself to let go of the voice.

- Another technique people find even more helpful is *number-mumbling.* As you read, have the little voice just keep repeating, "twenty, twenty-one, twenty-two . . ." You'll be surprised the first time you try this. You'll find you're able to get through the material quickly and easily. Then you'll get to the end . . . and be totally confused. You won't remember anything except, "twenty, twenty-one, twenty-two . . ."

  With a little practice, though, you will begin absorbing the material without hearing it. All you are hearing is the numbers. Finally the voice gets bored with the numbers and it stops. At this point your reading speed may jump ahead quickly. When you get beyond three hundred words per minute, the voice can't keep up, so you won't have a subvocalizing problem. However, keep in mind that hearing the numbers is just a temporary method to help you reach higher speeds.

• The third technique is *reading at higher speeds*. Test your reading speed. If you read under three hundred words per minute, subvocalization may be holding you back. If you read beyond three hundred words per minute, you don't have a subvocalization problem, so don't worry about it.

5. A[i]—*use subvocalizing*. Do this for difficult or technical reading. At this point it is good to make a distinction between reading and study. When trying to understand and remember difficult material, it's useful to see it, hear it, write it, and cover all the senses. When we discuss reading, however, we've been talking about that first exposure, where you simply need to see the words and take them in.

We also distinguish between light reading and difficult or technical material. If the material is especially difficult or technical, we can't go faster than three hundred words per minute, so don't worry about subvocalizing. In fact, there is a school of thought that believes that during difficult reading it is better to have the little voice carrying on an internal dialogue— questioning, anticipating, and massaging the material. It is primarily for lighter reading, where there are many pages or chapters to cover, that it's not necessary to hear the words.

6. K[i]—*learn to derive more pleasure from reading*. You, too, will gain confidence and pleasure with reading as you incorporate this key. If you don't feel initially motivated to read, imagine what it would be like if you were. How would you be sitting? How would your body feel? How would things look? Even if you initially just pretend you are motivated, this is often enough to get you started and make the process more pleasurable.

In summary, your reading key is shown in Figure 9.10

The simple techniques and modeling in this key increased my reading speed to five hundred words per minute. This is

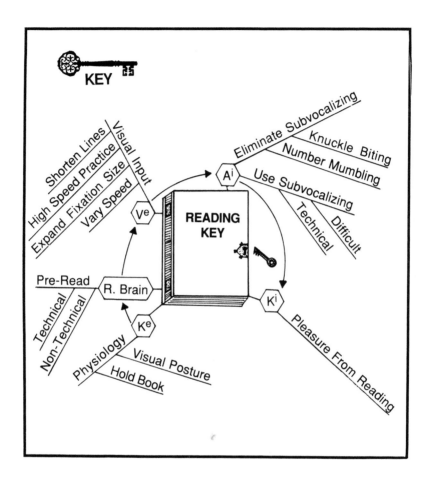

FIGURE 9.10

still better than the vast majority of our population. But if you really want to go for it—that is, if you want to reach the practical reading speed limit of eight hundred to nine hundred words per minute—use the collection of exercises in "Your Sixty-Day Reading Program" in Appendix Two.

EXERCISE 26: AFTERTEST

Once you have been using the techniques from the key for a week or two, you may want to check your progress against your previous pretest. As before, you will read an article, time your reading speed, and answer some questions to check your comprehension. Turn to Appendix Three for the aftertest.

CHAPTER TEN

*P*OWERSTUDY

When I works, I works hard;
When I sits, I sits loose;
When I thinks, I falls asleep.
—ANONYMOUS

The average university student is expected to spend about two thousand hours in class and another four thousand hours studying. That is equivalent to about forty hours per week of solid study for two years. Furthermore, high schools and universities assume that good study skills come naturally for students and make little attempt to teach students how to study and learn more effectively. As students we do the best we can and hope our strategies will work. Unfortunately, it's often not enough.

In this chapter we will examine strategies to overcome barriers to effective study and learning. These include getting started, remembering what we have read and studied, getting the most from study time, and improving understanding.

REMEMBERING WHAT YOU'VE READ AND STUDIED

Diane enjoyed showing off her custom home—a benefit of her years of study to become a successful lawyer. She especially enjoyed showing off her study with its impressive library of books, texts, and references. One evening after her friends had left, she wandered back into the library and had a strange thought: "I wonder what's in all the books I've read throughout my life." Of course, she knew generally what was there, but she wondered if she still remembered one tenth or even one hundredth of everything she had studied. I wonder if you have ever had a similar feeling.

An important part of reading and study is remembering it. This falls into two categories: remembering material from each part of a class or study session, and remembering material altogether after the class or study session is over. Memory from each part of a class or study session follows the Ebbinghaus curve we discussed in Chapter Six.

The shape of the curve in Figure 10.1 shows two peak memory times. The primacy effect shows best recall from the beginning of a study session, and the recency effect shows additional high recall at the end. This particular student remembered about 70 percent from the beginning of his study session. After three hours of solid study, however, his recall was down to only about 30 percent.

If he had taken a break after two hours, the recency effect could have increased the recall as shown in Figure 10.2.

Even so, he can still recall only about 40 percent of what he is studying by the end of two hours. Both these curves show unfortunate results, because they show that we study best at the beginning, when we are freshest. Isn't there some way to keep recall at the high level we start with?

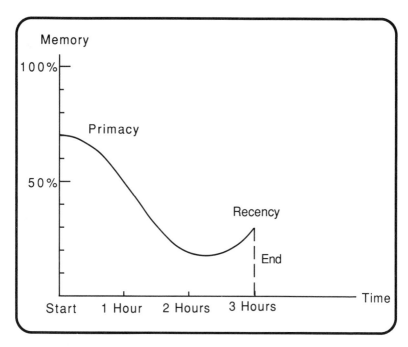

FIGURE 10.1

MODULAR STUDY

The trick to maximizing recall from a class or study session without having to employ the memory techniques from Chapters Six through Eight is to downchunk the material into modules: *modular study.* The German researcher B. Zeigarnik[1] surmised that the shorter the study session or class, the less the drop in memory, and the more relative benefit from the reminiscent effect. However, if the session is too short, downchunking inhibits seeing the broader whole picture, and the unit lacks sufficient meaning. If it is too long, recall and efficiency drop off. Many researchers[2] have observed that interrupting an extended learning session with a break at just the right time enhances memory and effectiveness.

Ideally, then, you should take a break every thirty to forty minutes. I did not say take a thirty- or forty-minute break; five to ten minutes is

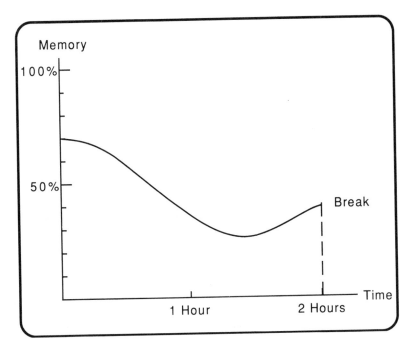

FIGURE 10.2

enough. That's enough time to stand up and stretch, splash some water on your face, or get a snack or some fresh air. The break should be relaxing and totally different from your session activity. (See the "Break Time Activities" box.) If the student in Figures 10.1 and 10.2 used this modular study with breaks, the memory curve would probably look more like that shown in Figure 10.3.

You can use this routine for hours because it helps maintain a high level of recall, and it also keeps your energy at a high level. The same is true on your job. A change of pace every thirty to forty minutes enhances efficiency.

On the other hand, suppose you are studying something especially difficult, such as advanced calculus. Perhaps you have been studying for two hours and it just isn't making any sense, when suddenly it starts falling into place. At this point, should you take a break, or keep going with your momentum? Many people guess that you should keep going a while longer to get into the flow. That's not the right answer. It would be better to take a break.

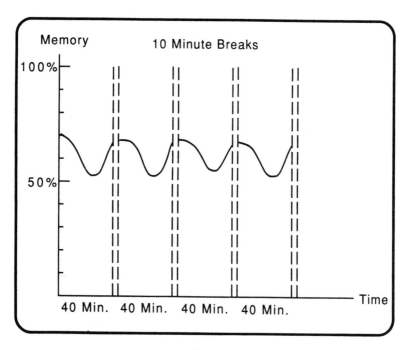

FIGURE 10.3

If you keep going, you may understand the material, but it's less likely that you will remember it. Haven't you had situations where you understood something, but on the test you couldn't remember it? Ideally, you want to have both understanding and memory. If you take a break, you'll look forward to coming back because you were starting to get the material, and now it is more likely you will remember it.

BREAK-TIME ACTIVITIES

During my five- to ten-minute breaks every thirty to forty minutes, I usually do several of the following:

- splash a little cold water on my face
- do a few minutes of stretching exercises
- get something to drink or a piece of fruit
- lie with my eyes closed for a few minutes
- step outside for some fresh air and sunshine
- juggle
- dance

Juggling is excellent during a break because it promotes mind-body coordination, promotes left-brain/right-brain balance, and provides a good metaphor for all we have to do in life. I teach juggling in my two-day seminars. Also, most novelty shops carry a kit called "Juggling for the Complete Klutz"—an easy way to start.

LONG-TERM MEMORY

Taking a break every thirty to forty minutes will help maximize recall from each part of a class or study session, but what about holding on to the recall long after the class or study session is over? Without reenforcement, recall might fall off along the general shape of an Ebbinghaus curve as shown in Figure 10.4.

For this particular student, recall increases slightly for about ten minutes after the study session—again illustrating the reminiscent effect. Then it falls off. After twenty-four hours, recall is about 70 percent gone, and from there it gradually disappears. However, there are two ways to keep the recall at the high level it was at the end of your study session: a series of four to five reviews, or a supermemory concert review.

Ten minutes after your class or study session and just after your

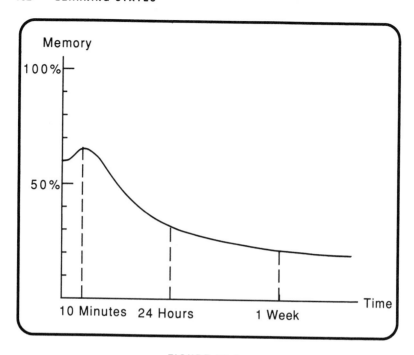

FIGURE 10.4

break, take your first review. This consists of rereading and revising your notes. For an hour's worth of class or study time, you might take five to ten minutes to reread and revise your notes. This ten-minute period is crucial in transferring information from short-term to long-term memory. Revising your notes might also take the form of organizing the information into a pattern discovery map. This technique always helps you to pull the information together to see the whole picture (V^i and right brain). Writing out the pattern discovery map also promotes kinesthetic involvement (K^e).

Take your second review one day later—after you have had a chance to process the material with a night's sleep. This time list the main points you learned twenty-four hours ago from memory—not all the detail, just the main headings or main points. Compare these with your original notes to see if you left anything out. Then add any missing main points. This second review might take another four to five minutes and should be sufficient to bring back the rest of the detail of what you learned.

Take your third review one week after the class or study session.

Follow the same procedure as your second review: Recall from memory the main points or headings you learned one week ago, and compare with your notes. This will take another five minutes or so.

The fourth and possibly last review occurs one month after the initial session and is just like the second and third reviews. It will take only four to five minutes. As an option, you can review the information again in six months; you'll probably find it is still there.

At this point you have invested a total review time of twenty to thirty minutes, which is very efficient to learn and retain an hour's worth of study material. Of course, you may be thinking that if you are taking four or five classes and try to schedule four or five reviews for each class, you could get into some serious bookkeeping problems. In this case I suggest leaving space between your classes if at all possible. In this way you can do the first review 10 minutes after each class.

For your second review, you might want to lump all of today's classes together and review them tomorrow in one sitting. Again, a week from today schedule a third review for all of today's classes. You can schedule the one-month review and the six-month review in the same way.

The forgetting curve without the reviews is now modified to look as shown in Figure 10.5.

For this student, the reviews added 30 to 40 percent to the study time but improved recall by 500 percent! This is a typical result and definitely not a bad investment of time. It would be like investing thirty-five hundred dollars to get back fifty thousand dollars!

If the material is particularly difficult to remember or if you are in a hurry to commit it to long-term memory, there is an alternative method to the reviews. Make a tape of the material in lexical units and do the six-step supermemory process outlined in Chapter Eight. In this way you don't have to extend your reviews over a longer time. If the material is not so difficult to remember, but perhaps you have a large volume of it, the four reviews would probably be easier. In that way you don't have to make a tape.

STUDY: YOUR KEY TO GETTING STARTED

The two biggest complaints I hear about study are (1) procrastination and (2) having enough time to study once you finally stop procrasti-

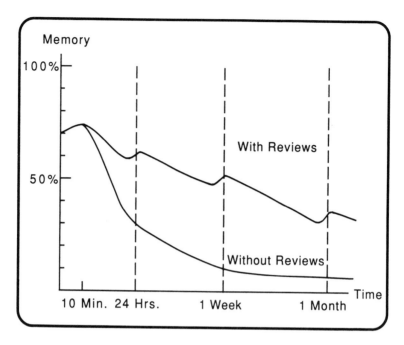

FIGURE 10.5

nating. Many of us have elaborate rituals to get started—a cup of coffee, spring-cleaning the room we'll be studying in, a walk to the store for a snack, or a nap. Of course, these provide ways to keep busy without getting anything done.

EXERCISE 27

Take a minute or two to list the things you don't like or perhaps find difficult about study. Go for quantity. Once you have the list, pick the three or four items that are most difficult for you. Stop reading until you have completed this.

My seminar participants frequently report the following. Are any of these on your list?

EXERCISE 27 (continued)

- I don't feel motivated to study.
- It's too much work.
- Study is boring.
- I have too many other things I'd rather be doing.
- It's a sure way to fall asleep.

The best way to ensure the success of a study session is to set up a brief study preparation phase. If you are having a hard time getting started, you might start with supermemory step 1—*State*. A few stretching exercises, physical relaxation, and internal suggestions can ease you into a more empowering state within about five minutes. On the other hand, if you're all fired up and can hardly wait to study, skip this step.

EXERCISE 28

Think back to a time when you were totally motivated to study and you were focused on and effective with that study. Think of a *specific* time and be back in that situation. Notice as much visual, auditory, and kinesthetic detail as you can. If you can't remember a specific time, just imagine what it would be like if you did have that focus and motivation.

Now take a few minutes to list personal benefits you would derive from being able to study this effectively. What changes would you be able to make in your life? How would you feel about yourself? How would you feel about new learning?

Many people have a hard time getting motivated to study because they hear a stern voice inside (A^i) telling them they *should* be studying now, or they *have to* start working on the assignment right away. They picture (V^i) what will happen if they don't do it. Their resulting state is a rebellion against that stern voice and feeling paralyzed by seeing the prospect of failure. A more useful approach is to use your motivation key from Chapter Two.

Once you have established an empowering state, the magic key shown in Figure 10.6 will help prepare you to get the most from your study time.

Let's go through this step by step:

1. K^e—*physiology.* A first consideration in preparing yourself to study is to make sure your environment will support focus and effective learning. The best temperature for study is cool enough to avoid drowsiness. A back support for the lower back promotes an alert visual posture and eases tension.

2. V^e—*optimize visual input.* Do this as you do with reading. The most ideal lighting is indirect solar light, coming from a window, outdoor shade, or a frosted skylight. At night, incandescent light is okay. Fluorescent is the worst form of lighting for this purpose.[5] Its spectrum is so distorted from natural sunlight that it promotes fatigue and makes it hard to concentrate. Studies show that fluorescent light even promotes hyperactivity in young children.

3. A^e—*minimize noise and distractions.* Setting up an environment free from distractions and interruptions improves focus and concentration. Agreement with roommates or family about quiet times for study is helpful.

4. Left brain—*decide the time and scope of material to cover.* Perhaps it's now 7:00 P.M., so you decide to study until 7:40 P.M. (Remember that thirty to forty minutes is the ideal length for a class or study session.) You might decide that one chapter in a text is a reasonable amount of material for your study session. You can even put a marker at the beginning and the end of the chapter. When you are that clear with your goals, the mind has a strong tendency to complete them.

5. A^i—*internal dialogue.* Take a minute or two to ask yourself what you already know about the material and what you would like to know when you are done. Maybe you'd like to know the

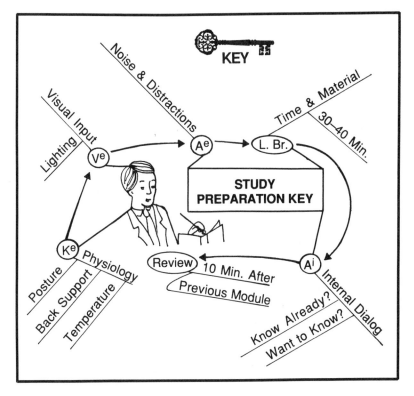

FIGURE 10.6

answers to the questions at the end of your chapter. Read the questions first. Even though they make no sense now, as you read through the chapter, the important points will jump out at you.

Another way to accomplish this is to glance through the chapter, take each section heading, and turn it into a question. As an example, if you are reading through an introductory chapter on physics and the first section is "Momentum," your question might be, "What is momentum, and what does it mean physically?" Maybe the next section is "Kinetic Energy." Your question might be, "What is kinetic energy, and does it relate to momentum?" This process actively involves you in the study.

6. Review. The last step is to *review* what you were doing just before the last break. Remember the ten-minute review from the previous section? It's a great idea to employ your super-

memory techniques from time to time during your study session. Then, tomorrow, twenty-four hours after your review, you'll have your study material in your long-term memory.

Beyond this key, having a routine time and place for study is freeing because you don't have to decide when and where to study. Of course, all of this is common sense, and I find that better students tend to incorporate some of these ideas instinctively. It is likely that if you follow these steps you will be more focused and effective and require less study time.

GETTING THE MOST FROM YOUR STUDY TIME

After the preparation, I recommend a four-step process for study. The technique is to go through the material four times, but reread only a fraction of the words[6].

1. *Visual preview.* If you need to study a book, glance through the whole book very quickly—the back cover, contents, preface, and introduction. Quickly thumb through the book to pick up pictures, a few headings, and to get a general idea of what it looks like—as though you were browsing in a bookstore. For a chapter or article, glance through the headings, the subheadings, illustrations, graphs, charts, and footnotes—not to understand them but just to see what they look like.
2. *Reading preview.* For an article or a chapter, go all the way through, reading the first one or two sentences of each paragraph. Along with this, read the introductions, summaries, and conclusions thoroughly. In Chapter Nine, this is what we call prereading. If you have not already done so, read the questions at the end of your chapter and turn section titles into questions. For technical information or difficult reading, read everything without trying to understand it the first time through.
   For a whole book, preread and read the first chapter. Then preread any internal chapter that seems to be a summary or transition, then read it thoroughly. Finally, preread and read the last chapter thoroughly.

3. *Study view.* Now go back and read the rest of the words with a deeper level of understanding. Skip or skim sections that seem unimportant. When you come to important sections, mark them with your visual aid (a soft pencil) as shown in Figure 10.7.

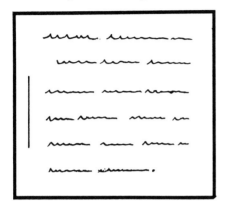

FIGURE 10.7

For sections that are confusing or difficult, mark them as shown in Figure 10.8

Do not underline or highlight the material—that is much too slow. For difficult or confusing material, don't stop or get bogged down. What is confusing on page 3 may be better explained on page 5. It would be a waste of time to get slowed down just now, but note for later reference the fact that it was confusing.

4. *Afterview and note-taking.* Go back only to those sections you marked as important or confusing, and now start taking notes. Many people take notes the first time through, without knowing what's important or not important.

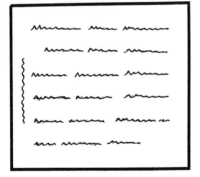

FIGURE 10.8

They usually take notes on everything. If you wait until later, you will see the important points and the confusing points. You will also have more of a vision of the whole. At this point you can likely reduce your volume of notes by 60 to 70 percent. Also, if you want to, set up your notes in pattern discovery map formats.

To secure what you have studied in long-term memory, follow the guidelines earlier in this chapter. Review your material ten minutes later, twenty-four hours later, a week later, a month later, and perhaps six months later. If something is particularly difficult to remember, use memory strategies from Chapters Six and Seven, or record a tape in lexical units and do a concert review of the material.

It is good to begin your study time with the most difficult or boring material—what you least want to do. You might also alternate contrasting subjects to maintain variety and interest.

If you have used elaborate rituals such as a cup of coffee, listening to music, or a walk to get yourself started, save these for break-time rewards, or rewards for when you have completed your study. It is also important to avoid marathon study sessions. These drain your energy, anchor stress and panic with learning, and aren't particularly effective.

REWARD LIST FOR STUDY

Here are some activities you might reward yourself with at various stages of achievement in your studies:

- running or jogging
- drawing
- listening to music
- taking time for your favorite sport
- going to a movie
- writing letters
- acting in a play
- buying new clothes
- meditating
- gardening
- playing with pets
- reading for pleasure
- playing with your kids
- doing yoga exercises
- shopping
- playing a musical instrument
- going to the beach
- taking time to do something you've always wanted to do but never had the time

LEARNING TIPS TO IMPROVE UNDERSTANDING

The methods we've discussed to this point promote good use of your time, ease in getting started with your study, effective reading skills, mental clarity, focus, and ease in remembering what you've read and studied. All this should produce a learning state more conducive to understanding what you've studied. In addition, we can incorporate a few more techniques from NLP to help you understand the more difficult material.

When we model successful students, we find they approach their course work aggressively. They get to know their instructors; they take advantage of office hours and discussion time to clarify their understanding; and they actively participate in class instead of being a passive sponge.

You will usually be most successful understanding difficult material if your initial exposure is in your primary modality—visual, auditory, or kinesthetic. Many instructors rely primarily on auditory presentations, with perhaps a little visual reinforcement. If you are finding the presentation difficult to follow, ask for clarification in your primary modality:

- *Visual:* "Can you help me *visualize* that idea?" or "I can't quite *picture* what you're saying."
- *Auditory:* "That *sounds* confusing to me. It would help to *hear* it in a different way."
- *Kinesthetic:* "Could you make that more *concrete*, so I can get a better *feel* for it (or get more of a *handle* on it)?

Then practice the material on your own, or in a small study group if you can. Be sure to incorporate your primary modality: picturing the ideas (V^i), explaining the concepts to others (A^e), or writing out the principles (K^e).

One final suggestion: Be careful where you sit in the class.[7] If the class favors the right side of your brain, sit on the right side of the class. Examples of right-brain subjects include art; music appreciation; and any class promoting vivid imagery, such as literature or occasionally psychology. Sitting on the right promotes right-brain functioning. If the class favors the left side of the brain—math, hard science,

English grammar, etc.—sit on the left side. This promotes left-brain functioning. If you want more balance, you might sit in the middle. Students instinctively prefer one side or the other in various classes. If you ask them why, they respond, "I don't know. I just like to sit here," or "I like to sit there." When you see where better students are, you will find a correlation between the side of the room and the type of class. If you aren't sure whether the subject favors one side of the brain more than the other, find out where the better students are sitting. You may want to join them. If it's a crowded class, don't tell everybody what you are doing.

The keys we have gathered for motivation, memory, reading, and study are the most powerful known. Our next step is to unlock barriers to personal power.

PART FIVE

*S*TATES

FOR

*P*ERSONAL

*P*OWER

THE COLOR OF TIME

> *Today is the tomorrow*
> *you didn't plan for yesterday.*
> —*Anonymous*

In *Powerlearning®* we have focused on developing thinking, memory, and learning skills with the philosophy that achieving the goals, dreams, and states we desire will involve learning. To the extent that we learn more effectively, we gain personal power—the ability to paint our desired destiny on the fabric of life.

We all have three primary colors with which to work: (1) time, (2) living life intelligently, and (3) living life with passion. These are the subjects of our concluding chapters.

INFORMATION OVERLOAD

Beyond air pollution, water pollution, and toxic wastes in our natural environment, most of us are now confronted with a new toxin that discolors our time: *information overload*, often in the form of "paper pollution." When I use the term *information overload*, I wonder if that rings a bell with you. Do you sometimes experience too much to do, not enough time to do it, and a feeling of being overwhelmed?

175

Below is an artist's conception of information overload. I wonder if you sometimes have days when you feel like the person in the middle of this next picture.

FIGURE 11.1

I'm sure we've all had days like this. From my research I am convinced that the three things that most discolor our available time are lack of knowledge on:

- how to custom-tailor our use of time
- how to manage power flow
- how to reduce or eliminate fatigue

Let's begin with time.

YOUR DIRECTION IN TIME

Time management is the art of making the most of the time we have. This can be crucial for those of us working in more than one job, taking classes, and maintaining family and friends while trying to maintain a balance of recreation and play, keeping up a household, and keeping up with rest and exercise. Life may seem like juggling with too many pieces falling on the floor.

The first step toward effective yet artful use of your time is to know clearly your direction through time. Following are some exercises I first encountered in Alan Laikin's pioneering work *How to Get Control of the Time in Your Life*. If you haven't done exercises like these in the past two or three months, it is very useful to do them *now*.

EXERCISE 29

Take a blank sheet of paper and spend not more than two minutes to list the things you would like to accomplish during the rest of your life. Write as fast as you can, and go for quantity. Be sure to include all of the playful, as well as practical, and even outrageous possibilities, like skydiving or that African safari— whatever you have ever dreamed of doing, even if it didn't seem practical or sensible. Do not spend more than two minutes making the list. Check your clock or watch and start *now*.

Once you have finished, take one more minute to go back over the list for additions or modifications.

EXERCISE 30

Take a second blank sheet of paper and for not more than two minutes list all you would like to do in the next five years. Some of these may be the same as items on your first list, some may be different. Again, go for quantity and avoid censoring the possibilities. When you are ready, *start*.

When the two minutes are up, take one more minute to go back over the list to make additions or changes.

EXERCISE 31

Take a third blank sheet of paper and spend another two minutes on the following. Suppose you knew you would be dead in six months. All of the funeral arrangements and legal matters have been taken care of, and money is not an obstacle. What would you do during these last six months? Again, go for quantity.

Again, once you have completed, spend one more minute to go back over the list to check for possible additions or corrections.

EXERCISE 32

Take one minute each to go back over your three lists in Exercises 29, 30, and 31 and pick the five items from each you would most like to do—the ones that are most dear to you. Start with the six-months list, then the five-years one, and finally the life list. Again, spend not more than one minute on each.

Once you have completed, this take a maximum of thirty seconds on each list to go back over your choices and verify that these are what you most want.

After doing the exercises, do you notice any patterns in your goals? How do the three lists compare? As you can imagine, the six-months list contains the things in life that are most important to you. If your life goals are fairly consistent with these, your direction in time is congruent. On the other hand, if your lifelong goals are very different from your six-months goals, you may want to take another look at your course in life.

CUSTOM-TAILORING YOUR USE OF TIME

Over the years as I have asked my seminar participants what they find most helpful in managing their time, the key shown in Figure 11.2 has emerged:

1. K^e—*physiology*. Make the best use of your best time. At what time of day are you most effective? Are you a morning person or a night person? When I get up at 4:30 or 5:00 A.M., if I work for an hour and a half right then and there, that time is probably equivalent to two and a half or three hours later in the day, because I am much more focused. If you aren't really awake until three in the afternoon, or if you are a night person, plan your day to make best use of your peak performance times.

   If you don't already know when you function best, monitor yourself for a few days to discover at what times of day you are most effective. The best use of your prime time is ideally for your most important and creative projects. It's also best if this time is uninterrupted.

   The other consideration regarding physiology is fatigue. If you experience fatigue, use principles in the last section of this chapter to reduce it or eliminate it entirely.

2. *Right-brain sensory planning.* A daily goal and activity list provides an external visual plan (V^e) as well as internally *seeing the whole picture** of how the day will unfold (V^i). This, of course, also engages the right side of the brain. Then as you go through the details of the day, it is easier to maintain perspective and balance. The writing itself is kinesthetic (K^e), and imagining how you will feel when your goals are accomplished gives an internal dimension (K^i). If you want an auditory dimension, you might talk to yourself as you make the list (A^e) and have that soft, soothing, sexy voice inside (A^i) invite you to enjoy the day's activities.

   The mistake many people make in daily planning is focusing

---

*Seeing the broader, whole picture is sometimes called *upchunking*—the opposite of downchunking, or breaking the whole into smaller parts.

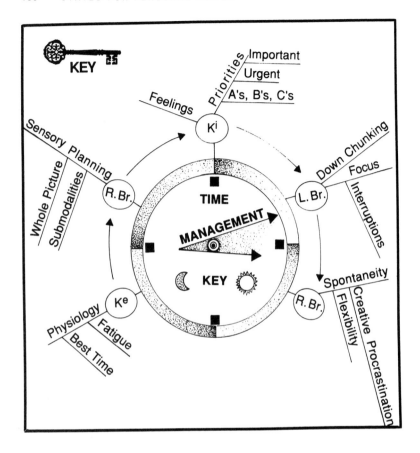

FIGURE 11.2

too much on the process or work of getting through the day, as opposed to imagining the outcomes. They often hear that internal scolding voice telling them what they have to do (A^i), feel the drudgery of the work ahead (K^i), and picture potential failure and missed deadlines. What gives power to daily planning is visualizing your success (V^i), hearing that inviting internal voice (A^i), and imagining how you will feel with your plans accomplished (K^i).

A list also frees you from having to remember all the work projects, classes, assignments, errands, and social commitments you want to do that day. If you number your list according to priorities, you never have to worry about what to do next.

If you write your list on a 3″ by 5″ card or a folded piece of paper, you can keep it with you during the day. In that way you can enjoy the reward of crossing off items as you complete them. Also, it will be convenient to add new ideas for today or tomorrow as you think of them.

Some people like to make their list first thing in the morning, to start with freshness and clarity each day. Others prefer to plan the next day at the end of the afternoon or evening. They find it helps them let go of unfinished tasks and gives a greater continuity from one day to the next.

What works well for me is to do both—to note at the end of the day what I did and didn't get done, and what I would like to carry over to the next day. The next morning, with a fresh perspective, I review plans I made the evening before. Along with a daily list, weekly and monthly lists together with a pocket calendar allow a broader perspective. They help you see the larger picture of your life.

3. K^i—*feelings about the day's activities.* This step involves being honest with yourself in deciding how you feel about each planned activity or goal.

- Which items are you most inspired to do, and which do not overly excite you? In particular, decide the one item you least want to do, and make sure to do that item first. We will come back to this point in the section on reducing or eliminating fatigue.
- Distinguish between which items are *important* (positive K^i) vs. which are *urgent* (negative K^i). I wonder how many of us spend most of our time doing urgent things—meeting deadlines, working on crises, putting out fires. What about the *important* things? What's important is what you want to be doing over the course of your life and what is closest to your heart—your shortterm, midterm, and long-term goals. Are you doing something each day to move you closer to these goals?

Most experts on time management agree that it is essential to spend some time each day doing something to move closer to your goals, even if it is just a few minutes or half an hour. At least you will know you are making small steps and progress. Otherwise, if the only thing you are doing is meeting deadlines, and solving crises, what's the point?

• *Prioritize items on your list.* A classic system is A's, B's, and C's. The A's are top priority—you definitely want to do them today. These are items you cannot afford to postpone until tomorrow—an assignment at school, work due today or tomorrow, or progress toward your most important goals. The B's have second priority. It would be nice to do them today, but the world won't fall apart if you don't. The C's are of lower priority and do not require immediate attention. They are often small, easy jobs—shopping for shoes or picking up a *Consumer Reports* article on a car you may buy in a year.

After you start the day with that one item you least want to do, then do the A's first. In that way, if there are things you don't get to on your list, you have the most important things out of the way. In fact, I like to make three separate lists: the A's, the B's, and the C's. I almost always get all of the A's done, most of the B's, and maybe some of the C's. At the end of the day, instead of focusing on what I didn't do, I can see the most important things I accomplished and how I made the best use of my time.

You can ask yourself two questions that can help you prioritize: "What would happen if I didn't do this item today?" and "What's the worst that would happen if I didn't do this item at all?" Also, you want to make sure that your activity is bringing you some degree of personal happiness, growth, and satisfaction.

C MANIA

A common pitfall in time management is to get distracted from the difficult A's you are working on in favor of accomplishing a number of easier C's. In the midst of working on a report due tomorrow, you suddenly find yourself compelled to reorganize your closet, change your spark plugs, or call the Army buddy you haven't spoken with in fifteen years.

C's are often more appealing than A's because they are easier to do, more familiar, and run less risk of failure. If you feel you might be getting sucked into C's, ask yourself if the job you are doing really needs to be done now. "Do I really need to be alphabetizing my canned vegetables, or would it be better to be working on my income taxes, which have to be postmarked in two hours?" If you catch yourself absorbed in C's, be easy with yourself and gently bring yourself back to the more important tasks.

4. *Left-brain focus and downchunking.* One of the best ways to promote focus is to *avoid interruptions.* This is especially important during your prime time to help maintain focus and concentration. You might tell people around you that you work alone at certain hours—for example, between 8:00 A.M. and 10:30 A.M.—and will answer phone calls and get back to visitors later. An answering machine that screens calls can be a great help in this regard. You can leave a message stating the best times to reach you and ask your callers to leave a detailed message. Also, if you're expecting one important call, you can screen the others and get back to them later.

Of course, that's not always possible, so some people hide out during their prime time. Others come into work an hour or more early to get an undistracted start for the day and their important projects. With their increased efficiency they can often leave work earlier with more done.

Left-brain focus can also help you power through those least desirable or tedious projects you have a hard time getting started on. As with modular study, break the project into smaller pieces through downchunking (i.e., sessions of thirty to forty minutes). If it seems so dreadful you can't even muster the energy for this much time, work on it for just ten or fifteen minutes.

There is a principle from physics: *Static friction is greater than kinetic friction.* It is harder to get an object moving in the first place than to maintain motion once you get it moving.

You might decide at first not to work on the project but simply to spend ten to fifteen minutes to bring together the materials you will need to do it, or to find out how you can learn what you need to know to do it. The next day you might begin the project with the stipulation you will spend no more than fifteen minutes on it no matter how much you are enjoying it. After the project gets moving and you feel the relief of finally having it under way, you can allow yourself the treat of extending the chunks to longer periods of up to forty minutes each.

5. *Right-brain Spontaneity.*

• *Maintain a sense of flexibility.* Have in back of your mind the question "What is the best use of my time right now?" Maybe you had certain plans this morning, but a number of distractions and interruptions came up. Now it is forty-five minutes before your lunch break, so what would be the best use of your time? You might want to change your previous agenda.

It's also a good idea to plan diversions during commutes and waiting times. Maybe you need to make a trip to the post office, and you know there is always a long line there. Reading a book while you stand in line is a marvelous way to improve the quality of your time. Likewise, travel and commuting times are excellent opportunities to learn a foreign language from cassette tapes. I'm learning several foreign languages during what might otherwise be dead time.

If you have the kind of job where you have to sit around from time to time, bring some of your own projects to work with. With all of these methods, you'll find you're getting a lot more accomplished with your life.

• *Schedule "creative procrastination" time.* In her book *Creative*

Procrastination, Frieda Porat suggests leaving some of your time unscheduled. When scheduled tasks take longer than expected or interruptions occur, this allows leeway. If everything goes as planned, you have time for an extended break, a walk or a hike, or time to be spontaneous and do something you hadn't planned.

Scheduled time should have a limit—perhaps until late afternoon or dinner. Having some unstructured time each day puts a limit on the potential tyranny of left-brain orderliness and the right brain to be spontaneous. Unstructured time is also essential for artists, writers, and other creative people. It can be a time to let your heart lead you into deeply fulfilling activity.

There is a story of a wealthy farmer who lived in New England during Colonial times. His neighbors were a poor Indian family who also farmed. One day, out of a sense of compassion, the farmer offered to give the Indian family forty acres of his land. The Indian husband thanked the farmer for his generosity but turned him down, saying, "If I have all that extra land to work, when would I have time to sing?"

Knowing that your scheduled structured time has a limit is often a motivator to improve your efficiency during that time.

TIME LINES

Think for a second about your past. If you could imagine a physical direction for events in your past, which way would that be: toward your left? behind you? under you? Point in that direction. Next, think about your future. If you could visualize a direction for events in your future, which way would that be? Point in that direction. Finally, notice which way you might imagine events in the present: right in front of you? below you? maybe over to one side? Point in that direction. If you don't have a clear sense for these directions, give it your best guess.

TIME LINES (continued)

To sort events from the past, present, and future—that is, to distinguish which events go where—we all unconsciously assign various directions for different time periods. Connecting those directions together gives a straight line or sometimes a curve we call our time line.

A person who "lives in the past" may literally have a time line with the past more visible than with the present or the future. In the same way, someone who lives for tomorrow ("future-oriented") may have a time line with the future more visible than with the past or the present.

Therapies based on working with a person's time line have evolved to help people with time perception problems—someone who never learns from the past, or the person who lives only for now and can't plan for the future, or a person whose future appears dim. Time line work also provides techniques to make your dreams and goals more compelling.

PAPER FLOW

A golden rule for paper flow is to handle each piece of paper once or twice at most. If you do this, you will make immediate decisions, and stacks of unattended papers will no longer have the tyranny of tying up your mental energy.

Whatever mail I keep from my college mailbox goes into three stacks on my desk. The A stack—whatever is top priority and must be done today—is the only one that remains on my desk. The B stack would be nice to do today, but it isn't crucial. These items get filed into a pending bin or a tickler file to do later this week. The C items are papers and correspondence I can't quite throw away. Maybe one day I'll need them.

The classic remedy for C papers is a C drawer. I don't even take the time to file these items. If I ever need them, I can shuffle through the drawer and find them. Periodically I purge the drawer to see if the items are still of interest.

One last point on paper flow is use of your desk. Ideally, the desk is a tool for processing only current priority items for today. That's all you should see on the top of your desk.

REDUCING OR ELIMINATING FATIGUE

One of the biggest causes of fatigue is procrastination. Besides having to do an unpleasant task, looking forward to it may be unpleasant as well—a second source of fatigue. As we have discussed, a classic way to deal with procrastination involves putting that one item you least want to do first on your daily list. Follow this by the most important "A" items.

I wonder if you've ever done that and noticed how you feel afterward. Most people feel a sense of exhilaration knowing that the most difficult item for the day is done. It may not even be that important—apologizing to someone or signing some papers—but for whatever reason, you've been procrastinating. When you get that task over with, it frees up a lot of energy.

Be careful that the item you start with is not too big a project. Otherwise you might not do anything else that day. If it's too big, downchunk into small unpleasant pieces as we discussed earlier, and start with one chunk each day. At home I keep what I call my "procrastination list"—all the undone tasks from the past few months. I find that if I start the day with one of those items, as the list shrinks, my energy goes up. It's a direct relationship. Sometimes the easiest way to get started on a difficult project is simply to bring together all the materials you will need to do it.

Besides this, other things you can do to reduce or eliminate fatigue are:

• *Exercise.* Some of the best exercises for fatigue are also the best for cardiovascular fitness: aerobic exercise as recommended by the American Heart Association. Follow their guidelines: Exercise three to four times a week on alternate days. The exercise should get your pulse up to a certain level, depending on your age and physical condition. It should also be something you enjoy so you will keep up the routine. Dancing, hiking, cycling, aerobics, and swimming are all very stimulating.

A good, consistent routine will not only reduce your tendency toward fatigue, but you will also find increased clarity of thought and focus. Exercise makes you feel better—physically, mentally, and emotionally.

• *Diet.* The most crucial meal to eliminate fatigue is lunch. Two items to avoid for lunch are high-protein foods, and fats or oils.[1] The suggestion about protein may seem surprising, but most of us eat much more protein than our bodies can possibly use. What the body does not require, it breaks down, but at an energy drain to the body. The average American diet is also far richer than necessary in fats and sugar—an unhealthy way to get calories.

Your best bet for lunch is to go with complex carbohydrates and fresh fruits or vegetables. Complex carbohydrates include beans, corn, pasta, breads, potatoes, and rice—what we used to call starches. A complex carbohydrate is a complex sugar that breaks down slowly and supplies energy gradually over a long time. This is one of the major ways marathon runners get their energy.

If you eat raw fruits or raw vegetables, it is best not to have them both in the same meal. Raw fruits and raw vegetables require different digestive enzymes, which interfere with digestion of the other. If either is cooked, however, it doesn't matter.

If you follow the old maxim "Eat breakfast like a king, lunch like a prince, and dinner like a pauper," you will feel better and be less prone to fatigue. Also practice "systematic undereating."[2] Eat to a point that you are just about satisfied but could eat a little more—and stop. Too much digestive activity makes anyone sluggish.

Breakfast is a good time for high protein, since you have the rest of the day to digest it. For lunch it is best not to stuff yourself and to stay with the recommendations above. A light and early dinner improves the quality and depth of your sleep. Obviously, if your physician or nutritional counselor has given you other advice, follow it.

• *An afternoon nap or meditation break.* I'm not sure if you have a couch or a bed in your office, but a short afternoon nap can not only perk up the rest of the afternoon and evening but also may reduce the amount of sleep you require. Meditation is also an excellent way to eliminate fatigue and energize yourself.

• *Alternate physical and mental tasks and take breaks.* Varying tasks and routine can take some of the drudgery out of what you are doing. And as we've discussed, taking a break every thirty to forty minutes helps maintain energy and improves memory.

• *Periodic rewards:* These might include snacks, some time doing something you especially enjoy, or taking a walk; these can help motivate you to get through tedious tasks, and add richness to your passage through time.

LIVING LIFE WITH INTELLIGENCE AND PASSION

*Ask yourself what you would do,
if you knew,
you could not fail*
—ANTHONY ROBBINS

Intelligence is a measure of the overall performance of our brain. It is the basis of contemplating atoms, appreciating art, mastering sports, or feeling religious devotion. It is the foundation of enjoying what we see, hear, feel, smell, and taste. It is also basic to higher love and fulfilling our dreams.

Passion is the juice of being alive. It is the fire within our dreams, the spontaneity of now, the power behind empowering states, a key ingredient of true intelligence.

This chapter presents some innovative methods for improving intelligence and living with life with passion—through empowering states—for peak performance in learning, sports, and enjoyment of life.

INCREASING YOUR INTELLIGENCE

Intelligence as measured through IQ testing has been thought to peak when we reach adulthood (at about seventeen or eighteen). Beyond that age it was thought to remain fairly constant, and to decline with old age. People also believed that our IQ was mainly inherited.

As it turns out, environmental factors as we grow up can have profound effects on our intelligence. We can also improve our intelligence at any age with appropriate physical activity, mental exercises, and visualization.

Because a bit of well-directed practice with IQ-type questions can significantly improve the results, IQ testing has come under some criticism. In addition, IQ testing leaves out some qualities that could make a big difference in a person's overall intelligence, such as:

- flexibility and creativity
- independent thinking
- appreciation of beauty and humor
- originality in dealing with novel situations

There are, however, other forms of testing that take some of these factors into account.

SIX SECRETS TO IMPROVE YOUR INTELLIGENCE

Since intelligence enhances our appreciation and enjoyment of life, and since each of us *craves* greater achievement and happiness, I have chosen the acronym, CRAVES to illustrate six secrets to improving intelligence. These are.

C: Circulation in your brain
R: Right-brain/left-brain exercises
A: Avoid dulling influences
V: Visualization exercises

E: Enrich your environment
S: Synchronize your brain waves

FIGURE 12.1

Let's consider each of these.

1. *Circulation in your brain.* Improve the circulation in your brain. Some researchers have speculated that Einstein's genius was in part due to enhanced capillary circulation within his brain.

   As we have discussed earlier, after age thirty we lose brain cells at an average of roughly ten thousand per day. The 5 to 10 percent of your neurons that do develop to their full potential (thousands of dendrites) are presumably the best nourished; the ones that die off are likely the least nourished.

   Aerobic exercise, recommended by the American Heart Association, improves circulation and extension of the capillary system throughout the body—including, of course, the brain.

   In a Canadian study,[1] three hundred school-age children participated in an exercise program. As they became better fit physically, their grades simultaneously improved. Other studies have also demonstrated that exercise promotes better emotional stability, memory, and clearer thinking.

2. *Right-brain/left-brain exercises.* There is a growing body of evidence showing that by working to improve one area of the brain, other areas simultaneously improve. The two halves of the cortex are specialized but not isolated. Each side complements and improves the performance of the other. My suggestion to right-brain professionals such as artists, actors, dancers, and musicians is that they can improve their performance by taking a course in algebra, computers, or science. Left-brain professionals such as engineers, accountants, or clerical workers can improve their left-brain skills by taking a drawing class, a dance class, acting, or perhaps learning to play a musical instrument.

When school budgets are tight, what is the first thing to go? Art . . . music . . . drama—all right-brain activities! The potential here is that we are crippling our children intellectually. In a classic study[2] in Mead School in the Byram section of Greenwich, Connecticut, children spent 50 percent of their time doing traditional schoolwork and a full 50 percent of their time doing right-brain activities. Do you know what happened? Of course, the right-brain skills improved, but so did left-brain performance in areas such as math, science, and English grammar.

As we discussed earlier, drawing is a powerful means to put you in touch with right-brain functioning. Acting is another powerful approach. The other right-brain shifters discussed in Chapter Five are also useful.

There are a number of good books on logical puzzles that allow you to enhance left-brain functioning. Books designed to prepare you for IQ testing will also help. The left-brain shifters—crossword puzzles, making up puns, asking detailed questions—are useful. Good mystery books are another aid.

In planning your daily schedule, if you alternate mental and physical activity as well as right-brain and left-brain activities, you can improve your effectiveness.

3. *Avoid dulling influences.* Drug and alcohol abuse can not only distort your mental functioning but also literally kill or pickle millions of brain cells. Smoking affects your brain for the same reason it affects your heart: breathing in excess carbon monoxide. A single puff has ten to fifteen times the concentration of

carbon monoxide considered dangerous by air pollution authorities. Treat your brain with respect and dignity. Remember that it is the most superb engineering feat we know of.

On the other side of the coin, you can promote sharp functioning of your brain by taking care of your physiology—with proper diet, exercise, and *proper rest*. Remember the dietary strategies from Chapter Eleven to reduce fatigue and increase energy.

4. *Visualization exercises.* Improving your powers of visualization will promote creativity, give you a clear internal picture of your goals and success, and perhaps develop the corpus collosum linking the left and right hemispheres. Dreams and images are the language of the right. Interpreting and understanding these images is a job for the left. The corpus collosum allows flow of thought back and forth. Make use of the visual thinking techniques from Chapter Five and the visual memory methods from Chapter Seven.

5. *Enrich your environment* (and your children's). Numerous studies[3] on gifted children show that intelligence is not so much hereditary as it is a result of a rich, stimulating environment, especially during the first few years. Julius Caesar began his schooling as a warrior riding into battle at age three with his uncle. Alexander the Great also started quite young.

In the early 1800s a German doctor, Witte, set out to give his son Karl completely enriched surroundings. Karl then entered the University of Leipzig at age nine, and received his Ph.D. at fourteen and his Doctorate of Law at sixteen.

Lord Kelvin, one of the great nineteenth-century physicists, began with a rich early home environment. He was admitted to the University of Glasgow at age ten and lived a full and productive life to age eighty-three.

Mozart was immersed in his father's music and instruments from birth. He was playing and composing by age five and composed his first symphony at age eight.

In 1952 Aaron Stern[4] in New York gave his daughter an enriched environment with classical music, flash cards with numbers and pictures, and frequent talking to her with *no* baby talk. By four she had read the *Encyclopaedia Britannica*; by twelve she had entered college; and by fifteen she was teaching higher mathematics at Michigan State University. Her IQ is about 200 (150 is considered genius level).

It is important to distinguish between providing a rich, stimulating environment as opposed to *pressuring* children to satisfy their parents' egos. The concept of early learning has come into question as a result of bad experiences children have had from excess parental pressure and the fear that early intellectual development will somehow detract from the child's emotional and social growth.

The fact is that when children grow up in an environment that is enriched, loving, and relaxed, they are not social misfits. They also don't tend to excel in only one field but do well in studies, artistic activities, leadership skills, and personal relationships. In one study,[5] Dr. Terman tested over a thousand people with an IQ over 135. He found their physical health to be better than the average population; their divorce rates were lower; and educational achievement was, of course, much better.

These results with children are well known. What has not been as well recognized is that adults might also benefit from enriched surroundings. Dr. J. Altman and Dr. Gopal Das[6] took a group of adults rats and set them up in a stimulating, enriched environment. The result after a few weeks was increased intelligence compared with the control group (biological relatives). Key areas of the brains of the rats in the enriched surroundings were observed to have improved dramatically in size and chemical functioning.

ACTIVITIES TO ENRICH YOUR ENVIRONMENT

- Try out new activities (things you've never done before).
- Take new courses of study.
- Cover all your senses when learning.
- Surround yourself with beauty, art, music, good lighting, and color.

ACTIVITIES TO ENRICH YOUR ENVIRONMENT (continued)

• Vary your routine.
• Travel.
• Test your personal values and beliefs by trying out viewpoints that contradict your own.
• Have an appropriate balance of right-/and left-brain daily activities.
• Each day ask yourself, "What did I do today that was new and different?"

6. *Synchronize your brain waves.* One of the more powerful methods to enhance your intelligence and to put yourself into a resourceful state is also one of the simplest. It is an ancient mental-relaxation and stress-reduction technique that has recently been "rediscovered."

The brain puts out weak electrical signals called brain waves, or more technically EEG waves. These vary in frequency. Both sides of the brain put out a mixture of frequencies; the side more involved with the activity at hand puts out a stronger signal. The less-involved half puts out a weaker signal with more alpha waves, indicating it is more relaxed.

BRAIN WAVE TYPES

Type	Frequency	Associated with
Delta	0.5–4 Hz	Deep sleep
Theta	4–7 Hz	Deep meditation and reverie—"twilight" level of consciousness
Alpha	8–14 Hz	Relaxed state or daydreaming
Beta	14–22 Hz	Wakefulness; wide awake or engaged in mental activity

A common characteristic of the signals is that brain waves on one side are very different from brain waves on the other. This indicates that the two halves of the brain are not synchronized or coherent.

During practice of the mental relaxation technique mentioned above, something very different begins to occur. Dr. J. P. Banquet[7] observed that the brain waves become purified in frequency and synchronized between left and right. The waves are not identical but are much more alike than normal. After people practice this technique over a period of time, some of the brain waves synchrony begins to carry over into activity. This would seem to indicate more of a balanced functioning between left and right.

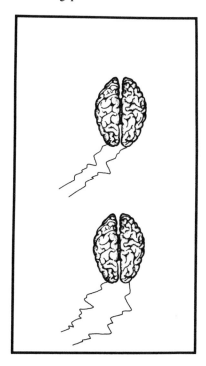

FIGURE 12.2

You might wonder what the advantage would be of sitting down, relaxing, and having your brain wave synchronized. Over six hundred scientific studies done on people experiencing this state of awareness have demonstrated some far-reaching benefits for memory, creativity, and intelligence.

Researchers have observed that when a person takes up this practice, both long-term and short-term memory immediately improved.[8] Comprehension and ability to focus also improve. Abstract reasoning (especially important in mathematics, sciences, and computers) improves, and creativity is enhanced.

Short-term studies have demonstrated an increase of intelligence as measured by field independence, and long-term studies[9] of three to five years show a steady increase of intelligence as measured by fluidity. This testing in contrast with usual IQ testing, is not altered by educational background or preparation.

Later studies have shown a synchrony among the back, center, and front of the cortex, as well as vertical synchrony within the brain. Synchrony between the back and center of the cortex would suggest improved perceptual motor activities such as sports and dance. A number of studies have indeed shown this to be the case, and many professional athletes now practice this technique. Vertical synchrony may also account for autonomic changes such as in blood pressure, respiratory rate, and pulse observed to be considerably lower than in deep sleep.

At this point you are probably wondering what technique I am talking about. I've been describing a form of meditation called *Transcendental Meditation*, or TM for short. I am most familiar with this form of meditation, since I have practiced it for about twenty years. If you meditate fifteen or twenty minutes twice a day, you begin experiencing better memory, clearer thinking, increased physical well-being, synchronized brain waves, and empowering states more often.

Other forms of meditation may produce similar benefits, but TM is the most researched form and the only technique I am aware of that produces brain-wave synchrony to this extent. Transcendental meditation is taught one to one by trained teachers at TM centers in most larger cities throughout the world.

Now see if you can reconstruct the six secrets to increase your intelligence contained in CRAVES.

AGING AND MEDITATION[10]

Our biological aging can apparently be slowed as a result of meditation. Dr. Keith Wallace and others have discovered that people practicing TM for five to ten years frequently have a biological age five to ten years less than their actual age.

We have known for a long time that aging is very individual. It is as though we each have an internal biological clock, each running at a different rate. Now we may have a way to slow our clocks down.

POWER ANCHORS

Don and Dorris were celebrating their twentieth anniversary at a romantic restaurant with candlelight, champagne, inviting aromas, and soft music in the background. Don got up to request a certain song from the band, came back to the table, touched Dorris on the back of her neck in a certain way, and suddenly she felt depressed.

I wonder if you have had a similar experience of going through the day feeling fine, when suddenly, for no apparent reason, you are depressed . . . or maybe the reverse, where you are in a lousy mood when "something snaps" and you feel fine.

In Chapter Seven we discussed *memory anchors*, wherein a strong emotion or physical sensation becomes connected with or anchored to a memory. Beyond simple memories, a visual, auditory, or kinesthetic stimulus can trigger an emotion or an entire state. Such connections are called *state anchors*.

Do you notice feeling a sense of serenity when you look at your favorite painting? Perhaps "our song" brings back romantic feelings you had with that special someone. Or maybe you notice a different emotion when that stranger on the highway gives you an obscene gesture because you're not going ninety miles per hour. Each of these perceptions—the painting, the music, and the gesture—are neutral by themselves. Somewhere in the past our brains have linked or anchored these with states.

State anchors naturally occur when a V,A, or K experience becomes unconsciously linked with a memory or state. There was a time when children taking piano lessons would get their knuckles whacked with a ruler each time they made a mistake. No one could understand why so many people developed a fear of playing the piano.

I remember a time when I made it a point to call my old girlfriend at the end of a weekend of leading seminars. I was normally feeling satisfied at successfully completing the seminars and anxious to hear her voice, yet very tired. After some time I began to notice something strange: In the middle of a highly energetic day I could call her to chat and suddenly find myself feeling tired. I was beginning to wonder if the romance was waning when it occurred to me that I had inadvertently anchored the sound of her voice with feeling tired. Some psychologists in fact feel that the downfall of many romantic relationships is a mismatch of thinking styles (VAK) and too many negative anchors from unpleasant arguments, anger, and hurt that unconsciously become anchored with the other's face, tone of voice, or touch.

Positive-/and negative-state anchors are naturally created unconsciously. When stimulated or *fired* in the future, they elicit various states—some pleasant, some not so pleasant. Thus many states occur beyond our conscious awareness. Is it possible, however, to neutralize negative state anchors and create positive ones for the states we desire? The answer from NLP is a resounding "yes." The connection of a number of empowering states to a single stimulus is called a *power anchor*, and power anchors are likely the quickest and most powerful ways to access empowering and resourceful states.

Suppose, as an example, you wanted to create a state in which you feel powerful and confident. Or maybe you would like a state where you feel happy and joyful. Or perhaps your would like a state where you feel especially creative and flexible. In each case, proceed with the following steps:

CREATING A POWER ANCHOR

1. Find a quiet spot where you can sit comfortably undisturbed. Relax and breathe easily.
2. Go back to a time when you were totally experiencing your desired state. Be in that situation as if it were happening *now*. Notice the sights, sounds, and especially the feelings from that experience.
3. Intensify the feelings from this state. Finding and adjusting the submodalities that are most significant for you can be helpful here.
4. When the feelings reach a peak, do a *unique* stimulus: Touch some part of your body in an unusual way, speak an unusual word, or look at something unusual. The most crucial part of the entire process is having the stimulus coincide with the peak of the experience.

CREATING A POWER ANCHOR (continued)

5. Change your state by standing up, walking around, or drinking something for a few minutes.
6. Test the anchor by firing it—that is, experience the touch, sound, or sight. If you do not go back into the desired state, redo steps 2 to 6 or use a different stimulus for your anchor.
7. Whenever you naturally find yourself in the desired state, you can *stack* your anchor by firing it at the peak of that experience.
8. You can create a power anchor by stacking a number of different empowering states using the same anchor.

You can also create anchors for other people—touching your lover in a certain way when he or she is in a particularly resourceful state . . . stimulating your child at a magical moment of delight or discovery.

PEAK PERFORMANCE IN LEARNING

A crucial step toward owning the knowledge we wish to master is to be able to use it in a performance context—passing a test, using the new skills in a tennis match, being at one's best during a job interview. You may have used the reading, study, or memory techniques from this book to learn the material, so now you want to set up a state of peak performance for using it.

A natural starting point is to begin with your physiology—getting enough sleep the night before, imagining how you would be sitting or standing if you felt totally confident and empowered, and perhaps a few minutes of stretching or light exercise.

A powerful way to engage appropriate IR's is through a method called the George Technique. Dr. Donald Schuster from Iowa State University suggests the following, which should take five to ten minutes:

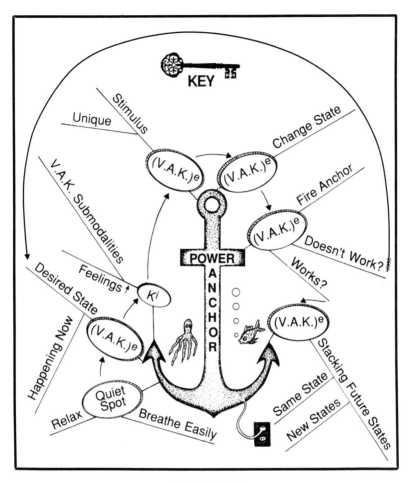

FIGURE 12.3

THE GEORGE TECHNIQUE[11]

The name George comes from an expression used in Colonial times. Whenever someone didn't want to do something or was procrastinating, the saying was "Let George do it."

The idea here is to give your unconscious a name: George, Georgette, or any other name to make this part of you more personal. Then when you have a stressful situation, such as a test, a job interview, a tennis match, or difficult learning, you can ask George or Georgette for help.

You can ask for help in two ways. One is to write a short note or letter: "Dear George (or Georgette): Here are the reasons why I would like to do well in this situation . . ." Then list the reasons. By doing this you are taking care of the left side of your brain with words, logic, linear thought, and reasoning.

For the right side of the brain, mentally project yourself into the activity. For example, if you are going to take a test, imagine yourself feeling confident and energetic. The adrenaline is starting to flow, and this leads you to peak performance. You are answering the questions, remembering everything, and working quickly. When test-taking in this easy state, what emotions do you feel? What do you feel in your body? How do things look? How do they sound? Finally, thank that unconscious part of you as if you had already succeeded.

You cover the left brain with the note and the right brain with the mental imagery. The sense of gratitude is also important. The more thankful you are for the help your unconscious provides, the more it wants to help in the future. In a very real sense, you are establishing the link between your own conscious and unconscious minds.

The last and most powerful step in establishing your state is to fire your power anchor. In fact, if you are pressed for time, it is enough just to do the steps for your physiology and use the anchor. If time allows, add the George Technique.

If your performance situation is a test, here are a few more suggestions:

- *Anchor success to the physical setting where you will be taking the test.* If possible, take some practice questions that you feel confident about into the same room where you will be taking the test. Gain the experience of successfully answering testlike questions in that setting. If that room is not available, see if you can find a nearby room that is reasonably similar in layout and setting.
- *Gain right-brain perspective and elicit unconscious help.* Read the test questions through before starting to work so you can begin to see the whole picture. Start on easier questions to begin the momentum of success. When you get stuck on a question, mark it, and return to it later. This allows your unconscious to work on the problem while you are successfully working on other questions.
- *Construct pattern discovery maps to help answer essay questions.* This is the quickest way to see the whole picture of how to organize your thoughts. The map also facilitates pulling missing chunks from memory.
- *In the event of test anxiety or panic, look up.* The problem with taking a test and experiencing anxiety is that you are looking down to answer the questions. This kinesthetic pose perpetuates more unpleasant feelings. To reduce or eliminate these feelings, change your physiology. Take a few minutes to assume a visual posture— sitting straight up and looking up. It is very difficult to maintain unpleasant feelings in this position. Beyond that you might briefly stretch or sharpen your pencil.

SIX SUCCESS SECRETS

The ultimate formula to achieve the success you want and deserve consists of six little secrets—SMARTS:

S: Specific goals
M: Motivation
A. Act
R: Reward system
T: Think clearly and powerfully
S: Stay with it

Let's see how each of these influences your success in learning, improving your relationships, changing your habits, or advancing your career.

1. *Specific goals.* Many failures in life come from lack of clear, specific goals. You need to know clearly the outcome you desire. If you get on an airplane and just start flying without a specific destination, you are liable to wind up anywhere. Even if you go to a travel agency and say you want to go to Hawaii, they can't help you. Hawaii is too nonspecific. Where in Hawaii? However, if you say you want to go to Honolulu on March 20, now you are getting somewhere.

Once you have a specific goal of *what you want, by what date*, the next step is to answer the following questions: How will you know when you have achieved your goal? What evidence is required? If, for example, you desire to be wealthy, how much money will it take before you consider yourself wealthy? If you want more happiness, what evidence will you use to decide you are happy?

With this specific information your unconscious can program you mentally to allow you to achieve that goal. Be specific and detailed in the results you want—not how you are going to achieve those results. The unconscious mind will generate creative ideas and plans you never dreamed of. Then you will become open to those occurrences and circumstances in daily life that will support your success. All you need is to know clearly what you want and how you will know when you have achieved it.

Choosing models whose success you would like to develop also helps. You might also write out your goals and post them in a conspicuous place as a daily reminder of your life's direction.

2. *Motivation.* It is essential that you cultivate desire and interest in your goal, whether it is getting an "A" in a computer class or getting twenty consecutive tennis serves in. The more motivated you are, the easier it is to learn to remember and to advance your skills.

The two most powerful ways to cultivate motivation are to use your motivation key and your power anchor. In addition, visualizing your success with the George Technique enables

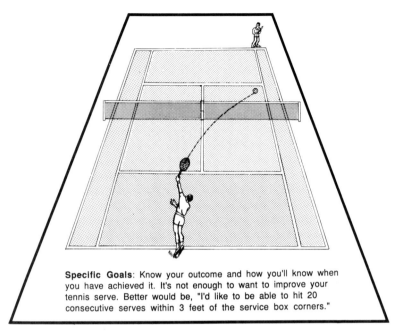

Specific Goals: Know your outcome and how you'll know when you have achieved it. It's not enough to want to improve your tennis serve. Better would be, "I'd like to be able to hit 20 consecutive serves within 3 feet of the service box corners."

FIGURE 12.4

your right brain to see the whole picture of achieving success, and your left brain to sort through details of the step-by-step sequence of events necessary to reach your goal.

You can also enhance motivation by adopting some of the beliefs of people you model. Of course, you only want to use those beliefs that will contribute to what you want to achieve. For example, I would love to have the skills and strategies of certain tennis stars, but could certainly do without their manners on the court.

EXERCISE 33: UNCONSCIOUS SUPPORT

One of the most crucial factors for effective motivation is to have 100 percent support from your unconscious. If part or parts of you are ambivalent about the goal, you are likely to self-sabotage your efforts. A powerful way to check for unconscious support and to resolve discrepancies is to answer and/or resolve certain questions about your goal honestly.

As an example, pick one specific goal and honestly answer and/or resolve these three key questions:

5. What positive benefits do you now have as a result of not having your goal?
6. Is there a way you can achieve your goal without having to give up these positive benefits? How can you do this?
7. Can you think of specific circumstances in which you would be better off without your goal? How can you resolve this?

Answering these questions may bring to the surface limiting beliefs that have been holding you back. It is important to examine the merits of these beliefs, how they may once have served you, and if you may now want to change some of them.

Setting specific goals makes your dreams concrete. Motivation fuels those dreams.

3. *Act.* Get yourself moving. Physics tells us that it is harder to get something moving than to keep it moving once it has started. Act without too much planning. Just get started.

A crucial first step toward action and change is to *accept yourself as you are now.* Only then do you have a clear reference point for change. Faith and self-trust are crucial to establish positive motivation and to undo your past negative beliefs or "learning blocks."

To build positive beliefs, concentrate your attention on your strengths, and acknowledge your successes as they occur.

Gratitude toward your unconscious mind is important here. The more you acknowledge your unconscious for its help, the more it is likely to help in the future.

4. *Reward system.* Set up a system of rewards or treats for achieving steps along the way for both short-term and long-term goals. This is a concrete way of expressing gratitude for the help your unconscious gives. Take time out for a movie, a picnic, a concert, or just free time to do nothing. Unstructured time can provide you with some of your most creative ideas.

Many people use rewards, but make the mistake of treating themselves well too infrequently. Some education specialists suggest at least once or twice per week. I agree.

Suppose you want to establish the habit of studying Spanish forty-five minutes each day. Psychologists tell us that it takes about twenty-one days to establish a daily routine as a habit.[13] To set up a reward system, divide twenty-one days into seven intervals of three days each. Then give yourself a gift or a treat at the end of each segment. Almost anyone can do an activity for just three days, and you'll be surprised at how quickly study becomes an automatic part of your routine. Using techniques in this book, you could learn about twenty-five hundred words and be conversationally fluent in Spanish or any other foreign language within about six months.

5. *Think clearly and powerfully.* Clear thinking and decision making can be clouded by strong emotions, including fear. The right-brain/left-brain shifters from Chapter Five allow you to shift easily away from any emotions that cloud movement toward your goals. Use visual, auditory, and kinesthetic thinking for appropriate situations.

Thinking powerfully also involves sensory acuity. Is what you are doing getting you the results you want? If not, take a different approach.

6. *Stay with it.* Specific goals start you moving, motivation fuels the process, but *persistence* and *flexibility* are what keep you on the path. Most people are too easily discouraged by what they perceive as failures. Consider this: Thomas Edison had nearly ten thousand failures before his first successful light bulb. Apparently he didn't even think of his first ten thousand tries as failures. Each one taught him how *not* to build a workable bulb.

HOW BEST TO USE POWERLEARNING

Powerlearning is in fact a philosophy of gaining personal power through enhanced memory, learning, thinking, and a collection of techniques. The methods are helpful only to the extent that we make good use of them. I suggest to my seminar participants that they are most likely to be successful if they implement the methods a little at a time.

Start with a few simple techniques in those areas of life that are most pressing, whether that be improving your reading skills, discovering and using your motivation key, improving your memory, managing your time and energy, or setting up a power anchor for yourself.

The uniqueness of Powerlearning is that we can experience the states we desire in dreams fulfilled as a means to achieve those dreams.

The value of improving your learning skills through Powerlearning is this: No matter what your goals, dreams, and desired states in life, achieving them always involves learning. To the extent that you can remember, think, and learn more effectively, you own your personal power—the ability and the choice to create what you desire.

READING PRETEST

FOR CHAPTER EIGHT

Record your starting time in hours, minutes, and seconds. To make things easier, wait for an even starting time such as: Hrs. <u>4</u> Min. <u>05</u> Sec. <u>00.</u> As soon as you have finished, record the end time and subtract to get the actual reading time. Later you will find a chart to get your reading speed. As soon as you are ready, record your starting time and begin.

	Hours	Minutes	Seconds
End time	——	——	——
Starting time	——	——	——
Reading time	——	——	——

"From Plankton to Whales" from Kon-Tiki by Thor Heyerdahl.[1]

It is certain that there must be very nourishing food in these almost invisible plankton which drift about with the current on the oceans in infinite numbers. Fish and sea birds which do not eat plankton themselves live on other fish or sea animals which do, no matter how large they themselves may be. Plankton is a general name for thousands of species of visible and invisible small organisms which drift about near the surface of the sea. Some are plants (phyto-plankton), while others are loose fish ova and tiny living creatures (zoo-plankton). Animal plankton live on vegetable plankton, and vegetable plankton live on ammonia, nitrates, and nitrites which are formed from dead animal plankton. And while they reciprocally live on one another, they all form food for everything which moves in and over the sea. What they cannot offer in size they can offer in numbers.

In good plankton waters there are thousands in a glassful. More than once persons have starved to death at sea because they did not find fish large enough to be spitted, netted, or hooked. In such cases it has often happened that they have literally been sailing in strongly diluted, raw fish soup. If, in addition to hooks and nets, they had had a utensil for straining the soup they were sitting in, they would have found a nourishing meal—plankton. Some day in the future, perhaps, men will think of harvesting plankton from the sea to the same extent as they now harvest grain on land. A single grain is of no use, either, but in large quantities it becomes food.

The marine biologist, Dr. A. D. Bajkov, told us of plankton and sent us a fishing net which was suited to the creatures we were to catch. The "net" was a silk net with almost three thousand meshes per square inch. It was sewn in the shape of a funnel with a circular mouth behind an iron ring, eighteen inches across, and was towed behind the raft. Just as in other kinds of fishing, the catch varied with time and place. Catches diminished as the sea grew warmer farther west, and we got best results at night, because many species seemed to go deeper down into the water when the sun was shining.

If we had no other way of whiling away time on board the raft, there would have been entertainment enough lying with our noses in the plankton net. Not for the sake of the smell, for that was bad. Nor because the sight was appetizing, for it looked a horrible mess. But because, if we spread the plankton out on board and examined each of the little creatures separately with the naked eye, we had before us fantastic shapes and colors in unending variety.

Most of them were in tiny shrimp like crustaceans (copepods) or fish ova floating loose, but there were also larvae of fish and shellfish, curious miniature crabs in all colors, jellyfish, and an endless variety of small creatures which might have been taken from Walt Disney's *Fantasia*. Some looked like fringed, fluttering spooks cut out of cellophane paper, while others resembled tiny red-beaked birds with hard shells instead of feathers. There was no end to Nature's extravagant inventions in the plankton world; a surrealistic artist might well own himself here.

Where the cold Humboldt Current turned west south of the equator, we could pour several pounds of plankton porridge out of the bag every few hours. The plankton lay packed together like cake in colored layers—brown, red, gray and green according to the different fields of plankton through which we had passed. At night, when there was phosphorescence about, it was like hauling a bag of sparkling jewels. But, when we got hold of it, the pirates' treasure turned into millions of tiny glittering shrimps and phosphorescent fish larvae that glowed in the dark like a heap of live coals. When we poured them into a bucket, the squashy mess ran out like a magic gruel composed of glowworms. Our night's catch looked as nasty at close quarters as it had been pretty at a long range. And, bad as it smelled, it tasted correspondingly good if one just plucked up courage and put a spoonful of it into one's mouth. If this consisted of many dwarf shrimps, it tasted like shrimp paste, lobster, or crab. If it was mostly deep-sea fish ova, it tasted like caviar and now and then like oysters.

The inedible vegetable plankton were either too small that they washed away with the water through the meshes of the net, or they were so large that we could pick them up with our fingers. "Snags" in the dish were single jellylike coelenterates like glass balloons and jellyfish about half an inch long. These were bitter and had to be thrown away. Otherwise everything could be eaten, either as it was or cooked in fresh water as gruel or soup. Tastes differ. Two men on board thought plankton tasted delicious, two thought they were quite good, and for two the sight of them was more than enough. From a nutrition standpoint they stand on a level with the larger shellfish, and, spiced and properly prepared, they can certainly be a first class dish for all who like marine food.

That these small organisms contain calories enough have been proved by the blue whale, which is the largest animal in the world and yet lives on plankton. Our own method of capture, with the little net which was often chewed up by hungry fish, seemed to us sadly primitive when we sat on the raft and saw a passing whale send up cascades of water as it simply filtered plankton through its celluloid beard. And one day we lost the whole net in the sea.

"Why don't you plankton-eaters do like him?" Torstein and Bengt said contemptuously to the rest of us, pointing to a blowing whale. "Just fill your mouths and blow the water out through your mustaches!"

I have seen whales in the distance from boats, and I have seen them stuffed in museums, but I have never felt toward the gigantic carcass as one usually feels toward proper warm-blooded animals, for example a horse or an elephant. Biologically, indeed, I had accepted the whale as a genuine mammal, but in its essence it was to all intents and purposes a large cold fish. We had a different impression when the great whales came rushing toward us, close to the side of the raft.

One day, when we were sitting as usual on the edge of the raft having a meal, so close to the water that we had only to lean back to wash out our mugs, we started when suddenly something behind us blew hard like a swimming horse and a big whale came up and stared at us, so close that we saw a shine like a polished shoe down through its blowhole. It was so unusual to hear real breathing out at sea, where all living creatures wriggle silently about without lungs and quiver their gills, that we really had a warm family feeling for our old distant cousin the whale, who like us had had not even the sense to stick up its nose for a breath of fresh air, here we had a visit from something which recalled a well-fed jovial hippopotamus in a zoological gardens and which actually breathed—that made a most pleasant impression on me—before it sank into the sea again and disappeared.

Now record your ending time and answer the following questions *before* computing your reading time and speed. Do not look back at the reading section to answer these. Pick the best answer for each question.[2]

1. Individual plankton are invisible.
   (T) True; (F) False
2. The net with which the author caught plankton was a funnel of fine silk, almost 300 meshes per square inch.
   (T) True; (F) False
3. Plankton seems to be more plentiful in colder waters.
   (T) True; (F) False
4. Not all plankton are edible.
   (T) True; (F) False
5. The definition of plankton that emerges from the article is
   a. strongly diluted, strongly smelling, brilliantly colored fish soup
   b. the basic food for every creature that moves in or over the sea

   c. a general name for thousands of species of minute organisms, both vegetable and animal, that drift near the surface of the sea

   d. tiny animals that live in the sea, mostly fish ova, larva, and shrimp, with an occasional jellyfish

   e. whale food

6. Plankton may be important in the future, the author suggests, because

   a. it can save the lives of castaways at sea

   b. it provides the basic food for edible fish in commercially important quantities

   c. we may learn to harvest it

   d. its presence or absence provides a map of the currents of the ocean

   e. none of the above is correct

7. Which of the following was *not* a characteristic of plankton?

   a. phosphorescence

   b. great variety of forms and colors

   c. a foul smell

   d. uniformity of flavor

   e. delicious flavor once you got up the nerve to try it

8. To the author, the most memorable feature of the whale they sighted was

   a. its size

   b. its blowhole, shiny as a polished shoe

   c. its breathing

   d. its jovial, harmless disposition

   e. its sudden, silent disappearance into the sea

9. To the reader, the most remarkable feature of the story of the encounter with the whale is

   a. the danger the raft was in

   b. the surprising safety of the raft

   c. the contrast between the danger the reader can imagine, and the light, matter-of-fact way in which the story is told

   d. the way the whale's "personality" is rapidly sketched

   e. the offhand bravery of the members of the expedition

10. The logical connection between plankton and whales, which explains why the author discusses them together in this passage, is

   a. the fact that humans will learn to strain plankton out of the sea for food, as whales have always done

   b. the fact that both whales and plankton are marine animals

   c. the contrast between the smallest marine life and the largest
   d. the fact that whales, the largest of marine life, depend for food completely on plankton, the smallest
   e. the fact that the whale appeared immediately after the men's first appearance with the plankton

Now to get your reading speed in minutes and seconds as well as in words per minute (wpm), consult the following table:

min.:sec.	1:30	1:40	1:50	2:00	2:10	
wpm	823	738	671	615	568	
min.:sec.	2:20	2:30	2:40	2:50	3:00	3:10
wpm	527	492	461	434	410	388
min.:sec.	3:20	3:30	3:40	3:50	4:00	4:10
wpm	369	351	335	321	308	295
min.:sec.	4:20	4:30	4:40	4:50	5:00	5:20
wpm	284	273	263	254	246	231
min.:sec.	5:40	6:00	6:20	6:40	7:00	7:30
wpm	217	205	194	185	176	164
min.:sec.	8:00	8:30				
wpm	154	145				

Record your speed on this page or on a separate piece of paper. Answers to the questions follow. If you missed one, your comprehension is 90 percent; two, 80 percent;, etc.

Your speed _____ wpm.
Your comprehension is _____ percent.

Answer key:

Question:	1	2	3	4	5	6	7	8	9	10
Answer:	F	F	F	T	T	c	c	d	c	c

Keep your results in a safe place to compare with a later test after you have practiced some reading techniques and exercises.

Y------------------------------- OUR SIXTY DAY READING PROGRAM

If you want to reach the highest reading speed available to most humans, take about ten to twenty minutes per day on the following set of exercises and suggestions. Make sure you have read Chapter Nine before starting this program, since these suggestions are based on the key presented there.

Keep track of your reading speed on the progress chart that follows the exercises. To compute your reading speed in words per minute (wpm), count the number of words on an average page. Read a number of pages and time yourself.

$$\text{wpm (speed)} = \frac{\text{number of pages read x number of words per average page}}{\text{number of minutes reading}}$$

By doing these exercises, you should be able to double and possibly triple your reading speed within sixty days. Comprehension should also improve significantly.

1. K^e—*physiology*. Whenever you read, practice:

- holding the material for an upright visual posture; if the book is heavy, support the weight on the front edge of your table or desk, or get a book holder
- use a visual aid (a pencil)

You can further improve the kinesthetic quality of reading through:

• *Metronome training.* If you have access to a metronome used for timing music, you can use it to establish and maintain a smooth, consistent reading rhythm. Set the metronome at a comfortable speed. Then let each tick correspond to one line with your visual aid. In this way you can avoid the slowdown that normally occurs after reading for a while.

Knowing the tempo allows you to know your reading rate. Over the sixty days you can gradually increase the tempo to push your speed ahead.

2. Right brain—*involve the right brain more through prereading.*

• For nontechnical or lighter reading, preread the first one or two sentences of each paragraph in the reading section or assignment except introductions, summaries, and conclusions, which you read thoroughly.
• For difficult or technical reading, read everything the first time through without regard to understanding.

3. V^e—*optimize the quality of visual input.* Do this through the following exercises:

A. *Eye swing warm-up (two minutes a day).*[1] The exercise that follows will help you improve the mechanics of moving your eyes across the page. It works primarily to reduce the number of stops your eyes make on each line of print, and to smooth out the rhythm of those stops. At the same time, if your reading habits include any eye movement uncertainty when returning from the end of one line to the beginning of the next, this exercise will help you eliminate that problem.

"Read" these pages by glancing very briefly at each bar, moving from left to right along each line. Work very quickly, or without being aware of it you will make more stops than the bars indicate. Be especially careful to make a fast return sweep from the end of one line to the beginning of the next.

Until you have tried it on several occasions, you probably will not feel that the exercise is comfortable. However, one "reading" is enough on any occasion. Practice this exercise just before reading each speed exercise in this manual.

Of course, in normal reading the stops you make on the line are determined partly by the phrases read, which may not be spaced as evenly as the bars here.

B. *High-speed practice.* Spend ten minutes per day reading much faster than your normal reading rate. Use any light material of your choice, preferably something of interest to you. Try for as much comprehension as possible, but know that this practice is primarily about speed.

C. *Shortening the lines by one-half inch.* Practice this technique, as explained in Chapter Nine.

D. *Phrase-flashing warm-up (3 minutes a day).*[2] This exercise expands your eye focus from the usual average of 1.1 words per fixation to the optimum level of 2.5 words with each stop. You don't necessarily take in a whole phrase per stop while reading normal text, but these exercises will broaden your peripheral vision.

The object of this exercise is to expand your eye focus. The phrases in the following material start short and get progressively longer. The object is to look at each phrase for the briefest possible fraction of a second, so you must read it in one glance. Start with Group A. When you can complete it without difficulty, go on to Group B, and so on.

With a sheet of paper, cover the columns you are not working with. Also, cover the column you are using with a 3″ by 5″ card. Move the card down to expose the first phrase and then back up again with the quickest possible flick of the wrist, so the first phrase in the column is exposed for an instant. Then tell yourself what you saw. If you are certain, guess, and then check yourself. Now do the same for the second word in the column, and so forth on down the column.

Group A

iconoclastic	a success story	the coal miners
on this spot	more and more	her purple dress
out on strike	get out of hand	strange question
beat them all	the grim reaper	It's not worth it.
ignorant of it	savage repartee	in the same boat
at high speed	once and for all	student rebellion
miss the boat	the other media	old acquaintance
came too late	bright and early	musical evenings
a key witness	being in fashion	lead him a dance
money orders	ulterior motives	He's impractical.
vital statistics	five months ago	not my fair share
thunderstruck	notwithstanding	source of income
the spare tires	before and after	far from accurate
along that line	better than ever	do the impossible
afraid to think	What time is it?	unusual endeavor
as they do say	in the meantime	graduate students
bacteriological	free information	an optical illusion
vegetable crop	finished product	whiskey and soda
our way of life	beyond question	They don't know.
old comic strip	He had seen me.	as clear as crystal

Group B

under suspicion?	The sky is clear.	take another look?
bigger and better	be that as it may	in the final analysis
largest molecules	get along without	acts like a chimney
I don't believe it.	as a matter of fact	a million and a half
basic significance	of real importance	relative instabilities
legal professional	the Panama Canal	world trouble spots
in the first quarter	it stands to reason	fencing instructions
incomprehensible	almost as much as	Start all over again.
no brighter future	from bad to worse	good administration
a perfect example	freedom of speech	molecular biologists
for the time being	a new lease on life	over and over again
so greatly in need	under construction	We are not amused.
the political scene	staggering problem	5 barrels of gasoline
a patent absurdity	extremely valuable	crude oil production
a flying laboratory	a standard practice	at your convenience
Council of Europe	inferiority complex	few and far between
the primary lesson	another application	at this time last year
bone of contention	a college education	a sharp straight nose
balance the budget	Second World War	will not be permitted
turn back the clock	theory and practice	to settle the question

Group C

effective operations
crude oil drilling rig
dissatisfied customer
partly for this reason
Take my word for it.
perfunctory applause
What a brilliant idea!
to explain these facts
manipulate the media
precision instruments
vote of no confidence
to add insult to injury
it now seems possible
It's too much trouble.
setting out poinsettias
unpolluted waterways
Estimate your results.
no fluorescent lighting
coal and iron reserves
psychological moment
He said nothing at all.
by the end of the year
change in temperature
three remarkable facts
the nineteenth century
of all the requirements
He bets on the horses.
It goes without saying.
unhappily disorganized
the local representative

Is he a reliable man?
millions of Europeans
based upon experience
How much did it cost?
devastating earthquake
produce the best result
overwhelming majority
throughout the country
a necessary adjustment
to play into their hands
It's not very important.
important contributions
make enough to live on
circumstantial evidence
It's a matter of custom.
a presidential candidate
because of bad weather
if the truth were known
throughout the universe
a serious miscalculation
big electrical appliances
in what has gone before
a problem of nationality
He rose from the ranks.
How fast can you read?
a reciprocal relationship
you simply can't impose
Roman Catholic Church
three different languages
You know what I mean.

Group D

first virus crystallized
a dramatic monologue
we lack the incentives
training and experience
this anarchistic outlook
What splendid animals!
an awkward disposition
the humanistic tradition
I shall be most grateful.
our analysis has implied
That accusation is false.
a rapid circulation of air
really needs overhauling
a personal responsibility
in international relations
under the circumstances
that you follow this plan
They can easily be seen.
a functional arrangement
great financial difficulties
take it into consideration
attorneys for the defense
no foreign correspondent
Supreme Court decisions
no mechanical difficulties
engineering achievements
noncommissioned officers
eighteenth-century novels
House of Representatives
United Nations Assembly

running around in circles
happily playing the piano
try to discover new ways
when all is said and done
it brings in the whole line
at the end of four months
This need not prevent us.
many years of experience
started moving cautiously
due to prior commitments
for some special comment
We have great confidence.
bewildered and withdrawn
the Union of South Africa
The verdict was "Guilty."
in three different countries
underground storage tanks
The whole thing is absurd.
many-branched candelabra
we may approach the work
an alternative interpretation
no hospitalization insurance
a Constitutional amendment
two political representatives
Governor of South Carolina
about the fifteenth of March
three wars in one generation
Mutual Broadcasting System
We may have made an error.
resume the military operation

4. A^i—*eliminate subvocalizing for nontechnical or lighter reading.* Practice these suggestion from Chapter Nine:

- knuckle biting; or
- number mumbling; or
- high-speed practice.

5. A^i—*use subvocalizing for difficult or technical reading.* Have the voice inside be questioning, anticipating, and actively involved.

6. K^i—*learn to derive more pleasure from reading*. This should be a natural outcome of using this key to improve your speed and comprehension.

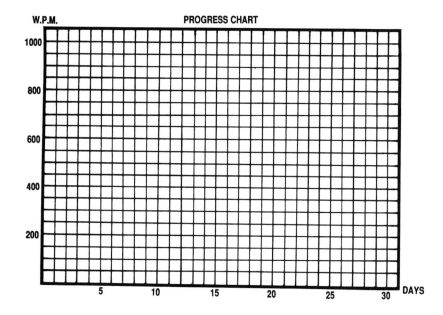

Reading Aftertest

FOR CHAPTER EIGHT

As before, you will read an article, time your reading speed, and answer some questions to check your comprehension. Be sure to use a pencil as a visual aid. The text is structured with vertical lines for "shortening the lines." Keep the visual aid between these two lines. Also, incorporate the prereading. Read only the first one or two sentences the first time through, then go back and read everything. Include both readings in your reading time.*

Record your reading time in hours, minutes, and seconds, as before. As soon as you are finished, record the end time. A table following the articles will again give your reading speed.

As soon as you are ready, record your starting time and begin.

	Hours	Minutes	Seconds
End time	____	____	____
Starting time	____	____	____
Reading time	____	____	____

---

*Sometimes including the prereading will result in an initial slowdown of your overall reading speed. With practice, most people can do both readings faster than a single reading before. The big advantage from prereading is increased focus and comprehension.

SURPRISING Rx FOR A RICHER, HAPPIER LIFE [1]

- Greg Haber, a college dropout, tried the Army as a career, but after four years realized it was not for him. He finally began to find himself as a real-estate salesman. But there were problems: depression, headaches, and heart palpitations that defied medical diagnosis.

  Today Greg, age forty-five, is free of his aliments. The wonder drug, he reports, is education. On a psychologist's recommendation, he enrolled in a weekend college course unrelated to his job that proved to be the only medicine he needed.

- Robertson Beck was suffering from a nervous breakdown, compounded by the loss of his job and the breakup of his marriage. His excuse for his failures was that he has had to abandon a promising architectural career because of his financial problems. "Go back to your studies," a family counselor advised the thirty-nine-year-old Beck. "Support your education with any part-time work you can get, but study as though your life depended on it—as indeed it may."

  Beck did just that. Today he has a degree and a new career. But he is continuing to take courses because they "sharpen my ability to concentrate and improve the mental stamina I need in my job."

- Emily and Ralph Peters, a middle-aged couple, were "bored to oblivion" by a calisthenics class. "Exercise is a bust when it becomes routine," explained Ralph, "so we salvaged our sanity by enrolling in something different—a course in archaeology. Every week we hike and climb and do various kinds of manual labor on field trips—more exercise than we ever got on that smelly gym floor. Our brains get exercise, too, so we end up feeling mentally fit as well as physically fit."

Adult education has long been on the upsweep, with millions of Americans of all ages going back to school—in the evenings, on weekends, while on leave of absence from a job, even during holidays and vacations. Yet only recently has there been evidence of correlations among continuing education, mental well-being, physical health, and, in some cases, even longevity.

Dr. Robert Samp, a physician and health educator at the University of Wisconsin Medical School, has for many years conducted research on why some people live longer than others. He discovered what he terms "a protective intuition" in old people whose lives remain meaningful. Based on his studies of more than two thousand older Americans, Dr. Samp says, "There is plenty of indication that taking courses is a beneficial activity, contributing to good health."

Dr. John B. Moses of Scarsdale, New York, a physician with long experience in the field of aging (among the young and middle-aged as well as the old), says, "Activity slows down the aging and hardening process in blood vessels. You may not think of learning as something 'active.' But it involves the entire body, including vision, hearing, other senses, motor activity, reflexes, and, of course, that mysterious attribute we call motivation. To me, the learning process and its demands all add up to a healthier existence—at any age."

The Academy for Educational Development (AED), a nonprofit planning and research organization, has conducted hundreds of interviews with people in their sixties and older who have returned to the classroom. Typical reactions: "It's the surest way to keep my mind active." "The classroom is the best medicine there is for an adult who wants to stay healthy and enjoy life." "These courses have made a new woman out of me."

"Education is a means for individuals to adapt to accelerated change," says psychologist James E. Birren, director of the Ethel Percy Andrus Gerontology Center at the University of Southern California. "Thus, continuing education over the life span is not only desirable; it may become essential."

Education is like exercise. You can improve your health by starting an exercise program after you retire, even if you never have done so. But you are obviously better off if you are continuing a program you started earlier.

Robert Adamson, director of the College at Sixty program at Fordham University's Lincoln Center campus in New York City, reports that older students likely to benefit most from structured college education "are those who have enjoyed learning all along. They have the healthiest mental outlook."

"Any program of study—formal or casual—that gets participants involved and motivated is likely to be beneficial," says Alvin C. Eurich, president of AED. "The most valuable programs, though, are those that continue over the years and develop lifetime learning habits."

William Berkeley is president of Elderhostel, a successful program of one- and two-week courses on college campuses for people sixty years of age and older. "You cannot imagine," he told me, "what a 'wonder drug' it is for older people to discover that not only can they cope with classroom demands, but many of them can perform as successfully as the other, younger students in their regular classroom sessions. Morale skyrockets; they see better, hear better, feel better. Education is the most effective tonic they could find."

This doesn't mean everyone must sign up for courses in adult education programs. Structured curricula are the most feasible for many because they offer specific sequences of study, cultivate regularity of activity, and often provide some form of evaluation. Yet the "mental jogger" who prefers to pursue education by himself can achieve the same benefits, if properly motivated.

The exact relationship between education and health may never be proved scientifically—there are too many additional factors. But evidence of learning's positive effects continues to mount. And meanwhile, as psychiatrist W. Beran Wolfe put it, "The cultivation of mental elasticity is the best insurance against melancholia, depression, and a sense of futility."

Now record your end time and answer the following questions *before* computing your reading time and speed.

1. Greg Haber had a successful Army career after continuing his education.
   (T) True; (F) False

2. Learning involves the entire body, not just the entire brain.
   (T) True; (F) False

3. To get the most benefit from learning, it should be related to your job.
   (T) True; (F) False

4. When Emily and Ralph Peters replaced their calisthenics class with a course in archaeology, they still felt the need for more physical exercise.
(T) True; (F) False

5. According to one quote from the Gerontology Center at the University of Southern California, "Continuing education over the life span is not only desirable; it may become essential."
(T) True; (F) False

6. According to this article, continuing education promotes:
   a. mental well-being
   b. physical well-being
   c. ability to concentrate
   d. longevity
   e. all of these

7. In interviews with people in their sixties who have returned to the classroom, which is *not* a typical reaction?
   a. "It's the surest way to keep my mind active."
   b. "I want to train for a retirement career to keep myself active."
   c. "These courses have made a new woman/man out of me."
   d. "The classroom is the best medicine there is for an adult who wants to stay healthy and enjoy life."

8. People who pursue education on their own can get the same benefits as people who take structured curricula.
(T) True   (F) False

9. The author feels that the *best* educational programs are
   a. any that get the participants involved and motivated
   b. ones that balance mental and physical stamina
   c. ones that provide specific sequences of study, cultivate regular activity, and have forms of evaluation
   d. ones that promote lifelong learning habits

10. In conclusion, the author feels that
   a. the relationship between education and health has now been proven.
   b. evidence of learning's positive effects continues to mount.

   c. cultivation of mental elasticity is the best insurance against depression.
   d. "b" and "c."
   e. "a," "b," and "c."

Now consult the table to get your reading speed. For example, if your reading time is 1 minute, 30 seconds, then your reading speed is 830 words per minute (wpm).

min.:sec.	1:30	1:40	1.50	2:00	2:10	2:20
wpm	830	750	680	625	575	535
min.:sec.	2:30	2:40	2:50	3:00	3:10	3:20
wpm	500	470	440	415	395	375
min.:sec.	3:30	3:40	3:50	4:00	4:10	4:20
wpm	355	340	325	310	300	290
min.:sec.	4:30	4:40	4:50	5:00	5:10	5:20
wpm	280	270	260	250	240	235
min.:sec.	5:30	5:40	5:50	6:00	6:20	6:40
wpm	225	220	215	210	200	190
min.:sec.	7:00	7:30	8:00			
wpm	180	170	155			

   Record your speed on this page or on a separate sheet of paper.

Your speed is ____ wpm.
Your comprehension is ____ percent.

Answer key:

Question:	1	2	3	4	5	6	7	8	9	10
Answer:	F	T	F	F	T	e	b	T	d	d

   If you got all ten correct, your comprehension was 100 percent. If you got nine correct, it was 90 percent; eight correct, 80 percent; etc. Compare the results with your pretest.

MEMORY RHYTHMS

ON YOUR OWN

MAKING A TAPE OF SHORT LEXICAL UNITS

As you were reading the suggestion that you make a tape, you may have been thinking, "I'll bet this isn't as easy as it sounds." Actually, it's much easier than traditional "brute force" methods. The only tricky part is synchronizing the time of speaking four seconds and pausing four seconds. One easy approach is to use a metronome. Set the metronome ticking in the background at one tick per second. Then when you are ready to record, speak your unit for four ticks and pause for four ticks.

If you don't have a metronome, the last ten minutes of side two of the *Learning Power* tape from Powerlearning® Systems has a recording of a metronome ticking. Then you can play this tape in the background while you make your supermemory tape. Every fourth beat has the crash of a tambourine. To setup the lexical units, it sounds like this. CRASH—click—click—click—CRASH—click—click—click.

Making your tape with this method requires two tape recorders. Use a small, inexpensive recorder in the background to play the metronome. Meanwhile, record your list into a better-quality recorder. Leave the first minute or two of the tape blank; then listen to the pattern of clicks until you are ready.

As the tambourine crashes, speak your first short lexical unit until it crashes again. Then pause. With the next crash, speak your next lexical unit until it crashes again. Then pause again, etc.

If you have only a few words in your lexical unit, speak a little more slowly. If you have eight or nine words, speak more quickly. If you end a little before or after the tambourine, it doesn't matter. The units should be *about* four seconds.

If you want to avoid the clicking on your tape, you can connect an earplug or headphones to the recorder with the metronome tape. Then you will hear the beat in your ear, speak perfect lexical units, and avoid rerecording the metronome. In fact, I strongly recommend that you use headphones. Otherwise the rerecorded clicking may distract you later.

MAKING A TAPE OF EXTENDED LEXICAL UNITS

If you are recording extended lexical units, the process is much simpler. Read the complete lexical unit into the recorder and then count inside your head, "one one hundred, two one hundred, three one hundred, four one hundred." Then speak the next unit, and count again. You may want to check your counting against a watch, but usually it's accurate enough. Of course, a disadvantage of the extended units is that you can't do the breathing pattern.

Remember, once you've recorded your tape, you have a choice. If the material is not too difficult to remember, making the tape is enough. If it is especially difficult, play it back, read along silently from the list, and do the breathing if appropriate. This completes setting up your memory rhythms.

MEMORY RHYTHMS WITH SHORT LEXICAL UNITS

Short lexical units (seven to nine words or less) can be spoken comfortably in four seconds. It's a great way to organize foreign words, short foreign phrases, short to moderate equations, technical terms, short to moderate spelling words, etc.

- List the units you want to memorize.
- Set a metronome, or play a recorded metronome on one tape recorder for your friend's timing or to record a tape.

On your own:
- If you are making a tape, use two tape recorders—one for the metronome and one for your voice. Leave the first one to two minutes blank, and then speak the first lexical unit. Remember to speak for about four ticks, pause for four ticks, speak for four ticks, pause for four ticks, etc.
- You can use an earplug or headphones with the metronome tape recorder to avoid rerecording the clicks.
- Record one or two minutes of faster baroque music at the end of the material. We will explain the use of music in later sections.
- If the material is not too difficult to remember, just making the tape is enough, and you are done with the active organizing.
- If the material is difficult to remember, play the tape back and *read silently from the list.*
- You can also use the breathing pattern. Hold in your breath while the voice is speaking. Then breathe out and in during the four-second pause.

With a friend:
- If you are studying with a friend, he or she reads one copy of the list aloud and uses the metronome for timing.
- You read along silently from your copy of the list and do the breathing pattern.

MEMORY RHYTHMS WITH EXTENDED LEXICAL UNITS

An extended lexical unit is a single point or principle expressed in one sentence. If the principle involves several sentences, each sentence is a single extended unit. Extended lexical units may include points from law, longer foreign phrases or spelling words, steps to solve an equation, etc.

• List the units you want to memorize.

On your own:
• If you are making a tape, leave the first one to two minutes blank. Then speak the complete lexical unit and pause for four seconds while silently counting, "one one hundred, two one hundred, three one hundred, four one hundred."
• Speak the next unit and again pause for four seconds, etc. Continue through your list.
• At the end of the tape, record one or two minutes of faster baroque music. Again, we will discuss the use of music later.
• If the material is not too difficult, just making the tape is enough. If the material is difficult to remember, play the tape back and read along silently from the list.
• With extended lexical units, do not use the breathing pattern.

With a friend:
• If you are working with a friend, that person reads from his or her copy of the script aloud while you read along silently from your copy of the list.

NOTES

CHAPTER ONE

1. Eric Jensen, *Student Success Secrets* (Woodbury, N.Y.: Barron's, 1989), pp. 17–19.

CHAPTER TWO

1. Tony Buzan, *Use Both Sides of Your Brain* (New York: E. P. Dutton, 1979). Buzan has coined the term *mind maps* for similar patterns. He has used them extensively as a tool for organizing notes, while Gabrielle Rico in *Writing the Natural Way* (Los Angeles: Jeremy P. Tarcher, 1983), has used a variation—"clustering" as a powerful tool to overcome "writer's block." Powerlearning uses this method as a way to display magic keys and other patterns of thought.
2. Steve and Connirae Andreas, *The Heart of the Mind* (Moab, UT.: Real People Press, 1989), pp. 155–165.

CHAPTER THREE
----

1. Peter Russell, *The Brain Book* (New York: Hawthorn Books, 1979), p. 36.
2. Tony Buzan, *Use Both Sides of Your Brain* (New York: E. P. Dutton, 1979), pp. 16–17.
3. Win Wenger, *How to Increase Your Intelligence* (New York: Dell Publishing, 1975), p. 35.
4. Jacquelyn Wonder and Priscilla Donovan, *Whole Brain Thinking* (New York: William Morrow, 1984), pp. 18–20.
5. Ibid., pp. 18–20.
6. Ibid., pp. 18–20.
7. Gabrielle Rico, *Writing the Natural Way* (Los Angeles: Jeremy P. Tarcher, 1983), p. 189.
8. David Lewis and James Green, *Thinking Better* (New York: Holt, Rinehart, & Winston, 1982), pp. 8–13. This book touches briefly on memory and learning but is primarily a pioneering work on critical and logical thinking skills. Three of my four fables (1, 2, and 4) are discussed here.
9. Robert True, "Experimental Control in Hypnotic Age Regression," *Science* 110:583–84.
10. Geoffrey Naylor and Else Hardwood, "Old Dogs, New Tricks: Age and Ability," *Psychology Today* (British), (April 1975), pp. 29–33.

CHAPTER FOUR
----

1. Some of the test questions are adapted and from several sources:

   • Jacquelyn Wonder and Priscilla Donovan, *Whole Brain Thinking* (New York: William Morrow, 1984), pp. 31–36.
   • Sharon Crain, *Self-Presentation for the Professional*, seminar and workbook (Palo Alto, Calif.: June 1985) pp. 1–16.
   • David Lewis and James Green, *Thinking Better* (New York: Holt, Rinehart, & Winston, 1982), pp. 149–50.

2. The labels "cerebral," "doer," "facilitator," and "expressive" have been used in other personality inventory tests. Wonder and Donovan, op. cit., were the first to interpret these in the framework of the right-brain/left-brain model.

CHAPTER FIVE
----

1. Sharon Crain, "Self-Presentation for the Professional" seminar and workbook (Palo Alto, Calif.: June 1985) and Jacquelyn Wonder and Priscilla Donovan, *Whole Brain Thinking* (New York: William Morrow, 1984). Dr. Crain discusses *fogging*, a well-known tool in the context of the right-brain/left-brain model. Wonder and Donovan discuss the problems of boredom and talking on the telephone, also based on the right-brain/left brain model. The love-letter technique has been successfully used for some years by the Catholic Church in their marriage encounter weekend. I have interpreted this technique and the problem of being stuck on a detailed problem in terms of the left and right sides of the brain.
2. Crain, op. cit.
3. Wonder and Donovan, op. cit. The authors present some of the techniques for right-and left-brain thinking in this and the next sections.
4. "Just How the Sexes Differ," *Newsweek* (May 18, 1981), and Jo Durden-Smith, "Male and Female—Why?" *Quest/80* (October 1980). These two articles discuss developmental differences in the sexes with age. These differences are interpreted here in terms of the left- and right-brain specializations and the thicker corpus collosum women generally have.
5. Tony Buzan, *Make the Most of Your Brain* (New York: Simon & Schuster, 1984), pp. 63–72. Buzan presents a nice discussion on hearing, listening, and memory. He touches on the concept of generalized vs. focused learning without calling it that.

CHAPTER SIX
----

1. Eric Jensen, *Student Success Secrets* (Woodbury, N.Y.: Barron's, 1989), p. 121.
2. This is quoted from Mark Van Doren in *Instant Memory* (Pacific Palisades, Calif: Institute of Advanced Thinking, 1972), p. 3.
3. *New Scientist* (October 9, 1980). Researchers at the University of Cambridge tested subjects at 10:00 A.M., 3:00 P.M., and at 7:00 P.M. on long-term memory. The subjects at 7:00 P.M. scored highest and the ones at 10:00 A.M. scored lowest.
4. These categories are adapted and modified from Peter Russell, *The Brain Book* (New York: Hawthorn Books, 1979), p. 237.
5. George Miller, "The Magic Number Seven, Plus or Minus Two: Some Limits in Our Capacity for Processing Information," *Psychological Review*, Vol. 63, pp. 81–97.
6. Hermann Ebbinghaus, *Memory*, trans. D. H. Ruyer and C. E. Bussenius (New York: Teachers College Press, 1913).
7. *American Journal of Psychiatry* (February 1978). Researchers from UCLA divided a group of smokers into two groups. Each member of the control group smoked a nonnicotine cigarette, while each in the experimental group smoked a regular one. On a memory test afterward, the experimental group scored 24 percent lower.
8. *Journal of Studies of Alcohol* (January 1980). Researchers at the University of Oklahoma Health Sciences Center studied young to middle-aged women before and after drinking. Memory was not only impaired by the immediate drink, but also the more years the subjects had been drinking, the greater the effect on memory. Some memory loss even carried into times the subjects were not drinking.
9. *Newsweek* (September 29, 1986), pp. 48–54.
10. Ibid.
11. *The Sybervision Foreign Language Series—Instruction Manual* (Pleasanton, Calif., Sybervision, 1988), pp. 2–14.
12. *Prevention* (February 1985), p. 123.
13. Colin Rose, *Accelerated Learning* (New York: Dell, 1985), p. 16.
14. George Korona, Organizing and Memorizing (New York: Columbia University Press, 1972).

CHAPTER SEVEN

----

1. P. McKellar, "The Investigation of Mental Images, *Penguin Science Survey* (London: Penguin, 1965).
2. Ralph N. Haber, "How We Remember What We See," *Scientific American* (May 1970), p. 105.
3. Gordon Bower, "Mental Imagery and Associative Learning," *Cognition in Learning and Memory* (New York: John Wiley, 1972), p. 69.
4. Several suggestions are adapted from Tony Buzan, *Make the Most of Your Brain* (New York: Simon & Schuster, 1984), pp. 63–72.
5. Jacquelyn Wonder and Priscilla Donovan, *Whole Brain Thinking* (New York: William Morrow, 1984), and SALT teacher training course (Summer 1982), Iowa State University, Ames, Ia. Wonder and Donovan cite research from the Center for the Advancement of Creative Persons and University Associates and from the Synectic Institute of Massachusetts as supporting these statistics.
6. Duncan R. Godden and Alan D. Baddeley, "Context Dependent Memory in Two Natural Environments: On Land and Under Water," *British Journal of Psychology*, Vol. 66, pp. 325–32.

CHAPTER EIGHT

----

1. Sheila Ostrander and Lynn Schroeder, *Superlearning®* (New York: Dell Publishing, 1979), p. 19.
2. S. Krashen and T. Terrell, *The Natural Approach to Language Acquisition* (Oxford: Pergamon Press, 1983).
3. Ibid., Chaps. 2 and 3.
4. Ostrander and Schroeder, op. cit., and D. H. Schuster and C. E. Gritton, *Suggestive Accelerative Learning Techniques* (New York: Gordon and Breach Science Publishers, 1986). The latter describes this step as an "active organizing" phase for teachers, while *Superlearning®* describes an organizing step for students to use the method on their own.
5. Colin Rose, *Accelerated Learning* (New York: Dell, 1985), p. 93.
6. Ostrander and Schroeder, op. cit., p. 125.

7. Rose, *op. cit.*, p. 102.
8. Ostrander and Schroeder, *op. cit.*, p. 51.
9. Lin Doherty at "Mastery of Magic," a presentation on NLP and accelerated learning methods for teachers, (June–July 1985), Santa Barbara, Calif.

CHAPTER NINE
----

1. Tony Buzan, *Use Both Sides of Your Brain* (New York: E. P. Dutton, 1979), pp. 35–47.
2. Eric Jensen, *Student Success Secrets* (New York: Barron's, 1989), p. 81, and Buzan, ibid., p. 31.

CHAPTER TEN
----

1. B. Zeigarnik, "Das Behalten erledigter und unerleddigter Handungen," *Psychologisch Forschung* 9:1–85.
2. P. Russell, *The Brain Book* (New York: Hawthorn Books, 1979) and Tony Buzan, *Use Both Sides of Your Brain* (New York: E. P. Dutton, 1979). Buzan and Russell each suggest this "modular learning" approach, with a break every thirty to forty minutes, based on Zeigarik's findings. Each presents the graph I have shown of how the memory curve is modified with these changes.
4. Russell, op. cit., and C. Rose, *Accelerated Learning* (New York: Dell, 1985). Russell and Rose each recommended the four to five reviews with the timing as I've suggested in this section. This pattern is consistent with research on how to improve the normal Ebbinghaus curve, and this timing facilitates transfer from short-term to long-term memory.
5. John Ott, *Health and Light* (Old Greenwich, Conn.: Devin-Adair, 1973).
6. Adapted from Buzan, op. cit., pp. 137–147. Buzan's approach is similar to SALT in establishing a broad right-brain perspective first and then focusing on finer left-brain detail.
7. With each eye the left half of the field of vision goes to the right

side of the brain, while the right half of each field of vision goes to the left side of the brain.

CHAPTER ELEVEN
----

1. P. Airola, *Are You Confused?* (Phoenix: Health Plus Publishers, 1971), Chap. 2 and p. 54.
2. Ibid., pp. 52–53.

CHAPTER TWELVE
----

1. *New Age Journal* (November 1977), p. 24. This article reports on a study of the mental and emotional benefits of exercise with school-age children.
2. "Why Children Should Draw," *Saturday Review* (September 3, 1977), pp. 11–16.
3. Win Wenger, *An Easy Way to Increase Your Intelligence* (Gaithersburg, Md.: Psychogenics Press).
4. "The Edith Project", *The Sunday Times* (London) (April 17, 1977).
5. C. Rose, *Accelerated Learning* (New York: Dell, 1985), p. 21.
6. J. Altman, "Autoradiographic and Histological Studies of Postnatal Neurogenesis: II. A Longitudinal Investigation of the Kinetics and Transformation of Cells Incorporating Tritiated Thymidine in Infant Rats, with Special Reference to Postnatal Neurogenesis in Some Brain Regions," *Journal of Comparative Neurology* CXXVIII, (1966); Gopal D. Das, "Autoradiographic Examination of the Effects of Enriched Environment on the Rate of Glial Multiplication in the Adult Rat Brain," *Nature* CCIV (December 19, 1964).
7. J. P. Banquet, "Spectral Analysis of EEG in Meditation," *Electroencephalography and Clinical Neurophysiology* (1975), p. 35.
8. Allan I. Abrams, "Paired–Associate Learning and Recall: A Pilot Study of the Transcendental Meditation Technique" (Berkeley: University of California), *Scientific Research on the Transcendental Meditation Program: Collected Papers* (New York: MIU Press, 1975).
9. Arthur Aaron, David Orme-Johnson, and Paul Brubaker, "The Transcendental Meditation Program in the College Curriculum: A

Four-Year Longitudinal Study of Effects on Cognitive and Affective Functioning," *College Student Journal* 15 (1981), pp. 140–46.

10. R. K. Wallace, M. Dillbeck, E. Jacobe, and B. Harrington, "The Effects of the Transcendental Meditation and TM Sidhis Program on the Aging Process," *International Journal of Neuroscience* 16 (1982), pp. 53–58.

11. D. H. Schuster and C. E. Gritton, *Suggestive Accelerative Learning Techniques* (New York: Gordon and Breach Science Publishers, 1986).

APPENDIX ONE

----

1. Thor Heyerdahl, "From Plankton to Whales," *The Kon-Tiki Expeditions* (George Allen & Unwin: 1950) reprinted in Horace Judson, *The Techniques of Reading* (New York: Harcourt Brace Jovanovich, 1972), pp. 30–32.

2. Judson, *op. cit.*, pp. 32–33.

3. *Ibid.* p. 475.

APPENDIX TWO

----

1. Horace Judson, *The Techniques of Reading* (New York: Harcourt Brace Jovanovich, 1972), pp. 54–56.

2. *Ibid.*, pp. 476–479.

APPENDIX THREE

----

1. William Cross, "Surprising Rx for a Richer, Happier Life," *Reader's Digest*, vol. 120, April, 1982, pp. 138–140.

P OWERLEARNING ®

SYSTEMS

We all want to live our lives to the fullest. Everyone wants to learn new things . . . a foreign language, a new hobby, computers, university course work, or how to advance our careers; yet many of us feel blocked. We have in the human brain the gift of nature's most superb engineering feat, but we were not given an instruction manual.

Powerlearning® Systems offers seminars, consultation, books, and tapes that provide the most advanced technologies available today to accelerate learning and have fun in the process.

For information on available services and products write to

Dr. Don Lofland
Powerlearning® Systems
P.O. Box 496
Santa Cruz, CA 95060

• Corporate Seminars
• In Service Trainings for Teachers
• Individual Consultations
• Accelerated Learning Books, Tapes, & Resources
• Foreign Language Courses.

Compliments of the

GREATER WASHINGTON
Board of Trade

Are You Fascinated?
The four people you need to succeed

Ken Tucker

2008

Are You Fascinated?

Acknowledgments

This book, each chapter, each page, is authored in great part by the people who helped and continue to help me succeed. People like my high school teachers, Brother Aaron Kraft and Mr. Vincent Ferguson, who were the first to confront me with my potential. By others like Ed Allen, Stunce Williams, Myles Munroe and The Visionaires, Lee and Edward Watson, Henry O'brien and Clarence Williams, who at various times instilled in me the hope and guarantee of a God-ordered life. And others like Dr. William "Rudy" Lewis, Dr. Keith Terry, Dr. Wayne Samuelson, Dr. Gladys Styles-Johnston, Jim Grotrian, Jerry Fox, Ken Lee and many others at University of Nebraska at Kearney, who opened wide doors of knowledge and opportunity for me. My fellow travelers, including Donald McCartney, John Harris, Dr. Jack Huck, Judy Shonerd, Jeannette Volker, Linda Heiden, Ted Suhr, Jose Soto, and Larry Meyer, who helped me examine and at times, reexamine possibilities.

My thanks to my editor, Clea Simon, without whose hard work and exacting standards this book would not be possible. To my associates, Angela Ho-Sang, John Harris, Rudy Lewis, Van Brown, Sharla McDaniel, and Sandra Adkins, who demanded this book because of their constant pursuit of excellence in serving our clients. And, my deepest thanks to my wife Judy, my daughters, Kendra and Kristen, my son Kenny, Anthony Fykes, my son in law, and to my brothers Freddie Tucker and Kersch Darville, all of whom endure being the testers and subjects of my most recent research and discoveries. Finally, and most of all, to my parents, Vernon and Dorothy, Gloria, and Eric, who gave me my life and my start in life.

Foreword

There is an old African adage that states: "It takes a village to raise a child." The principle buried in this statement is still true for our cyber-space, high-tech, computer-driven culture of contemporary society. The only difference is that the village today is made up of people we choose to allow to "raise us" on our road to success in life. It is my deep conviction that all of us, whether we fail or succeed in life, are a sum-total of all the people we have known and who have impacted or influenced our lives. The powerful affects of people in and on our course to our destiny is inevitable and we must understand, appreciate, and recognize the type people required to be sure our journey is successful.

No human was designed to succeed alone. No success is an individual success. We are created to need others. As a matter of fact, the first defect in man recognized by the creator was summarized in the statement: "It is not good for man to be alone." This divine verdict forever settled the issues that any or all measure of achievement in life is a corporate effort. Everyone needs others to succeed.

It is this reality that makes me excited about this book, "Are You Fascinated?" by Ken Tucker. This work identifies the four most important people you need in life to succeed and the role they play in the process of your success. In his profound yet thought-provoking style, he leaps over complicated psychological jargon and delivers practical precepts and principles that we can all embrace and apply.

Ken, in this fascinating work, identifies the important people we all need in our lives to achieve any measure of true success such as; The People-Picker, The Possibility-Vendor, The Dream-Maker, and The Leader-Leader. This book is essential for all to read and will help the individual who wants to succeed intentionally and not as a haphazard social experimentation.

This is destined to become a classic and will be re-read many times because of its practical and vital content. I commend this work to all and hope you will be as inspired and fascinated as I was.

Dr. Myles Munroe
BFMI International
Nassau, Bahamas

Introduction

A re you fascinated? When we are fascinated, we are engaged in the world—and the world becomes both more fascinating to us and more fascinated by us.

Look around you, at the leaders, the mentors, all those we admire. Behind their confidence and decisiveness. Behind their power to hire and build careers. Behind their uniforms and badges, behind the duties and the deadlines, there is a real person—a person who is increasingly doing more, being more, because he or she is fascinated. And behind every one of these people, behind all their success, are several people who helped them find their fascination, who sparked the fascination within their own dreams. Who helped them take that fascination to the next step in business and in life.

Think of the teacher who first heard a young Mozart play. Think of the first mathematician who encouraged young Einstein's eager questions. Think of, in our times, the father who noticed the gifts of young Tiger Woods or the latent skills of Venus and Serena Williams.

These mentors, these teachers who guide us toward our fascination come to us at all stages of our life—and of our success. Think of the executive who first heard the insightful musings of the novice Peter Drucker, and then provided him with an opportunity to share his ideas with still more people. Think of all those who heard the dream of a young Winston Churchill, Billy Graham, Mahatma Gandhi, Martin Luther King Jr., or Nelson Mandela. Most importantly think of your own life, your own success, and the people behind that success. Then look ahead at your coming life—and the dreams and achievements to come. How will you realize those dreams and achievements? What fascinates you? And who are the people who have helped you in the past? Who are the people in the present who help you? And who are those who, in the future, will help you find your fascination?

You may know some of them. They are out there, and they are in you, too. They are the People-picker, the Possibility-vendor, the Dream-maker, and the Leader-leader. They are the four people we need to succeed.

Dedicated to the four people in my family who help me succeed:
Judy, Kendra, Kristen, and Kenny

Chapter 1.

The People-Picker:
The First Person You Need to Succeed

They choose us.

I remember so well that day so long ago, in beautiful Nassau. Nassau, the capital of the Bahamas and my hometown, is tropical, lush and full of life. When I was growing up, playing under the shadows of the coconut palms, it was more rural than it is now, more of a rustic village than a city. That meant, in many ways, life was simpler. When I got hungry, for example, I'd simply pluck a ripe mango direct from the tree. For lunch, perhaps I'd pick a sapodilla and savor its soft, brown flesh, choosing the fruit that I wanted for myself. In many ways, this life was idyllic. It was like living in paradise.

In some ways, I was. But I remember being particularly happy one day. That day, I was going to see my favorite aunt, my mother's sister, and not just for a typical visit. I was three years old, and I was about to be adopted. Even now, years later, I can clearly remember how that day played out. I'd been living with my mother, and that day she and her new boyfriend called for me, from her new Volkswagen Beetle. As I clambered in, I was so excited I could barely sit still. They drove me to my aunt's house and almost before the car was stopped, I'd jumped out, bursting with excitement. I remember running toward the house clutching a pillowcase that my mother had filled with all my earthly possessions. Waiting for me, there on the porch, were my aunt and uncle, arms open to receive me. I raced up to the porch of their one-bedroom clapboard house and into their loving arms. That instant, I became their first and only child.

I am fascinated by how life mixes the bad with the good, the sad with the happy, and the failure with the success. This was certainly the case the day of my adoption. That day, I was both the product of an unplanned and unwanted pregnancy and, at the same time, I was also a dream-come-true for first-time parents, the object of both love and joy for Vernon and his bubbly wife, Dorothy. Vernon, an ambitious man, tall and strapping, was always building, always moving forward. From his chicken farm, he moved on to running a small fleet of fishing boats. He had plans—for his life, for our family—and he set out to accomplish these plans with the support and affection of his wife, Dorothy, shorter, softer, and mischievously funny, but no less vital in the functioning of what would become our family. They had dreams, ideas for the future, and those dreams included me. That day, I was picked, like a choice fruit. That day, I was chosen.

I'm so glad my parents—as I now think of Vernon and Dorothy—picked me back then. They had choices, and they chose me. Even as a three-year-old that thought—the realization of being chosen—was important to me. Because how old we are doesn't matter; being chosen is important to people of all ages. Throughout our lives, we are chosen by others. We are chosen as marriage partners. We are chosen as business partners and employees. We are chosen for promotions. We are chosen to lead groups, and so forth.

Being chosen is important. It helps us to feel valued. *We* are special. *We* are the ones! While others are left behind, *we* get to move forward—into the job, the position, the family.

> ** It is important to be chosen! Being chosen confirms our sense of worth.*

Being chosen, however, means more to us according to who is doing the picking. In my case, as much as the act of my adoptive parents choosing me meant—and still means to me—the necessity of that choice remains. I was only available to be chosen by my parents because my "real" mother— that is, my birth mother— had not chosen me. This fact, this rejection, haunted me constantly in my youth. As an infant and a toddler, I yearned desperately for her to pick me up, to cuddle me. To choose me. During my school years in particular it bothered me that my "real" mother was not present to collect my report card. I felt ashamed, rejected. It was this shame, this nagging sense of being a "throw-away" kid that contributed to many of the bad decisions I made in those years, the bad behavior that nearly derailed me.

For once the sad yearning of early childhood had passed, the hurt of rejection began to take a stronger form. It turned bitter inside of me. Feeling unwanted—un*chosen*—I began acting out, acting badly, and this behavior won me a certain degree of notoriety by the time I reached my teens. Years later, in 2005, my high school dean of students, Vincent Ferguson, wrote an article reminding me of those years, specifically, who I had been and how much I had changed.

> About two and a half months ago a business leadership conference was hosted at one of our hotels on the Cable Beach strip. It, by all accounts, proved to be quite successful and extremely stimulating as a result of talks and mini workshops given by the several local and foreign experts. One of those visiting experts was a young man who attended St. Augustine's College, Fox Hill more than 30 years ago.
> At St. Augustine he and another student of his era were well labeled as the most incorrigible students on campus. Even though they had done well to gain entrance to this academically and athletically prestigious school, their behavior and academic performance did not endear them to their teachers. To make matters worse, they did not demonstrate much in the way of athletic prowess either. Their greatest badge of notoriety was their penchant for being expelled from classes and sent to the Dean of Students (Senior Master in the British tradition) for appropriate corrective measures. In those days of my early teaching years the rod of correc-

tion was interpreted quite literally, and so applied. Almost daily these two restless souls were sent for their medicinal or therapeutic dose of transformational procedure, but nothing seemed to work. Day in and day out the stinging swats of corporal stripes to the protruding buttocks as they bent with elbows in a chair, not the many push-ups, long hours of counseling and pleas, nothing seemed to work; but for the most part we didn't give up. If only we had at our disposal the benefit of brain research that is now available, how much more could we have helped students like these in their mode of learning!

Kenneth Tucker, who, more than John, used to wear his sadness of soul on his face in his early teen years, has really soared to high heights internationally. He has become a seminar leader and managing consultant in the United States.

On his visit for that leadership conference alluded to above, a friend who knew that he was once a heavy cross of mine, shared her joy, no exhilaration at participating in the conference. She was especially moved to pride and joy at seeing and hearing Ken who was once a student of hers also; and through her I was able to contact this miracle of a man by phone at his hotel the night before he was to return to the U.S.

During the course of our reminiscences, I found out that Kenneth is not only an inspirational speaker, but also an author.

It all only goes to show that parents and teachers should never give up on children. Sooner or later they could find their niche in life, all because of the faith, trust and support we give them, especially during their lowest moments.

Sadly, what Mr. Ferguson wrote was all true. And he was kind. He could have gone into detail about my past. He could have cited the times I took the juice of the monkey tamarind tree, a juice guaranteed to make anyone's skin itch, and rubbed it on my teachers' chairs. He could have talked about more serious problems, as well, such as my fist-fights with teachers, the suspension from school, and other acts of sabotage to school property and to others.

The truth is, by the time I entered my teens, I had become a proper young thug. Although we were not as organized as gangs are today, my friends and I had a gang of sorts—the "purple gang"—and our misbehavior quickly escalated to more than childish pranks. A fan, early on, of Rothman cigarettes, I was soon breaking into stores, stealing cigarettes and small items just for the thrill of it. But my behavior didn't stop there: Whenever there was a soccer game—"football" to us—or a gathering for music or any other social outing, the "purple gang" would be there. My parents probably thought I'd be heading out to watch the game or to enjoy the music. I'm sure they had no idea of the kind of sport I engaged in. But it was true, wherever people gathered, we would soon be there. And instead of looking for innocent fun, we'd be looking to fight. To mix it up with other youths and show our strength to other gangs. I can only thank God that guns were not the norm in those days. My weapon of choice was a steel bar, and I still carry some of the marks of those long-ago fights.

But those days are long gone. Mr. Ferguson did lose track of me. For these many years he has been unaware of a miracle that had quietly begun during the last part of my high-school career. That miracle came when Aaron Kraft, a brother in the Catholic tradition, entered my life. Brother Kraft, just like my mom and dad did, chose me. A short man, his small stature belied by his firm voice, Brother Kraft was my speech teacher, and he picked me as his special project one year. He, like all of the teachers, knew of my shenanigans. Knew, in fact, that my bad behavior had crossed the line to become truly criminal. He couldn't help but know: In the twice-daily announcement made over my school PA system, my name came up constantly as the subject of discipline, detention, or worse. But this did not matter to him—or rather, it was only a side effect to him, a bad outcome of potentially good traits. Brother Kraft was, as befit his calling, a Godly man, fair and just. But he was also a no-nonsense man, a serious educator—and an expert people picker.

Expert people pickers are rare. But they may be found in many places. Expert people-pickers can be parents. They can be executives or managers, nurses or teachers. There are expert people-pickers among the employees of any industry you could name. What distinguishes these special individuals is their knack for choosing the right person at the right time. Expert people-pickers have the uncanny ability to spot talent, even in the most unlikely candidate. Even, in the case of Brother Kraft, when the right person might be an angry teenager, a "throwaway" kid with the bad habit of terrorizing his teachers and fellow students!

Brother Kraft was not fooling himself. With his serious, bespectacled gaze, he saw what I was, and he recognized my problems. But—more importantly—he also saw my potential. He knew what I *could be*. In my bad behavior, he saw the force of my will, the energy that I was putting into anger, and he realized how that energy and will could be redirected. He saw my fearlessness, my bravery, and knew that if I were not looking for a fight, if I were not anticipating violence, I could use those same characteristics for a different, a better purpose. Perhaps above all, he saw my hunger. I wanted more than I'd been given, and I would get it—even if I had to steal or beat someone up to attain my goal. He saw that hunger in me and saw how it could help me grow, mature, and, finally, succeed. Expert people-pickers are good at that kind of foresight. They have the talent to accurately identify the appetite, aptitude, and ability a person has and can apply to perform a task or function. They are also extremely talented at designing opportunities that will draw out and develop that person's talent. Expert people-pickers possess the will, courage, and strategic prowess to help the people they choose succeed.

Brother Aaron Kraft was all that for me. His first strategy was to teach me American Standard English. When he met me, I spoke the Bahamian dialect, which sounds like Standard English with a very thick accent. As my speech teacher, he took me in hand.

"The word is pronounced 'they,' not 'dey,'" he would tell me. " 'Them,' not 'dem.' Put your tongue between your teeth until you can feel how the sound should be pronounced. Practice saying it in front of a mirror. Make sure your speech will be comprehensible to the world."

He was like a hawk, watching me during our one-hour class. Coaching and correcting, he was teaching me new ways to refine my speech, all the while slipping in lessons that would also influence my thinking, particularly the way I thought about myself.

"You are every bit as smart as the announcers you see on TV." That was one of the messages he drilled home, and it has stayed with me to this day. "The only difference between you and those announcers is that they speak proper English—and I will teach you to do that, too."

This fascinated me. Not long after I began speech lessons, my friends began to accuse me. "You tryin' to sound lik Amerikan," they said. "You tink you on TV or sometin', eh?" But this taunting could not get me to stop. Brother Kraft, expert people-picker that he was, had chosen me wisely and I was already feeling his impact. Secretly, I began to dream about someday becoming a television news anchor. My behavior began to improve. He had seen what I could be, and he had put me on the path.

> ** Expert people-pickers can see a person's appetite, aptitude, and ability—and they know how to turn those traits into positive productivity.*

But even though I had been chosen, there was still some of the "throwaway" kid in me. At some level, I was still the boy whose mother did *not* choose him, and I had some acting out still to do.

Some of those last misadventures came about in the company of my best friend, a young man I'll call Joey. Joey was a charismatic youth. Even though he was chubby—a real little

doughboy—he had striking green eyes and the kind of personality that drew others. It drew me, certainly, and when I would
come home from school—away from Brother Kraft's influence—it was all too easy to follow along with Joey.

The problem was, Joey was an angry young man. Angrier,
even, than me. Together, we got into some bad scrapes. We were
like brothers, only one month apart in age, and we hit our teens
in the 1970s, when the drug culture was on the rise. It wasn't long
before we and most of our neighborhood friends, our "gang,"
joined the party. For me, this time was a low point, the period of
the most fights, the most violence, and the most serious crimes.
My parents were blissfully unaware of what was going on, I have
no doubt, or else they would have taken me firmly in hand. I
know they would have been disappointed in their "choice." But
I was lucky, Brother Kraft's outreach helped pull me through.
For Joey, this same era was the beginning of the end.

Things started to get really bad for Joey after we stole his
stepfather's car. We were 15 at the time, and looking for trouble.
Joey's mother and stepfather had gone away for the day, leaving his stepfather's powerful five-speed convertible sitting out
front. It was too much temptation. Although by this time, I was
fully aware of my options, and I knew I was doing wrong, the
temptation of that jazzy little sports car, white with its black
"rag top," was just too much. Joey and I searched his house until
we found the keys. We took the car out, not expecting anything horrible to happen. We simply drove it to the movies and
enjoyed the attention we got in the flashy vehicle. But on the
way home, Joey and I went too far. The power of that sports
car's mighty engine was simply too much for a pair of troubled
15-year-olds. With my urging, Joey floored the gas, wanting
to see how fast we could make that car move. But we hadn't
counted on having to stop—and so when a stop sign appeared,
Joey pushed the manual shift hard, shifting down from fifth to
second gear, promptly burning out the clutch. It was a juvenile
mistake, one that wouldn't have happened if we'd been driving
carefully, slowly, or under supervision. As it was, it took us five
hours to push that car home. His neighbors knew what hap-

pened and told his parents. Shortly after that, Joey was sent to live with his grandparents, and we lost touch.

My life took a turn then. In truth, that day was a turning point for us both. I became a Christian soon after and graduated from high school. Joey, I later learned, never finished school. Instead, his anger and his drive—the same traits that Brother Kraft identified in me—dragged him down. Following his increasing taste for drugs and trouble, he ended up moving from the Bahamas to the States, and into a life of crime. He died of spinal meningitis in a prison in Florida.

Now, I am not saying I would have followed his exact path. I am not saying that I would have come to such a sorry end. But at one point, Joey and I were "running buddies." We got into trouble together. But then our paths diverged, and we went our separate ways. Why? Because I was chosen—first by my parents, and then by Brother Kraft.

Even after this crucial turning point, expert people-pickers have continued to have a great influence on my life. In my case, as I became a young adult, I was fortunate to meet two expert people-pickers working together. Ed Allen was a religious broadcaster and Stunce Williams a businessman. Ed, a pastor, was a true fatherly type. The epitome of his calling, he could speak and teach, and reach out to anyone. He certainly reached out to me. Stunce was a businessman, strong and smart. I'd been out of high school for a year when I met both Ed and Stunce, and their timing couldn't have been better.

This was a dreary time for me. After the excitement of my high school turnaround, I had begun to feel that I was wasting my time, facing up to a life underutilized and, really, underlived. I was working, no longer a criminal, but I was bored. The only job I could find was as a "beach warden," a kind of security guard, patrolling the beaches of Paradise Island in Nassau. Mind-numbing work, and not what I had dreamed of in Brother Kraft's class at all.

But there was a common thread running through my life, and once again, I was plucked out of obscurity. Like Brother Kraft, these two men were expert people-pickers. They spotted in me the same talent that Brother Kraft had not only identified, but had helped me hone: my ability to speak. And because I already intuitively understood the idea of the "expert people-picker," I was able to grasp the possibilities these two men put in front of me. They chose me, and I grasped eagerly for what they offered. Soon, Ed had put me to work introducing his global religious radio broadcasts. Stunce recruited me to host his radio and television programs. Soon, I was hosting a weekly Sunday morning religious radio broadcast and, each quarter, a one-hour television program aimed at young viewers, called "Encounter. "

In addition, Stunce, as the local director for the Christian Prison Fellowship, also enlisted me to visit inmates at a maximum security prison. Again, I knew the value of his choosing me, and I accepted the challenge eagerly. One day as I was visiting cell to cell, I came upon two inmates I knew. They were former friends, young men with whom I'd gotten into various scrapes. And now, I was visiting them—bringing them light and news of the world outside. I was outside, a rising professional, on a mission of mercy. They were both incarcerated, awaiting sentencing for murder. As I sat with them, and as I read the Bible with them, I was keenly aware of how close we had once been—and how our lives had diverged, thanks to a few special people, those expert people-pickers.

I was fascinated then—by the way our lives had diverged and by the way I had been chosen, picked from the flock. I am fascinated still. Are you fascinated? I am fascinated by the concept of people-picking, by the very existence of expert people-pickers.

Expert people-pickers are life changers. They are angels, messengers from God who deliver people from lives of crime or simply from boring, dead-end jobs. They are our saviors and partners for success. They bring messages of hope and purpose. Do you have an expert people-picker in your life? Are you an expert people-picker? Do you have what it takes to be an expert people-picker?

Expert people-pickers have been around for as long as

humankind has existed. In historic times, these people may have been the magicians, wisemen or women, shamans, priests or royal advisers. Whatever the title or position, the expert people-pickers were held in esteem, endowed with authority and obeyed. Samuel, the prophet, a notable example, chose both the first king of Israel, Saul, and the second, David. In both of the men he picked to be king, he identified the appetite, aptitude, and varying degrees of ability necessary for a king. Samuel knew and saw exactly who they were and what they could be long before they were king. Samuel, like all expert people-pickers, possessed the will, courage and strategic prowess to bring about their kingship.

Steve Jobs, for a more contemporary example, is known around the world as the mastermind behind Apple computer, the man who made the iPod a force in popular culture. But in truth, it was another Steve, Steve Wozniak, who started the technical breakthroughs that made the company. What Jobs had was the expertise, the vision—the ability to expertly people-pick—and he chose Wozniak. Although the two had long been friends, it was Jobs who had the vision for a revolutionary company. He chose Wozniak, and convinced the techie genius to devote his energies to their partnership. By picking a technical genius, someone whose skills would complement his own, Jobs made possible a company that has changed the way we live.

In our times however, most expert people-pickers and expert people-picking are not so valued. Jobs is famous because his company has made him wealthy, and we tend to overlook his people-picking skills and credit him for Wozniak's work. In general, unless they end up getting the credit for their protégé's accomplishments, we tend to overlook the people pickers. We are unlikely to hear about the adoptive parents, the teacher, the minister or the business person who identified and influenced the Nobel or Pulitzer honoree or even the employee of the year. As thankful as we are when we have the good fortune to work for a great manager, we rarely think to look behind the scenes to celebrate the person responsible for blessing our career in such a rewarding way. Who chose the person who made our life better? Who was his or her expert people-picker? Who brought that person into the company or the brotherhood, and thus started a chain of events that made our life better?

I thought about this the other day when I thought about Kyle. When I first met Kyle, I wasn't impressed. He looked too casual, like a superannuated college student who has never learned to shave properly or put on a suit.

I met Kyle by accident. I was walking through the Dallas-Forth Worth airport when I came upon a comfortable-looking place to sit and wait for my flight. As a professional speaker, this has become routine: Another flight, another city. The story of my life. As I sat down, a waiter approached me, and I realized that I'd sat in a café with waiter service. I'd have to pay for my seat by ordering something. I ordered a coffee, and—when that ran me more than four dollars—I realized I wanted a little more than just a hot beverage for my investment.

I waited till my server, Kyle, shambled over, looking sort of disorganized and too old for the job. And then I asked him, "Are *you* fascinated?"

He blossomed. "Absolutely!" Kyle said, his face lighting up at the thought. "Absolutely?" I questioned. "Yup. Do you realize the interesting people I get to meet doing this job?" Kyle said, clearly enjoying the opportunity to talk to yet another new person. "I mean last week I met Donovan McNabb." Using gestures he outlined the size of the football player, his face animated and his voice engaged. "He is big. Big! He is like three persons across," he said, stretching out his hands to illustrate. "And even though he's huge and famous and rich, he took the time to talk to me." Kyle glowed with the memory. "He was truly a nice person." But that wasn't all. "Then I met Miss America. She is beautiful on TV but in real life she is drop-dead gorgeous." He sighed, his face going dreamy. "Yeah, this is a great job, and what you just said—that's the perfect way to describe it. I am fascinated."

Who was his expert people-picker? Who knew that this seemingly dull job would be a focus of fascination for someone like Kyle? Who knew that the opportunities to meet the public—even if just to bring them an overpriced beverage—

would make this no-longer-young man come alive? Someone saw that potential in Kyle. Someone saw that appetite, that aptitude and that ability—and Kyle found himself.

  * *When we are fascinated, we blossom.*

People like Kyle serve their companies and customers well because they are fascinated by the work they do. And, thus, they do it well. I did not realize that I wanted a slice of pie with my coffee until I met Kyle, but after I had ordered one from him, I thought about Kyle—and about the expert people-picker who had chosen him for this job, in this organization. Who was the wonderful people-picker in his life for this organization? Organizations are people-picking all the time. Most organizations have entire departments specifically devoted to people-picking. Their problem is that few of these departments have bona fide people-picking experts assigned to the function. A recent study conducted at Harvard University concluded that 80 percent of employee turnover could have been avoided, had it not been for mistakes in hiring. What does this mean, in terms of institutional expense? Dr. John Sullivan, the executive director of the California Strategic Human Resources Partnership—a consortium of Fortune 500 executives, has done the calculations. The cost of a "bad hire," he found, can run a company more than a million dollars. Picking the wrong CEO can mean a loss of as much as 10 million dollars.

  * *Bad hiring practices—also known as poor people-picking—hurts an organization.*

All business-minded professionals agree that staffing—people-picking—directly affects the productivity and performance of their organizations. Putting the right person in the right position is vital. Yet most organizations entrust that responsibility to persons who lack the expert people-picker gene and genius.

Who are these people? Expert people-pickers are a combination of who they are and what they do. I have been blessed by meeting quite a few. Cheryl Beamer, an executive at the Gallup Organization is the quintessential expert people-picker. A tall, elegant woman, Cheryl has a friendly manner that immediately puts newcomers at ease. It's that refined ease, as well as the bounce in her step and the pep in her voice that lets you know she loves people—and that she is fascinated by people. And Cheryl can spot talent a mile away moving at 100 miles an hour.

"It's fun," Cheryl says, "helping people unlock what they do well. Wow, it's amazing." It's more than that—Cheryl's skill at people-picking, her fascination with people, is life changing. I am fascinated today because of Cheryl's impact upon my life. She was one of the leading decision-makers who decided to offer me a job at Gallup.

Let's review: Expert people-pickers are rare. An executive can be an expert people-picker, but so can a manager or a nurse, a teacher or a parent, as well. Expert people-pickers identify the appetite, aptitude, and ability a person has to perform a certain task or function. Expert people-pickers develop opportunities for the person to increase and multiply his or her talent. Expert people-pickers possess the will, courage, and strategic prowess to help that person succeed.

Chapter 2.

The Expert People-Picker and Your Success

Hire the pizza guy!" Duncan said to his call center manager, a sense of urgency creeping into his voice. "You've got to hire the pizza guy!"

Duncan Wallace, director for a global call center enterprise, was visiting the Indian location of his division, when something activated his people-picking radar. That something was the pizza delivery person, and Duncan was quick to figure out why. The new delivery guy, Sunder, wasn't the kind of young man you'd notice. Just another lanky Indian youth, working his way through tennis school by delivering food with a smile. But despite his casual manner, his slightly unkempt hair and delivery-boy clothes, there was something special about Sunder.

"He was not just delivering pizza," Duncan said. "He was actually spreading joy."

The way Duncan describes it, every time the young man came by with a hot lunch for the employees he acted on the entire staff like happy electricity. "Every pod of employees he stopped at instantly came alive with laughter and friendly banter," recalled Duncan. "He would remember a name, tell a joke, ask about how the day was going and so forth. After discreetly watching him work his magic, I was anxious to talk with the staff about this magical young man. So I walked around just casually asking questions about Sunder, "the pizza guy."

"What I found out confirmed my hunch. He had not been delivering the pizza long, they told me, but what a change he was from the last pizza guy! People throughout the division went on to describe the new pizza guy as smart, intelligent, caring, helpful, and fun to be around. So later when my call center manager complained about having difficulty finding the right employees—and in particular the right kind of managers—I told him: Hire the pizza guy!"

"Hire the pizza guy?" The manager asked, not believing what he had heard.

"Yes," Duncan told him. "Hire him first, because he has the customer service gene. Then hire him, second, because he has what it takes to be an effective leader. He has the ability to recruit followers."

I remembered the story of the pizza guy when I began to work on this book, and I loved what it told me—not just about young Sunder, but about Duncan. And so I called Duncan to ask him about it.

"Do you remember the story you told me about the pizza guy?

"Yes." Duncan was a little puzzled. "Why do you ask?"

"Because what you did for the pizza guy is fascinating." I told him. "So fascinating that it is one of the core topics of my new book, *Are You Fascinated?*" I explained to him the idea behind the book, that it focused on the four people that each of us need to succeed. "In the pizza guy's life," I told him, "*You* are one of those four vital people."

Duncan was slightly taken back. "That's kind of you," he said. "But all I did was spot his talent. He was the one with the spark—he obviously possessed that customer-service gene. In fact, he has gone on to become the operations manager of a Fortune 500 company. Success was in his cards. I didn't do much!"

"Ah, but that's my point!" I told him. "You *did* do much! You did more than anyone else could do for him at that time. Expert people-pickers, like you, come into people's lives at specific times—at turning points—and change things when we need them changed. Too often, people miss their opportunities, miss their chances. They miss their moment to change their lives.

But when an expert people-picker picks you, that gives you that chance.

"Call it serendipity or Karma or God's will," I told Duncan. "But expert people pickers are always there when we need them. And expert people-pickers are always on time." As I told Duncan, and as I stress here: Duncan did a lot. He gave that young man a chance to change his life.

How can you spot the expert people-pickers in your life? Expert people-pickers share five traits. These traits are as follows:

1. **Expert people-pickers are success-intuitive.** As Duncan did instinctively with the pizza man, expert people-pickers sense accurately and immediately what it is we do well. They sense the aptitude, appetite, and ability that we may not even be aware of. They also intuitively connect what we do well to what looks like success to us.

I didn't know Hesketh Johnson personally, when I met him one day, on my way to work. I'd heard of him—that he was a successful businessman who had reached out and was now known for his work with drug addicts and his youth advocacy program. But I had my own concerns that day. To anyone else, I was just another commuter, making my way through the crowd, when this strange white man came up to me. If anything, I probably looked less promising than the busy crowds around me. They were wearing suits, I was in my Beach Warden uniform. But he stopped me, and said to me: "You will be a great businessman for God someday. I just wanted you to know that."

I shrugged off this encounter. What a nut! But almost 30 years later, my immigration lawyer Kathy Sullieman—a smart, savvy woman—said something similar. Kathy, who had herself emigrated from Persia and made a success of her life here in the United States, had gotten to know me well as a student and as a client. So when she talked, I believed her.

"Ken," she said to me one day, with moist eyes, "I have to tell you this. You are going to make important contributions to our nation someday. I want you to know, someday you are going to be living in Washington, D.C., doing something important." I remember when she told me this, I remembered Hesketh's words, and I confess I began tearing up as well.

Expert people-pickers are like that; they get these moments when something otherworldly happens. As farfetched as it may seem at the time, they see in concrete images what we can be.

2. Expert people-pickers are placement-aware: Expert people-pickers know exactly where we fit best, whether it is a particular position within a team or as an individual performer.

Take the case confronting Max Trotz, a case I've often used when I speak to executive groups. Max, the young manager of a Walgreens store, had a below average employee working the store floor. The employee seemed to be trying, but she was never where she should be. A little overweight, a little older than some of the other employees working on the store floor, she seemed to always be lagging behind, never quite catching up. Although she seemed friendly toward the people who came in, always happy to chat and friendly toward everyone, she was just a little slow helping customers find what they needed and always a little behind stocking the shelves, and that meant a significant drag for the busy all-purpose pharmacy and household goods outlet. Max was a new manager at the time, but he had that insight that distinguishes expert people-pickers. So after a few weeks, he put her behind a cash register.

When I told a large audience of Walgreen executives this story, I heard a collective gasp: The sound of 7,000 executives waiting for the other shoe to fall. Well, this story has a happy ending. Almost immediately after Max made his move, everyone could see the difference. Behind the register, his employee didn't have to run around—and there her social skills were a positive asset. She was a natural at asking after customer's needs and making smart suggestions. In just a few months, she became one of the district's top suggestive sellers. Simply by repositioning her, Max helped her progress from a below average employee to an exceptional one. Expert people-pickers like

Max do this for people all the time. They position people for success!

3. Expert people-pickers are future-oriented: Expert people-pickers have a very clear picture in their minds of what success could look like for us in the future. They use this picture—this image of future success—to develop a road map for us in the present, a road map that can help us get to that picture and make it our own. Ed Allen, a great mentor, teacher and people-picker, is one of two key people who helped me find my own success. Ed primed me as his protege. When I was just starting out, a young speaker working for him, he assigned me the task of rewriting the sermon notes he had scratched out on table napkins, scraps of paper, and virtually anything that was nearby when inspiration struck. He knew I would learn by doing this. As I was copying these notes out, I could see how he used such literary devices as alliteration and captivating titles, how he used rhetorical questions and other skills to captivate listeners. It was an education I needed. By having me copy out these notes, he was showing me how to write my own speeches. Rewriting these notes, and the outlines he used to string his brilliant thoughts together, taught me the skills I needed to develop my own succinct and compelling message.

4. Expert people-pickers are unselfishly opportunistic: Expert people-pickers are on the prowl looking for opportunities—for us! They use these opportunities to position us for increasingly greater success. Don Clifton, the other key person in my speaking career, whom I will introduce more fully in a later chapter, was this kind of person, always looking for opportunities for others to succeed.

"Every leader, manager, spouse and friend, should look at the person sitting opposite them," Don used to say. "Look at that person and ask yourself, 'How can I help him or her discover just how good he or she can be?'"

"How can I help that person discover just how good he

or she can be?" Indeed that was Don's motto, and his gift to me. Don and his son Jim, the CEO of the Gallup organization, gave me opportunities. One such opportunity engineered by both Don and Jim came early in my career at Gallup. It was November, 1999. Gallup was holding its first CEO symposium at the famous Waldorf Astoria Hotel in New York City. Marcus Buckingham, then one of my colleagues at Gallup, was going to speak about a new book he had co-authored with Curt Coffman, called *First Break All The Rules*. The preparations were well underway by the time I got a call from Jim's office requesting me to attend a meeting with him and Don. During the meeting they gave me an assignment—and a wonderful opportunity.

"We want you to speak along with Marcus at the upcoming symposium," Jim said, looking me in the eyes. "You can do this, Ken, and you can do this well. And when you do this well, there will be other opportunities for you."

5. Expert people-pickers are time-conscious: Expert people-pickers know that the doors to success only stay open for a brief time. And they know that these doors open in sequence: The requirements for success today will not be the same requirements needed tomorrow. Therefore, they sense the urgency to help us now—and they know that the more successful they are in launching us now, the more independent we will become, the more strengthened and able to tackle our own success in the future.

I can look back on my last face-to-face interaction with my beloved mother Dorothy, and I know this was the case with her. I had stopped by to visit her in Nassau on my way to speak at a conference in Orlando, Florida. I walked up to her door dressed in my suit and tie, and when she opened the door, she gave me that same mischievous smile that I had long ago come to love, the same smile I got from her anytime she was going to surprise me for my birthday or with that special toy I wanted for Christmas. This smile, too, was to be a special gift.

"You knock 'em dead, don't you?" she said, looking me over

in my business attire. "I can see you take control. That's what we saw in you as a baby," my mother said to me. "Me and Vernon knew you were going to be special, more special than all the rest." In that moment I knew that I was only special because my Mommy and Daddy, Dorothy and Vernon, had chosen to give me their very special kind of love, the kind of love that only comes from sincere and committed parents. Dorothy died one week later, Vernon had died 14 years prior, but they left me with a unique gift, the gift of all expert people-pickers: self-worth. She looked at me, her son, that day and she passed the baton. It was as if she was signing off. Her mission—"rescue the throwaway kid"—had been accomplished. Expert people-pickers know when their work is done. They know how to let go, so that their one-time student can become the teacher.

How can I benefit from an expert people-picker?

Although we are all people-pickers, most of us are not *expert* people-pickers. Therefore partnering with an expert people-picker from time to time can greatly enhance our lives. However, in order to get the best and most benefit from an expert people-picker, the expert people-picker needs to be someone with whom you have an established and trusted relationship. Here are some ways you may utilize the expert people-picker in your life:

1. **In your career:** Specifically, use expert people-pickers to help you determine the ideal characteristics of the right job for you. This discussion with the expert people-picker should focus not so much on your technical expertise or qualifications but more so upon whom they know you to be as a person. Let them help you clarify the job-related activities that fascinate you. Some of the subjects you may want to discuss with them are:
    a. What regular habits do you observe in me which would indicate the type of job that would fascinate me?
    b. When I talk about work, what obviously excites me about my job?
    c. As we spend time together, what do you gather is my ultimate ambition for my career?

2. **In your relationships:** Helping you to understand your relationship-patterns and behavior is one of the most significant and potentially permanent ways that your personal expert people picker can help you. Choosing the person with whom we spend a great part, or the rest, of our life with is life impacting. Here are some questions you can pose to your expert people-picker to help them help you:
    a. Do you see any obvious patterns in the people

I choose for friendships or significant relation-ships?

b.　Have you observed any pattern of behavior, which are repeated over and again in my relation-ships?

c.　Is there a certain type of person that I obviously enjoy and who brings out the best in me?

3.　**In defining your purpose:** Expert people-pickers are gifted at seeing beyond career and relationships. They see how we fit into the universe. They are able to see the calling and potential in us, and they want to point us in that direction. Here are some questions that will help the expert people-picker in your life help you to clarify your purpose:

a.　Amidst all that you have seen me accomplish, do you believe that I am fulfilling my purpose?

b.　Throughout the time you have known me, is there any specific instance or example that you recall which points to what may be my life's pur-pose?

c.　Why did you choose me? What vision did you have of what I could become or contribute?

Celebrating the Expert People-Picker

What is your fondest memory of being selected or chosen

a.   In your family?   Who was the people-picker?

_____   _____

b.   In your school career?

_____   _____

c.   At work?

_____   _____

Note of appreciation to the people-picker in your life:
Dear _____, thank you for choosing
me. Because of your choice I am who I am today.

Chapter 3.

The Possibility-Vendor:
The Second Person You Need to Succeed

They charm us.

I dare you to do it!" My cousin Deborah put a sting in her words. "I dare you! Grab it!"

I was a seven-year-old daredevil, and I felt the lash in her language. Nobody dared *me* to do something and had the pleasure of seeing me back down! And so I did it: Ignoring the wild buzzing of angry insects and my own sense of danger, I thrust my tiny hand into the dense foliage of the hibiscus-flower tree and wrapped my fist around the wasp's nest within, tearing it from the tree and presenting it—triumphantly—to my astounded cousin.

My hand was swollen to twice its normal size for two weeks after that. But I didn't care. I'd faced down the taunting of my cousin and our extended family and friends, and faced down my own fear, as well. I had not backed away from the challenge, and I was satisfied.

That was me throughout my childhood and well into my early adult years. In fact, that same sense of daring—of never backing away from a challenge—underscored many of my adventures, and misadventures, of my high school years. So it was really quite uncharacteristic of me to back down from a challenge in the years following high school. And yet, that is what I did.

In the ten years following high school, as I worked and built a marriage and family with my beautiful wife Judy, I backed down over and over again from the challenge of education. Despite the fact that both Judy and I knew the next step for me was to pursue a college degree, even when we'd been married for five years with three wonderful children—Kendra, Kristen, and Kenny—I couldn't do it.

Judy had gotten her college degree. We had discussed numerous times and at length how good it would be for both of us to continue our educations, ideally going off to the United States together. There, she would get a master's degree—and I would finally go to college to earn my first, my bachelor's degree.

It seemed so simple, so much less painful than grabbing an angry hive full of wasps! And yet, each time we talked about it, I faced the reality of having to give up our comfortable life. I faced the option of starting all over again, in a new place and with all new challenges, and I was discouraged.

Some things in life seem harder as you get older, and this was one of them. We were comfortable. I had experienced a small degree of success as a businessman. I was selling insurance, running a landscaping business, and also serving as assistant general manager for a chain of jewelry stores. I didn't bring in a lot, but we were comfortable. We were able to pay our bills with a little leftover.

And we were settled in. There, in the Bahamas, we had a four-bedroom house, thanks to a mortgage, and drove two relatively new cars. We also had an income property: a one-bedroom condo on the canal at Port Lucaya—the site where Disney's Big Red Boat docked—that we regularly rented out to tourists. In addition, we had an acre and a quarter with 188 foot of waterfront right on the canal. We had plans for that property, and had just dug the foundation for a new house—a 5,000 square foot house. With so much going on, with so much already invested in our current life, it seemed foolish, perhaps, to risk it all. To dare, yet again, for something bigger.

And yet, I was not satisfied. I had a gnawing, haunting feeling that there was more for me—that life was calling on me to do more. To be more. However, the price seemed too great—the challenge too difficult. Until, that is, Henry O'Brien, a possibility-vendor, came into my life.

Expert people-pickers, as we learned in the last chapter, position us for success. Possibility-vendors, like Henry, whet our fascination with the impossible. They charm us applying never-ending gentle pressure to urge us toward our dreams, dreams they may have suggested, sticky ideas of futures and of goals that they may have implanted. But wait...

A word of caution, dear reader! Stop now! Stop reading, right now, if you have ever had an ambition that you have suppressed. Stop now if, deep down inside, you know that you are not living up to your potential. Stop now, if there is somewhere, deep inside, a tucked-away vision of what you *could* be, a vision that every now and then pops up into your consciousness. Stop now—unless you are ready to awaken and stir up that forgotten fascination, to revive that fascination with what seems impossible. Unless you are ready, stop now!

Possibility-vendors disrupt our "normal" lives with dreams of the impossible.

For me, the point of no return came in so softly. It was a Saturday morning, and I was busy planting begonias for one of my landscaping clients. Machete in hand, sweat on my forehead, I was content doing a simple job, a physical task, and I had not a serious care in the world. Then Henry crashed in with a disruptive, but sticky idea.

Henry had come by to visit my client, his friend. He and I had not seen one another for many years, and we were both surprised to run into each other like this. We played catch up for a bit, and then he went into the house to visit, while I returned to my planting.

All was peaceful, digging and planting, until I heard a voice. "Ken, you got a minute?"

I turned around and saw that Henry was coming up behind me. His face was serious, his manner solemn.

"Yeah, man. What's up?

"Have you ever considered going off to college?" Henry had an education, having graduated with a master's and post-master's degree in school psychology from the University of Nebraska. But this wasn't a conversation we'd had before. His question—seemingly out of nowhere—disturbed me, and intrigued me all at once. How did he know my secret wish?

"Yes, I have." I answered slowly, a little afraid of what I was getting into. To myself, I added: "And what business is that to you?"

"I have an idea that I would like to share with you," he began. And for the next hour or so, I listened to him and found that his idea echoed and supported my own suppressed desires. It was as if he were speaking out my thoughts and dreams—the dream of a college degree.

But I lived in the real world, the here-and-now. The reality of our financial commitments and our hard-earned comfort were still more compelling than that old dream. With that in mind, I carefully stowed that desire back into the dark compartment in my mind where it had already been stored for decades—since I'd graduated from high school. But I'd run into a possibility-vendor, and, true to his calling, he had planted an idea. He had made the idea of my going to college "sticky," or hard to discard. A sticky idea stays with you, never quite leaving your consciousness. It is to our good fortune when life's circumstances work behind the scenes to bring us back to such ideas over and over again. By reviving that hope—once again suggesting that "sticky" idea—Henry had kept that dream alive.

* *Possibility-vendors deal in "sticky" ideas: dreams that will not die.*

That's what happened for me one Sunday afternoon, when the next possibility-vendor came along. My buddy Simeon "Sim" Lockhart and I were out fishing, as we were most weekends.

Our practice was to swim out about a mile or two from shore, wearing face masks and snorkels, big flippers on our feet, and armed with Hawaiian slingshots, spears, and a net to carry our catch. Sim was the stronger swimmer, so he led the way.

We'd had a good day thus far. We'd speared a few large fish and moved onto hunting the spiny lobsters that are a Bahamian delicacy. As we swam along, I held the net, full of the wounded and bleeding fish. We were swimming peacefully when I saw something large pass in front of me. I didn't get a good look at it, but I saw that it was dark grey—and moving fast. I stopped swimming and brought my face up to the surface for a better look. To my despair, I saw two dorsal fins, slowly circling. Sim, meanwhile, remained blissfully unaware and continued to swim on ahead.

My throat went dry. My life was flashing before me. I was moving my fins just enough to keep from sinking, and I did not dare call out to Sim. I didn't want to do anything—make any noise or vibration—that would attract attention from those deadly fins. This pause lasted only about two minutes, but it seemed like an eternity before Sim realized I was no longer behind him. Then he did something that only a true and brave friend would do. He came back. He came back and—while the sharks continued to circle, getting ever closer—he reached over and pulled the net, with the bleeding fish, away from me. Holding the net out of the water, he reached inside and pulled out a fish—and he threw that fish as far as he could. He pulled out another, and threw it—and another and another, until each of the wounded fish were gone. Thank God, it worked. The sharks swam after the bloody fish, and Sim and I swam in the opposite direction. We'd had enough "sport" for the day! That afternoon, while we sat reflecting on how close we'd been to a shark attack, Sim the hero became Sim the possibility-vendor. "That was a miracle," Sim said. "There is no explanation for why those sharks didn't go into a frenzy. There was blood in the water all around you and the fish in the net were alive and wounded. Sharks attack everything and anything in that kind of environment. There is something more, something more important, that you are supposed to do with your life, Ken." This time, I got the message. It took two possibility-vendors, two sharks (possibility-vendors of a different kind), and almost two years, but finally—I got the message. Life was calling me to live a different life than the one I was now living. Life was calling me to change.

* It may take time to accept what the possibility-vendor offers, but the ideas and dreams will not let go until you do.

Let's review: Possibility-vendors deliver the sticky ideas that are hard to ignore. They charm us by providing constant pressure, keeping the dream or goal—the sticky idea—alive. These ideas tickle our fascination with the impossible. They stimulate our imagination and challenge us to move out of our comfort zones. They disrupt our lives. That is exactly what this did to my family. I went back to Henry and picked up the conversation we had left off two years earlier. And after that conversation, Judy and I had a talk. This time, the topic wasn't *if* we would go back to school, but how could we make it possible for our family of five to go to college!

It wasn't going to be easy. We arrived at the conclusion that we would have to sell everything. We would sell the house, and pay off that mortgage. Sell the property, and give up our plans for our gorgeous new house, and pay off the balance on that. Sell one of the cars, too. We would hold onto the rental property, as a source of income—albeit small—and Judy and the kids would move into a rented two-bedroom apartment for a short time, while we waited for her leave of absence from her job, at the Ministry of Education, to come through.

This began one of the saddest seasons for our family. We were tearing ourselves away from so many things that we held dear. Every item we sold was something we had valued, something we had purchased with care and love. My oldest daughter to date will mention the pain of watching us sell her toys, in particular a Cabbage Patch doll she had named Judy, after her mother. But it all went: We sold furniture, treasured wedding gifts, favorite books, and fishing gear. We were giving up the life we had come to know. We were giving up the life we already owned in order to pursue a new life, the one we hoped for, even though we didn't really know what it would be like.

Some people would call this faith. Others would label it foolishness. I call it fascination: Fascination with the impossible! Thanks to the possibility-vendors in our life, we as a family became fascinated with the impossible.

Yes, we felt a deep and very real sadness over the loss of our former life, giving up things and a way of life we had come to hold dear. Yet, at the same time, we shared the real and great anticipation of what was going to happen next. This is what the possibility-vendor will do. He—or she—will turn your focus forward, away from past accomplishments and already achieved goals toward looking instead at what is next, the big or seemingly impossible goal that you can pursue. Possibility vendors plant the sticky ideas that change our focus from looking *back* at our accomplishments to looking *ahead* at what we may yet accomplish.

* Possibility-vendors turn our focus forward—and ahead.

Author Lance Secretan speaks about such ideas in his book, *Inspirational Leadership*, calling them "the grand Cause." "The grand Cause," he writes, "speaks—or more accurately sings, croons, cheers and shouts—to the soul."

This sticky idea, this Cause as Secretan puts it, makes such a connection with our hearts, our minds, and our souls that it speaks to our inner knowing—to our spirit. To something that is not of this world. Indeed, that was our feeling as we made the choice to give up the life we knew, to leave our homeland. In many ways, we were like the original Pilgrims or like so many of the hopeful who landed at Ellis Island, beckoned by a beacon of hope. We had come to believe that the goal we were pursuing—the "something more" that was calling to us—was worth the sacrifice of all we had possessed and formerly treasured.

That is how possibility-vendors inspire. They awaken or implant a sticky idea—an idea that, if allowed, becomes a consuming passion, a cause. That is how Henry O'Brien inspired me.

"Ken, go to the University of Nebraska," he said to me. I remember his exact words. "The University of Nebraska will be good for you, Ken. And you will be good for Nebraska." And so I did: I made the trek north to Nebraska, leaving my wife and wonderful children behind, in the Bahamas.

Possibility-vendors are all around us. Where ever people interact—in families, schools, churches or social organizations—there are possibility-vendors. Too often, however, we ignore their voices. We ignore their call to action—and with good reason—possibility-vendors sell sticky ideas to us, and those ideas require great sacrifice.

The possibility-vendors in my life sold the sticky idea of college to me, but it was then up to me to find a way to fulfill that vision, to realize that dream. Always, once we have bought the idea that the possibility-vendor presents, that idea becomes part of us—and that means we must struggle to achieve its complete fulfillment.

A possibility-vendor can inspire us, but we must do the work.

We did struggle. Our family's original plan was that Judy and the kids would join me after the first semester or, at worst, at the end of the first year. But before we were ready a year and a half had passed. All the funds we had raised selling our properties and possessions had run out. Judy even began baking muffins at night to bring in an additional $40 each week.

She never complained. Friends and family members, however, saw her struggle, on her own, with our children. They began sending me messages, urging me to quit. To give up my dream. "Do what is right," they said. "Come back home and take care of your family."

By the end of my fourth semester, halfway through my degree, guilt-ridden by being an absent father and husband and fully aware of the toll my absence was taking on my family, I came to a tortured decision. I would quit school and return to the Bahamas. I drove my $650 barely-functional college car to an isolated parking space at the airport, left the key under the bumper, and boarded a plane back to my family.

I felt like a failure. My plan had seemed so well thought-out. I hadn't gone to Nebraska on a whim. I'd been accepted at other prestigious schools.

But Henry had convinced me, when he said, "Nebraska will be great for you. And you will be great for Nebraska." On that flight back, I was convinced that had been a mistake. In fact, I'd begun to feel like the entire venture had been a devastating mistake. After all, I had sold off all our assets. I had given up a good position, one that had carried the likelihood of promotion. I had "deserted" my family for two years. Now, here I was, traveling back to the Bahamas with nothing to show for it all. This was the shadow side of fascination. This was the flip side of anticipation—of daring to reach for the impossible dream. This was hopelessness and defeat.

When dreams seem impossible, the possibility-vendor sees how they can be made possible.

"You have to go back," my friend told me. "No question about it, you absolutely must go back." The friend who was certain was Donald McCartney, executive vice president of Princess Properties, educator, a disciplinarian, and a God-given possibility vendor. We were sitting in his library, back in the Bahamas, and he was glaring at me over his glasses.

"I can't go back," I whined. "My family is suffering. I need to be here for them. Going to school for a married man with three kids is impossible." There, I'd said it.

But the key to a possibility-vendor is that he—or she—sees the word "impossible" in a different light. "It is impossible the way it is at present," said my friend Donald, nodding. "You cannot continue to live and study and be the best student you can be, while living apart from your family. Nor, obviously can your family continue to suffer as they have been in your absence. We need to come up with a way to solve that problem."

Possibility-vendors are like that, they focus upon the possible within *im*-possible. I explained to Donald how one of our biggest stumbling blocks had been Judy's job. I told my friend that we had done all of the necessary paperwork, filed it all in a timely manner. But although we had applied more than two years before for her to get a leave of absence, we had not received any reply—not any kind of acknowledgment. Not even a rejection! Being familiar with how governments work, Donald arranged for us to speak directly with the Minister of Education, the Honorable C.A. Smith. Once he was involved, the mystery quickly became clear. The honorable minister discovered that Judy's application had been received but had not been processed or forwarded on for consideration. The minister was livid. This kind of shoddy handling not only had nearly defeated our dream, it made his office look bad. In response, for both our sakes, he immediately had Judy's application processed and reviewed. Within two weeks, Judy's application was approved—and that August, I was on a plane back to Nebraska. This time, with Judy and the kids. The entire Tucker family was going back to school!

Possibility-vendors, like Donald, influence our thinking. They change our mindset. They engage us in critical thinking to bring about solutions. The best managers do the same for the employees in their workgroups. They are possibility-vendors. They plant the sticky idea that each employee is a solution provider with countless opportunities to challenge the impossible—to change the automatic default employee response from "can't do" to "can do." This was the case for Pearce Fleming, CEO, of Summerville Medical Center, and his team. Pearce was appalled to discover that, on a survey, the majority of the center's employees reported that they felt either emotionally disconnected from their organization or frustrated at work. And yet, they intended to stay with this hospital for at least another five years! This disconnect did not set right with Pearce and his team, and in response they conducted focus groups with the employees to explore this further. They found that too many employees accepted apathy and low morale as the standard. This was simply "how it was at work"! Disconnection, frustration: That was what they expected, how they thought work always had to be.

Sadly, this is not that uncommon. In fact, it is the case in many organizations. Managers and employees accept that work is either painful or disappointing. They no longer seek connection, satisfaction, or fulfillment. Not so when the manager is also a possibility-vendor. Pearce and his executive team believed that employees could feel good about work and be fascinated about what they do, so they set out to address this problem. At the time of the survey, various indicators confirmed low morale was directly affecting performance. One place where the negative impact was clear and acute was in the emergency department. This is how Pearce describes the situation and the subsequent action he and his team took to turn it around:

"The leadership team was determined to put a stop to this de-motivating and unresponsive situation. That spring, we began hiring nurses with a unique appetite for the challenge of the emergency department. Then we tied their performance to the metric of Left Prior to Medical Screening Exam, which at the time was 11.9 percent. That went down to 2.9 percent after 3 months. How did we do it? *We changed our focus from looking at the situation as impossible to instead focusing on what was possible.* We could not change, over night every employee's attitude nor could we change the pace and the volume in the emergency room. But, we could change our expectations and which nurses we put in the emergency room to work. Other managers and departments quickly caught on to this strategy of focusing on what was possible instead of being de-moralized by the seemingly impossible. By the time the next survey came around 12 months later, our hospital was among the top 10 percent in employee attachment and performance out of 200 hospitals."

Let's review: The possibility-vendor redirects your attention. The possibility-vendor makes you look away from what you have now, and what you had, and toward the future—what you can have. What you can be. What you can do. The possibility-vendor does this by implanting sticky ideas—the seeds of dreams—that encourage you to look beyond what you have always thought was possible. The possibility-vendor charms us, and makes it easy to start thinking about the *im*possible. Although you may have to struggle, the possibility-vendor will give you the seed, the idea, of the future that you want to grow.

Chapter 4.

The Possibility-Vendor and Your Success

I had just started my career as a physical therapist when I came in contact with a young boy, who had been in a horrible car accident," Mic Adams, a burly, warm-hearted physical therapist—and a real possibility-vendor—stated as he shared his story with me. "He'd had a head injury that rendered him comatose," he continued. "With serious damage that his doctors were saying was permanent. I volunteered to work with him, to help move his legs to keep his muscles from atrophying and to keep his legs supple. He couldn't wake up from that coma, and over a period of three years, doctors tried different procedures to help him. One procedure in particular seemed to hold great promise, but after two failed attempts, the doctors declared him beyond recovery. Permanently comatose."

But Mic refused to see improvement as impossible. He kept looking for the next step that would take that boy, his patient, just one step more toward possible.

"As I continued to work with the patient," Mic continued, "I found myself reading about these kinds of brain injuries. Looking at the research, at what new procedures were being tested. Finally, I suggested to his mother that we find a surgeon that would put a shunt in the boy's brain. She agreed and we began our search. We found ourselves a new doctor, Dr. Ashbargatie. He had developed a new procedure that had proven effective on other patients. He agreed to take this boy on and he implanted the shunt in his poor, injured head. Two weeks later, after being in a coma for three years, the boy awakened.

"It was truly amazing," Mic concluded. "To see that boy come back to life, as it were, was absolutely fascinating. I am extremely fortunate to have experienced that miracle with that boy and his family."

Mic did not give up. He could not shake the idea that something, something even seemingly impossible could happen for the boy and his parents. Mic had discovered the possible within the impossible. Similarly, although not as dramatic, the idea of getting that degree, the idea that possibility-vendors Henry O'Brien, Simeon Lockhart, and Donald McCartney brought to my attention over and over again, would not let me go. The idea was sticky—it was caught in my mind—but these possibility-vendors wouldn't let me even try to forget it. Possibility-vendors lure us, cajole us, prod us, and sometimes even coerce us in five distinct ways:

1. They enchant us: Once I had become enchanted by the sticky idea of getting my college degree, it began to call to me, to lure me to a different life from the one I was living. It didn't win me over immediately. I took my time and, even after I had started, I gave up momentarily in defeat and doubt. But as soon as I did, another possibility-vendor miraculously appeared, rekindling my fascination with the idea, even though it seemed impossible. In true possibility-vendor fashion, Donald McCartney showed me once again how much I loved this idea, enthralled me once more with the idea of pursuing a different kind of life.

2. They disrupt our lives: It is quite reasonable to see how I could have lived out the rest of my life in the Bahamas, without uprooting my family, without selling all our possessions, without starting completely over in search of a dream. Everyone else in my family and in Judy's family were perfectly happy with such a life, "normal" and stable. Very predictable.

No wonder, then, that they were incredulous when we announced that we had decided to sell everything and take the entire family off to college.

"You must be crazy!" Some of them shouted. Others took

the subtle approach, pulling Judy aside and quietly counseling her: "Speak some sense to that man!" Together, they were vehement—and determined. They yelled; they cursed. They called us foolish. They pleaded. And when all that failed, they tried to use guilt. "What about your kids?" they asked. "Think about how they will feel, separated from their family, from everything they've ever known."

We tried to explain that this was only for four years, at the most. Just long enough for us to both finish our degrees. But still they argued: "Take them to the States? They will lose their culture," they said. "And then you are going to lose them! Think about how they treat black people over there. At least here, in the Bahamas, you know that color does not matter."

When all the begging and pleading, the threats and the guilt didn't work, they reluctantly gave in. But they still begrudged us the move. "They'll be back," they muttered. "When they've had a chance to see how things stand, they'll come home where they belong."

We did more than disrupt our lives, we disrupted our entire families when we made our move. But we did it because there were milestones yet to be accomplished. We did it to achieve something beyond the life we were already living. We accepted what the possibility-vendors told us, we listened to the dreams that had been so long in the backs of our brains. We were convinced that in order to have peace and fulfillment later, instead of regret, we had to disrupt our lives.

3. **They whet our fascination:** "Why do you do it?" she asked. "Why do you do this work, Ken, cleaning the grease drains, mopping floors, and dumping garbage?"

Mary was the manager of the student cafeteria at the University of Nebraska, and I was a mere custodian. Still, my answer came immediately—and confidently. "I do it because it is part of my journey. Not the destination," I told her, without having to stop to think. For me, getting up at 5 in the morning to face the high plains' subzero wind chill and trekking over to the student commons to report to work as a combination dishwasher, floor-cleaner, and all-around handyman was a necessary step on my journey to an as-yet unclear, but grand destination.

It wasn't easy work. Many times the tears froze on my face as I made my way over to that job. Often, these were tears of embarrassment from when fellow-students from the Bahamas who knew of me, knew of my relative affluence back home, saw me doing such menial labor. I was not immune to the pain of the journey, nor oblivious to the humiliation. Not at all. But I was truly fascinated by the thought that somehow what seemed improbable, even impossible at times, was in God's time going to come to pass. In every class, I earned an A grade. Each semester was another 4.00 GPA. Why aim so high? Why work so hard? Because, I was enthralled, fascinated with the quest of achieving the impossible!

4. They re-focus us: "Have you ever thought of speaking to the Minister of Education?" asked Donald. This was such a simple, such a reasonable question. But it was one that I had never thought to ask.

Why hadn't I? I had become immobilized by fear of the impossible. I had succumbed to the idea that I was trapped, that I was out of options. That I was stuck. Once we give in to that kind of despair, we are not likely to keep looking—and thus not likely to find, for ourselves, the way to get to the possible that is buried within the *im*possible.

That is why we need the possibility-vendor to succeed. Possibility-vendors help us to find ways into the impossible, breaking down what seems un-doable into do-able, approachable steps. Donald did that for me. "Let's find out what happened to Judy's leave of absence application first," he said. "Then you can determine what your next step should be." It was such a reasonable thought, identifying the possible step that would lead us toward what had seemed impossible. And steps like this one position us to accomplish the impossible.

Possibility-vendors don't see walls; they see hurdles to leap over.

5. They enlarge expectations: What is the next big event coming up in your life? What do you expect? Horace, the Roman poet and philosopher, put it marvelously when he said, "Life is largely a matter of expectations." I agree!

Life provides us with the raw material, but it is our expectations that determine the product we craft from that material. How big are your expectations? Are they limited to what has happened before? Are they limited to your present experience, to the level of your past accomplishments? *What do you expect?*

Our expectations have a direct impact on our future. In my life, the body and genetics I inherited at birth through my biological mother's decisions and her behavior, gave me the raw materials I had to work with. I thank her for that. However, the expectations—the hopes and dreams—that transformed this raw material into something absolutely fascinating, came through the amazing people-pickers and possibility-vendors in my life. Together these people helped me begin to change my discarded self, my "throwaway child" self, through a journey of expectations into something fascinating. These people helped me expect—and find—miracles.

* Things impossible in the present, are quite possible in the future.

How can I benefit from the possibility-vendor?

Possibility-vendors stretch us. They push us to reach for what seems impossible. Many times, because of our own disbelief, they have to convince, charm, or coerce us. Partnering with the possibility-vendor will help us accomplish things that we never imagined being able to do. However, as before, to get the best and most benefit from the possibility-vendor we need to establish a firm and trusting relationship with the possibility-vendor. Here are some ways you can build that relationship and open yourself up to the sticky ideas of the possibility-vendor:

1. In your career: Possibility-vendors incite us to live according to a larger vision. To do this, they will nudge us out of our comfort zones. In order for them to help us become fascinated with the impossible in our career, we have to give them permission. Here are some permission-giving statements to encourage the possibility-vendor to challenge you:

a.   I want a more fulfilling and satisfying experience in my job, brainstorm with me as to what I can do in my present career to increase fascination.

b.   I am satisfied and contented with where I am in my career, help me determine if this is complacency or my destiny.

c.   There are limitations I see in my career path, help me with ideas on how to overcome those limitations.

2. In setting expectations: "Life is largely a matter of expectations," says the philosopher Horace. I agree. So does the possibility-vendor in your life. Possibility-vendors enlarge our expectations. They cause us to expect more, expect it sooner, expect it bigger and better. And, they feed our expectation with sticky ideas. To do this we need to provide the ready and fertile mind. Here are mind-clearing thoughts which help prepare you to be receptive to the possibility-vendor:

a. Is there a disruptive or compelling sticky idea that I am suppressing?
b. Is it possible that this sticky idea is my entree into the life I am supposed to live at this time?
c. Are the apparent blockades that have me stumped actual detours that are guiding me to a safer, more direct, and more instructive path to my destination?

3. In pursuing life goals: Possibility-vendors help us to look forward and ahead to what we have yet to achieve. They push us towards a new chapter in our lives. Here are some statements you can make which authorize the possibility-vendor to disrupt your life:

a. Life is calling me to live a different life than the one I am living, suggest steps I can take now to begin that journey.
b. I will tell you what it is I have always wanted to do but have always shied away from because I see them as impossible. Show me the possible in the *im*possible.
c. Point out to me some of the possible regrets I will have if I do not pursue the goals that I have been/am suppressing.

Celebrating the possibility-vendor

Who helps you strive after the big hairy audacious goals?

a.   In your career? (Give an example of how they do this)

_____

b.   In your expectations?

_____

c.   In life-goal setting?

_____

Write a note of appreciation to the possibility-vendor in your life:

Dear _____, thank you for whetting my fascination. Because of your sticky idea, my life and vision are bigger and fuller.

Chapter 5.

The Dream-Maker:
The Third Person You Need to Succeed

They convert us.

Our dream had come true, at least partially. Our family was together and everyone was studying hard at their various schools way up north in Kearney, Nebraska. But, are you familiar with the old saying: "Be careful what you ask for—you may get it"? Well, that certainly applied to us.

Maybe it is always true that everything we desire, every dream we yearn after, comes with some unforeseen price tag. That was the case for us, and what a price it was. "Our family will be attending school in the States," we'd told everybody, enjoying the hubbub that this glamorous statement caused. But the glitz and glitter of that rich-sounding pronouncement quickly faded in the face of the reality.

Life in Kearney was hard. Both Judy and I were spending too much time at our studies to work at more than odd jobs. For the first two years, we were barely able to pay the rent and keep enough food on our table for our three growing children. We were grateful for the kind church folks we met, generous people who would often drop by with packages of food they had collected.

But then things got worse. Judy finished her two-year master's degree and in accordance with her contract returned to the Bahamas and to her job at the Ministry of Education, to which she'd be committed for two years. As a result, I became a single parent, working 88 percent full time and, with my bachelor's under my belt, rounding the corner to a master's degree. Things were tough. Judy would fly up to Nebraska when she could, but these would only be short weekend breaks. And these visits were hardly what you would call relaxing for any of us. While here, she would cook as much shepherd's pie and lasagna as the fridge would hold then have to turn around and return to the Bahamas. At the end of two years, at the completion of her contract, Judy rejoined us.

But even though we were all happy to be reunited, financially things got worse. I was making a very modest salary, but Judy could not work and we sorely missed her Ministry of Education paycheck. Once again, we were living far below the poverty line—a situation that continued for seven years.

Things got so bad at one point that in order to do something more just to feed our family, Judy had to get inventive. Being the industrious woman that she is, she found a solution in FoodNet. As members of the FoodNet program, we would collect discarded food. We would go to the super K Mart and other food stores and collect bottles of milk that were damaged but not pierced. We would collect bags of oranges in which one orange was rotten. Sometimes we would collect dozens of eggs from cartons where one egg was broken. We would also get cakes and pastries that were one day beyond expiration. It was a harvest of food that would otherwise be wasted, and what we found was perfectly healthy and of fine quality.

In fact, we started to get so much food and we saw so much truly good food going to waste that Judy came up with the idea of sharing this "second harvest" with other neighbors, and other neighborhoods. We began re-packaging this perfectly good food and delivering it to needy neighborhoods in Lincoln, Nebraska. It felt great to be doing this—not only having enough for ourselves, but being able to help others who also needed a lift. Still, it was a rough time for us all. Up to this point, reality was nothing like we had imagined or dreamed. That is, until life again provided us with another one of the persons we all need to succeed.

That third person—the third you need to succeed—is the dream-maker. Dream-makers help us convert dreams into reality. Dream-makers clear obstacles out of our way. Dream-makers put our talents to work. That was the case with Jack Huck, President of Southeast Community College. Jack became my boss when Southeast Community College hired me as a part of the administration. A tall, studious, and giving man, with a keen sense for getting impossible things done, Jack was a sincere and willing dream-maker.

"Ken, I am going to nominate you," Jack said to me one day. "The Kellogg's Leadership Program and the League for Innovation in the Community College, are soliciting nominations for a year long Kellogg's Fellows program. I am nominating you."

"Thank you," I said, flattered by his interest. "What do I have to do?"

"They will provide that information upon receipt of my nomination. Of course, you realize that this is a highly competitive event," he continued. "Your chances are slim. Only 20 nominees from all around the country will be chosen, based upon academics, outstanding accomplishments, and innovative programs designed and implemented within the community college. But I believe in you," he said. "And I'm going to nominate you!"

Dream-makers help us take that next step, making our dreams reality.

Jack, like the true dream-maker, was putting my talent to work in concrete ways, and in putting my talent to work he was helping me make my dreams come true. People-pickers choose us; they spot our talent. Possibility-vendors charm us; they whet our fascination for the impossible. Dream-makers, however, convert us. They help us take the next step. They convert us into believing partners with them. They focus their power and influence on making our dreams come true, and they put our talent to work. And I did work, a lot of work. With my bachelor's and master's completed, I started on a doctorate degree, while also working on my Kellogg's Fellowship—and on achieving permanent residence status.

This was the other part of my dream, and in it I had another dream-maker helping me along, my immigration lawyer, Kathy Sullieman. One day Kathy, a very encouraging dream-maker, came to me with an idea. "Ken," she said, "you have a very unique perspective because of your cultural background, you should develop a program for young people in Nebraska that will help them experience other cultures. Make it fun, but make it life-changing." That made sense to me—as a part of my Kellogg's fellowship program I was required to develop and implement a community-wide event. I developed a program called "I Can See Clearly Now," a multicultural student leadership retreat. This was conceived as a two day event, and we were able to involve the renowned Jane Elliot, who had developed her own innovative multicultural program, called "brown eyes/blue eyes," while a teacher in Iowa. Once again, call it serendipity, call it Karma, or call it God, but the people we need to help us succeed always show up on time. Not only did Kathy start me going, and Jane later invited me to co-facilitate with her, delivering her program around the mid-west. But also, while soliciting funds for the retreat from local organizations, I came into contact with the Gallup Organization, and, in particular, Irene Burklund.

I remembered Irene years later. I'd had a difficult day. I was sitting in my office, looking at the silent phone. I had just hung it up, after hearing bad news. I was sitting there, dejected, trying to recover from the disappointment of not being selected for a job I had applied for while simultaneously trying to figure out what other job could I pursue. I had worked with Jack Huck and Southeast Community College for three years, but life was again calling me to try a different path. That was the moment Irene Burklund came back into my thoughts. Immediately, I picked that phone back up and called her—and she was able to get me an interview with her organization.

Two weeks later, I had to travel to Miami, for the Kellogg's program—when it hit me: My interview was supposed to be that day! I had double booked and had totally forgotten the job interview with Gallup. Abashed, I called to apologize to Irene for missing the interview and explained what had happened. I knew I had to apologize, but I figured that would be it. I'd blown my chances. But in true dream-maker style, Irene did something that changed my life yet again. "No problem, Ken," she said. "We like busy people. I will schedule another appointment for you." That was the day my love affair with the Gallup Organization began.

About ten months into my job at Gallup, we were living our dreams and, in ways, the American Dream as well. In the months prior to Gallup, while still making my modest income from my job at a community college, Judy and I would drive past one certain neighborhood. Someday, we would tell each other—looking at the beautiful landscaping and the multi-level houses, someday we will live here. Thanks to Gallup, that was possible. We bought our dream house and moved in. We were living the dream.

Then it happened. The letter arrived. Not just any letter, but a letter from Immigration and Naturalization Services, in a red envelope. The letter which I still have today stated in part, "You have 45 days to leave the country." Apparently an error in timing on my part had resulted in me endangering my legal resident status. In order to remain in the United States, I would have to return to my previous job, if I could, or leave the country and wait for immigration approval, which might or might not be granted, before I could return.

My world crumbled. I sat there alone with that letter in my hand, asking myself impossible questions: "How could I break this news to my wife and kids? How could I tell them that after all of the years of struggling and sacrifice they had given, how do I tell them that my impatience had cost us our dreams? And where is God? Did He set us up for this disappointment? Did He bring us this far to leave us?"

I held onto that letter for a week without telling Judy.

During that week I called my immigration lawyer, Kathy, only to discover that it had been years since she had given up her law practice in order to work in her husband's medical practice. I was alone in despair. I finally broke down and told Judy. She was flabbergasted. We both were. Our dream had been completely deflated. Enter Amy Peck, my second immigration lawyer and a dream-maker extraordinaire. Remember what dream-makers do? They convert our dreams into concrete reality, helping us see how in daytime reality our dreams do come true. That was not the case with Amy at first. As opposed to Kathy's easy-going poise, Amy's approach is no-nonsense and, at times, painfully straight to the point. In fact, one of our earliest conversations went like this:

"Ken," said Amy, cutting right to the chase. "I have looked over your immigration file and you have two options. One, you can go and ask your former employer for your old job back. Or two, you can leave the country and we will try to get a visa for you to return."

While this was discouraging, I owed her nothing less than the truth. "I can't imagine why my old employer would take me back seeing as I left them," I told her. "They were not thrilled when I resigned. I do not know that it is impossible, but, it is certainly not likely. And as far as going out of the country, we only recently bought this house, I have a mortgage to pay."

Amy was silent for a moment, mulling over what I'd told her. "Well, you think about your options for a few days," she finally said. "And call me back."

This was one of those moments in life when you are forced to look at your cosmology, that is, how you make sense out of life. For us, faith is the answer. In this time of crisis, we turned to prayer. After we broke the news to the kids, each morning and evening we prayed specifically that God would intervene on our behalf with INS. A week after our first conversation, Amy, immigration lawyer and dream-maker called back. This time, the conversation went much better—and with a surprising twist.

Without any salutation or niceties Amy spoke: "Do you believe in God?" she asked.

"Yes, I believe in God," I replied immediately, speaking straight from my heart. "We have been praying ever since you gave us the news."

"Well, maybe that has had some effect. You see, Ken," she continued, "I have been troubled by your case. So, I have been doing some digging and I believe I have come across a law that has been tabled by Congress in the past, but that President Clinton is now reviewing. If he decides to sign that bill into law, you have a chance. So hang in there, Ken, and I will keep you informed."

I hung up the phone and cried. I cried, because I realized that it was God all along, in His mercy and by His grace, putting in my life the people I need to succeed. It was, He, calling me to live a life that was different from the one I had known. Amy called a little while later to inform me that the bill had indeed been passed into law, clearing the way for us to become American citizens. Dream-makers convert us into believing that dreams can come true. They remove obstacles so that we can succeed. The best managers in an organization are dream-makers. They are effective at removing obstacles so that employees may live their dream jobs. They convert employees into believing that dream-jobs really do come true.

> ** Dream-makers build bridges that get us over the gaps in our faith.*

Do you know the popular "Dilbert" comic-book character? Or perhaps you're more familiar with his UK counterpart, "Alex"? These comic creations are office sad sacks, popular because they put a funny face on a common misery, bemoaning the frustration so many employees experience on their jobs—misery inflicted most often by clueless, insensitive bosses. Sadly, the situation they make fun of is too often true. Research shows that 70 percent of good employees leave organizations because of a nightmare manager. Dream-making managers, on the other hand, are rare. They are rare because most managers and most people do not position themselves to be dream-makers. Most people simply focus on themselves, their own dreams and goals. "It's all about me," is today's common theme. We're the "Me" generation. "If I am going to make any dreams come true," popular sentiments seem to say, "it is going to be my dreams for me."

But even if these me-firsters are in the majority, they have not completely taken over. There are some—and maybe you are one of them—special and self-less people around us. These people, thank God, are looking to help others live their dreams. I have met some of them; you probably have also. In Illinois, for example, if you were to go to a specific privately owned bank there for a loan, you would not be introduced to a loan officer. Instead you would be introduced to a dream-maker, a loan professional whose sole purpose and mission is to help make your dreams come true. This bank has a greater mission than lending money. Its mission is to make their customers' dreams come true. That is what all dream-makers and the most successful organizations do. They make dreams come true for their customers *and* for their employees. In my work with organizations, the really worthy ones create the type of environment in which employees are able to live their dreams in the work they do. We all have dreams. And, we all have images of our dream-jobs and dream-careers.

* Dream-makers put our dreams first.

"I have always dreamt of becoming a singing star someday." Jennifer Hudson, recent Oscar Award winner and one of the hottest singing stars today said in an interview with Barbara Walters. Jennifer started singing at age seven when her grandmother, Julia, had her join the church choir. Jennifer's quest to live her dream drew national attention when she competed on the popular TV show *American Idol*. She gained special—unwanted—attention, however, when after one of her performances on the show, Simon Cowell, put her down, telling her, "You are way out of your depth here." Shortly after that, her

American Idol dreams were dashed; she was voted off the show by the viewers. But did she give up? No.

Disappointment, adversity, circumstances or difficult people, I have learned and she did, too, should not be seen by us as blockades to our path. At worst, they make us detour on our path to happiness and success. Jennifer Hudson learned that lesson during the two years after her disappointing shot at television fame. Unwilling to give up or give in, Jennifer continued to pursue her dreams, only in a different way. Her life was changed and her dreams realized when Bill Condon called to tell her that she had been selected to play Effie in the movie *Dream Girls*. That role gave Jennifer a chance to show the world—and Simon Cowell—what she could do. Fame and an Academy Award came soon after.

"I attribute everything to my grandmother," Jennifer said to Barbara, "I feel like this was her gift to me, I just want her to be proud, she would be in heaven shouting right now." With people-picking precision, Julia, Jennifer's grandmother spotted her talent. Through his dream-making intervention, Bill Condon turned her dreams into reality. That is what dream-makers do; they turn our dreams into reality and in so doing convert us into believing that dreams really do come true.

Let's review: Dream-makers convert us: They help us to believe that dreams really do come true. Dream-makers partner with us: They focus their power and influence on removing obstacles. Dream-makers help us build our future by putting our talent to work, and making our dreams become real-world realities.

Chapter 6.

The Dream-Maker and Your Success

M y mother came into your hospital with her wedding ring and now we can't find it," the caller said to Bill Adams, CEO of a large hospital in Virginia. "I want to make an appointment to discuss this with you."

Bill made the appointment and prepared for what he thought was going to be an angry and accusatory meeting. He was pleasantly surprised, he admitted, when he met the caller in person, and she turned out to be sad, but calm. Rather than being angry at him, she explained in a quiet voice, that she wanted to see him in person because she was hoping for his help. She then went on to explain that her mother had died a few days earlier as a result of cancer. With moist eyes, she described how her father and mother had been married for 50 years and what a wonderful loving couple and caring parents they had been together. Then she told Bill how the day before, her dad, with tears in his eyes had said to her, "It would mean so much for me to be able to slip that ring back on her finger before we bury her."

"So," the woman continued, "I was hoping that there was some way you could help me fulfill his dream of putting that ring back on my mother's finger. Is there any one you can think of who may be able to help us find that ring?"

Bill was deeply moved by the woman's story and her sad, but calm manner, and he promised to do all he could to locate the ring. "In my heart I yearned for a way to help them," Bill told me. "I left my office and stopped by the ward where the lady had spent her final days. The staff told me how the deceased had lost so much weight during the time she was there that they suspected her ring might have fallen off her finger. They were completely sympathetic to the poor woman's family, and I believed them," said Bill. "I mean, they told me they had done a thorough search. They had looked on the floor underneath the bed, around the room and in the bathroom. They had searched everywhere they could think of, but it was all to no avail. I went back to my office disappointed. But I was restless and not ready to give up. I just had this strong sense that there was something more I needed to do. Then I got an idea. I went into the basement of the hospital and located the laundry chute. I climbed into the bin and tumbled amidst the wet soggy dirty laundry. To my surprise, I found the ring. I almost cried right there and then. I will never forget the look on that woman's face or on her father's face when I handed them the ring the next day."

Bill could have given up. The nurses had done a thorough search. The ring was lost. Valuable items are often not recovered. Dreams go unfulfilled all the time. Not so in this case. Bill Adams the dream-maker was present. Dream-makers, like Bill, make our dreams come true. And, in making our dreams come true, they convert us. They convert us into believing that dreams still and often do come true.

Who are the dream-making partners in your life? Whose dreams have you helped to come true? Are there any dream-makers in the organization where you work? To spot the dream-makers in your life and in your organization, look for them to do three things particularly well:

1. They pursue our dream with us: Dream-makers are committed partners in the pursuit of our dreams. They take our dreams and make our achieving them their own personal goal. To bring that goal to life, they focus their power, influence, and energies on helping us capture those dreams. Bill quickly owned that daughter's dream of finding her mother's ring. He owned that dream with her, and he was not satisfied until he had done all he could to make that dream real for her and her father.

2. They remove the obstacles: Dream-makers run interference for us. "What is your most important job as a manager?" I asked a group of managers of a Fortune 500 organization. The answers the group came up with were more or less just what I expected. Some said their top job was to ensure that the organization's interest was protected and promoted. Others replied that they wanted most to help employees get their work done in efficient and productive ways. Still others responded that their highest responsibility was to select quality employees. Then as the responses quieted down, one lady in the back of the room spoke up, quietly but assertively. "To use the authority and leverage we possess to make our employees' dreams come true," she said. There was a hushed silence. No one moved. It seemed that everybody there was holding their breath. Then that breath came out in a collective sigh: "Wow." That was it—exactly! Although they might occasionally be distracted by how they do it, all those top managers there—some of the country's most effective managers, dream-makers themselves, recognized what the core drive was behind their primary job. To remove obstacles so that employees may live their dream-jobs. To be a dream-maker, so that people may live their dreams.

3. They build the future: Dream-makers pay forward, that is instead of trying to pay back those people who helped them; they help others by sharing their own experience. One day while driving in Oklahoma with Rudy Lewis, Rudy, an executive leadership coach took a detour to show me the small towns of Stratford and Ada, where he grew up. One building he pointed out to me was rather rundown. "That," he said, pointing to the site, "was where I had my first real job." As we looked out at the building, Rudy—an experienced higher education upper management professional who serves as a consultant with Fortune 500 companies—continued with his story, and his history revealed why he now invests so much time helping people like me make our dreams come true.

"H. B. Mount," Rudy explained, looking out at the ramshackle building. "That building used to house the most prestigious men's clothing store in this small town of Ada. People would come to shop in that store from all over Oklahoma. After returning home from military service, I was still very green and without any work experience per se, when I noticed a 'help wanted sign' in the store window. I went to Mr. Mount and asked him for the job."

Rudy paused at that point, obviously remembering a passage that was of great importance to him. "To my surprise he put me to work the very next day," he said, picking up the thread of his tale. "I was surprised because at the time Mr. Mount hired me it must have been obvious to him that I did not know the first thing about dressing. At the time, I did not own a suit or a decent pair of dress shoes. However, in spite of my rough edges and inexperience, he picked me. Mr. Mount believed in me. He took time to teach me the business and how to dress. He polished me up. Most importantly Mr. Mount invested his time and used his power and influence in an unselfish way to help me. He was a partner in making my dreams come true."

"After a few years, after I had graduated from college and was still working for him part time, Mr. Mount learned of my political aspirations. This is why I count him as one of the most important people in what I am today. Mr. Mount volunteered his time, money, and his influence to help me campaign. It was because of him that I was elected to the school board, and because of that entree I went on to make a career in education. Mr. Mount and others like him helped me realize my dream," Rudy explained to me, his voice filled with respect. "Because of people like him, I am honored to play whatever part I can, if any, in helping others realize theirs."

Our dreams are promises we make to ourselves. When dream-makers help us live up to that promise, it teaches us to look to do the same for others.

Our dreams are promises we make to ourselves.

How can I get the most benefit from the dream-maker in my life?

Dream-makers run interference for us. They remove obstacles from our paths by focusing their power and influence to help us. In doing this, dream-makers model for us how to pay forward the generosity we have received by helping others live their dreams. However, in order to follow the lead established by the dream-makers in our life, we need to make sure that we possess the mission, motive, and make-up of the genuine dream-maker. Here are some questions for introspection:

1. **Do I care enough?** Dream-makers care. They care enough to participate in the life of another. Even at the risk of diluting the time and resources they have for themselves, dream-makers care enough to take on a shared ownership of our goals. Do you care enough to be a dream-making partner to others? Here are three questions to help you process your answer:

    a.   Do I value what the dream-makers in my life have done to help me succeed enough to help someone else succeed?

    b.   If I were to help someone, do I need to know that helping them will benefit me in some way?

    c.   Am I likely to continue to act as a partner in helping another's dreams come true, even when it costs me?

2. **Do I have enough power and influence?** Helping others requires having the wherewithal to help. Dream-makers are equipped to help. They have the power and influence to make a difference within the realm of the dream. This power does not always have to come from a formal position; the dream-maker does not have to be a CEO or manager, or even any other kind of recognized power-broker. The power and influence to be a dream-maker may stem from the respect and honor you have as a person of integrity and wisdom. It can also be the power that comes from being recognized as a trusted expert or hardwork-

ing and honest employee. Chances are you already have the power and influence you need to be a dream-making partner to someone. Here are some ways to discover where your dream-making power and influence lies:

    a.   If I think long and hard enough, can I conceive of ways in which I am in a position to help another person realize his or her dreams?

    b.   In what role—be it at work, in the community, or else-where—am I a respected or highly valued contributor?

    c.   With which decision-maker(s) do I have influence or decision-making impact?

3. Do I have dream-making candidates in my life? The dream-makers in our lives make themselves available to help us. They are also alert and on the look out for those persons whom they may help. Likewise, if we are to be dream-makers, we ought to be alert and looking for the persons, our own dream-making candidates, whom we are uniquely equipped to help. Here are some ways, if you are willing, in which you can begin to identify the dream-making candidates in your life.

    a.   They are the person(s) to whom you make yourself available to help. Everybody meets and interacts with people all the time. There are those people with whom we develop a quick and easy connection. Many times this fertile environment makes it easy for you to build a dream-making partnership. There are also, however, those times when the initial interaction is not so smooth. In fact the introduction to each other may be uncomfortable or awkward. Yet, as a dream-maker, you sense that this is a person that you not only can help but whom you want to help. Dream-makers *choose* to become partners in helping others realize their dreams. Likewise, dream-making managers—the truly great managers—choose to make themselves available to help each employee experience more and more of their dream-job.

b. They are the people/employees who invite you to participate in their life and dreams. Sometimes people will invite you by choosing to tell you their hopes and dreams. Other times they will invite you by asking for your assistance long term. Many times they will invite you by asking for advice, which is asking for assistance in the short term. Most people develop a sense for who is willing and able to help them. Sensing that you are such a person or such a manager, people/employees will give you clear invitations to partner with them. The question you must ask yourself then is do you, *will* you accept?

c. They are the people whom you feel you can trust with your promise. Whenever, as a dream-maker, you choose to help someone and that person accepts your help, there are mutual promises made. You are promising that you will be that person's partner for a particular instance. Following that first promise, you are also promising to continue assisting them should challenges or difficulty arise in achieving the goal they are pursuing. Finally, you are also making the implied promise that in the future they may call upon you again to help. They, on the other hand, are making the promise that you can trust them to do their part in making their dreams come true. Dream-makers and dream-making candidates mutually commit to a partnership.

Celebrating the Dream-maker

What are some of your dreams that have come true?

1. _____
2. _____
3. _____

Who helped you to realize those dreams?

1. _____
2. _____
3. _____

How can you pay forward what your dream-makers did for you?

1. _____
2. _____
3. _____

Note of appreciation to the dream-maker in your life:
Dear _____, thank you for lending me your power and influence. I promise to partner with others to help them realize their dreams as you have done for me.

Chapter 7.

The Leader-Leader:
The Fourth Person You Need to Succeed

They confirm us.

K enneth, go up in the bow and do exactly as I tell you," my father, Vernon, said to me. I was 11 years old. He was a tall, strong man, my hero, but something in his voice made me look at him with a tremor of fear. We were on his fishing boat that day, far from shore, and when I looked up at him, I could see the worry on his face. "There is a storm coming," he was telling me. "It is going to get pretty rough for awhile. Do exactly what I tell you, when I tell you. Working together will get us out of this alive."

Was this the first time I had ever seen him worried? I don't know, but I can tell you that I remember exactly what he sounded like, what he looked like, and every other detail of that day. We'd taken his 18-foot smack boat, the Abaco Slim, out about 20 miles, deep into the dark navy blue waters that extend 100 miles between Andros Island and New Providence. This area is called "The Tongue of the Ocean," and offers many opportunities to fish. But because it runs from 10 feet deep to more than 6,000 feet deep it is also quite dangerous for the lone boat, unprotected and vulnerable. Even before my Daddy called me to stand in the bow, my pre-teen imagination was already running wild.

"I need you to be alert, son," my father said to me, his lean face stern and serious. I nodded to show I heard him, and tried not to look—tried not to even *think*—of the unique characteristic of the so-called smack boat. Designed for fishing, it had a hole smack in its middle that allowed sea water to flow into the boat, up to the sea level. This was called a live-fish well, and served to keep our catch alive until we returned to harbor. But as I made my way up to the front of the boat, my imagination kicked into high gear. Fear almost overcame me as I looked to the horizon in all directions and saw no land anywhere. Just then Daddy spoke again.

"I need you to grab hold of the anchor rope," Daddy said. I continued gazing off at the horizon, searching for land, as the boat began rocking violently from side to side. "Son, look at me, look at me!" The urgency of his voice pulled me back, away from the sea—away from my worst fears. I came back to life and grabbed the anchor line. "Good." Daddy nodded his approval. "Now when I say pull, you pull on that anchor rope with all of your might, and you keep on pulling, son, until you have the anchor on deck. Keep your eyes and hands on that rope. Do not look around at me, do not look anywhere but at that rope in your hands, and when I say pull, pull hard."

And so I stood in the front of the boat, waiting, while he maneuvered our small craft and readied it to run for shore. I heard the outboard engine roar to life and knew my moment was coming. And when he called to me, I pulled. I pulled until I thought my arms would break. I kept my eyes on the rope, watching it as it came arm-length after arm-length, out of that deep water. I tried not to notice how already the storm was upon us, how the water would fall away, as if the entire ocean were draining. I kept pulling. I tried not to notice when that water came rushing back, making a wall high enough to completely overshadow the boat. I kept hauling on that line and after what seemed like an eternity, the anchor came up. And with it, the boat—riding over those mountainous waves like a cork, the Evinrude outboard straining and growling as our little boat crested each wave and the rotors found air instead of water.

And because of my Daddy, what he did and—more important to me—what he told me to do—we rode out of that storm, and back into the safety of the harbor.

I could never forget that day, and that's the day I fondly recalled some years ago, when I spoke at the funeral of my Daddy, Vernon A. Cooper, the only father I ever knew. I eulogized him that day as I knew him. I knew him as my father, and—as was perfect for a true father—as the first leader-leader in my life.

If you've been blessed with such a parent, you will recognize the leader-leader. The leader-leader is the fourth person you need to succeed. The leader-leader helps you experience leader-moments. That day, in that storm, with Vernon focusing me upon what had to be done, that day my Daddy was a leader-leader to me.

"You did well." Vernon, said to me, after we had reached the safety of the harbor. "You did well. You did what I could not do. I needed you to get that anchor out of the water fast." With his calm, deep voice, he explained why my role was so vital. What I had done to save us both. "I could not handle the anchor," he said, "because I needed to stay back in the boat's stern to steer and regulate the power on the engine in order to get us safely over the waves. If you did not get that anchor unmoored, we would have capsized with the very first of those 12-foot waves."

In that moment, I was no longer a scrawny little boy. I was a hero. That is what the leader-leader does for us. They allow, many times they create leader-moments, wherein we are challenged to act upon the leadership capacity that is latent within us. Many conventional leaders miss this opportunity to develop others. Instead, they tend to take those leader-moments for themselves. They become known for their heroic acts. Not so with the leader-leader. The leader-leader nudges us to step up to the plate, delegates the important task—the major decision—so that we may develop whatever level of leadership ability and appetite we possess.

Everybody has some leadership capacity. Some people

have enough to become formal and life-long leaders. Others, most people in fact, have the kind of capacity that can best be applied in certain situations. Not every one is a leader, but everyone is equipped to lead from time to time. And for all of us, even those of us who may have limited leadership capacity or appetite, even for those of us who only step up into this role on rare or special occasions, this opportunity can be life changing. Being a leader, even for an hour, gives us confidence, builds our strength, and our sense of self.

The leader-leader gives us this. The leader-leader helps us become expert at recognizing and utilizing our leader-moments, giving us the confidence to act when we have to. The leader-leader confirms us in our sense of ourselves by showing us that we can take the reins. That we can take charge and trust our inner convictions, our inner leader, both in that moment of leadership—and in the rest of our lives.

> * *The leader-leader gives all of us the chance to become heroes.*

Remember Rudy from the last chapter? He told me about H. B. Mount, a dream-maker in his life? Well, Dr. William "Rudy" Lewis, educator, friend and business partner today, helped me tap into many of my leader-moments while I was a student at University of Nebraska at Kearney. A few years ago, I was reminded of one such moment he provided, when I engaged in an unexpected conversation during a trip to New York City.

"Hi, remember me?" I asked. I was shaking the hand of Roger H. Sublett, director of the Kellogg National Leadership Program and a program director for the W.K. Kellogg Foundation. He held my hand still and looked at me for a moment.

"Kearney?" He asked.

"That's right," I said. "What a great memory you have."

We were standing in the great hall of the Waldorf Astoria Hotel, the New York landmark. I had met Roger 10 years earlier when I was a student at the University of Nebraska at Kearney. He was the graduation ceremony keynote speaker. It was my job, working for the University public relations office, to chauffeur him around. Now here we were, thousands of miles and almost a lifetime away. I stood there in the great hall in the Waldorf that day and I was grateful. I was grateful for Roger and, most of all, for Rudy. Roger had been a willing participant and Rudy had truly been a leader-leader with me, helping create a leader-moment, an opportunity for me to "step up to the plate" by taking charge of Roger, however briefly.

The leader-leader, the fourth person we need to succeed, provides us with personal-contribution encounters. They force us to answer the questions: What am I meant to contribute right now? How am I meant to do it? Ten years earlier, while driving Roger to the Omaha airport, Roger helped me to examine those questions. Now, standing there, I found myself answering those questions, again, as we conversed.

"So what brings you to this event?" Roger asked.

"I will tell you in a moment," I replied. "But first let me test your memory further. Do you remember what we talked about while I was driving you to the airport?" I did not wait for him to answer. "We talked about what it meant and what was required to participate in the Kellogg's Fellowship Program."

"Yes, that's right," he chimed in, his broad face opening up in a smile. "I remember we talked about whether the fact that you were from the Bahamas prevented you from being nominated."

"Well," I said, "three years ago, I was invited to participate in the Kellogg's Fellowship Leadership Program and I am happy to tell you that I am very proud to be a Kellogg's Fellow."

"Wow, that's amazing." He said, "Who would of thought that we would be here like this today?"

"I am absolutely fascinated." I said. "Fascinated by the questions you put to me, fascinated by the spark you passed onto me — and fascinated by where it has helped me to travel. And, to answer your earlier question, I am one of the two keynote speakers you will be listening to today."

"Excellent. I am looking forward to what you have to say." Roger said looking me straight in the eyes with that big broad smile on his face. I was deeply moved as this life moment sunk in for me. Here I was experiencing, a decade later, the fruition of a leader-moment I had as a student driving Roger to the Omaha airport.

Rudy Lewis afforded me that life-changing, leader-moment, just one of the numerous times he did so starting with the very first day I met him. That day sticks in my memory. I was taking a class in public relations, and Rudy—that is, Dr. William Lewis, came to my class as a guest speaker. I was nearly done with my undergraduate degree by then, and looking about for what to do next when Rudy came to speak. I listened with great interest as he talked about his work in University Relations, but my interest really piqued when he said, "My office is devoted to developing leaders now for the future. We are interested in developing a diverse set of leaders, who are up to the challenge of leading in the 21st century."

After he finished his presentation, I excused myself from class. An hour or so later, when Dr. Lewis arrived back at his office, I was there waiting for him. He hired me and entered into my life that day as a long-term leader-leader. Although I did not know it then, he was doing for me what H.B. Mount had done for him. I resigned immediately from my floor-scrubbing, student cafeteria job. Rudy, as he is affectionately called by those of us—and there are many of us—who have been blessed by his leader-leading ability, provided many such opportunities for me and others, during his tenure as Vice-Chancellor of University Relations. Leader-leaders, like Rudy, help us increase our awareness of how we are equipped to lead and when we should lead.

The leader-leader helps us discover our leader-moments.

Let's review: The expert people-picker chooses us. He—or she—spots our talent. The possibility-vendor charms us. They whet our fascination with the impossible. She—or he—encourages our dreams of the impossible, often implanting the sticky idea that will grow into a goal. The dream-maker converts us into believing that dreams do indeed come true. He—or she—

gives us the concrete opportunities to make our dreams come true by putting our talent to work. The leader-leader, like Rudy, confirms us. They confirm that, in certain situations, we are all uniquely equipped and called upon to lead.

This role, this special person, is an essential for organizations. In his book, *Co-Leaders: The Power of Great Partnerships*, Warren Bennis sums up the vital role of the leader-leader this way; "In our hearts we know the world is more complex than ever and that we need teams of talent—leaders and co-leaders working together—to get important things done." Important things get done, and done in a different way when leader-leaders in an organization create an environment where more employees understand and own the opportunities they are equipped and called upon to lead in.

To explain the role of the leader-leader within the corporate world, I'll tell you the story of a CEO, whom I will call John, and his organization. John is the president and CEO of a large health system. He is one of the most insightful and innovative leader-leaders I have had the privilege of meeting. His special gifts became apparent from Day One.

To explain, upon coming into his job, John took over a new team. On that team, he found employees who were, in his words, "trampled down and depressed because they had been disrobed of the dignity, respect, and sense of calling that employees need in order to lead effectively." John immediately set out to change that. He did what the leader-leader does for their organizations; he created an environment where more employees could freely experience their leader-moments.

John acted on a plan. That plan had him identifying the leader capabilities on the team, and then delegating—letting *them* experience their leader-moments. I'll let him explain: "When I take on a new position," he explains, "I give myself 90 days by the end of which I want to have less control of the day-to-day operations of the organization than I had day one." John told me. "During those 90 days I am identifying the talent, skills, knowledge and experience of my employees. I do this because in 90 days I need to know into whose hands I am willing to place my trust, my job and my future. The challenge was, I discovered, that these employees were punished for failure under their previous leader. As a result, they lacked confidence in their personal capacity to lead. Their willingness to take risk was very low. So I gave them permission to fail."

"I told them that going forward the only failure they needed to worry about was the failure to do something. 'Do something, anything, but do it big, I told them, the risk is upon me.'"

Can you see what John did? By giving his employees *permission to fail* he gave them the tools they needed to grow, to become leaders on their own. The effective leader-leader within the organization makes it easier for employees to try out their leadership skills. They do this by helping employees view their area of responsibility as a safe zone where they can identify and grow their capacity to lead. Everybody has some ability to lead, but few people have jobs, or leader-leaders for that matter, that make it easy for them to take on the risk of leadership.

> * *Leader-leaders provide safe zones for risk-taking leader-moments.*

The leader-leader does not have to be, nor are they in most cases, a formal leader. Take for example, Bill Pilson, a soft-spoken, analytical and studious and normally reserved-type person. Bill was introduced to me as an engineer in a medium sized hospital. I later learned that Bill was far more than that; Bill was the quintessential leader-leader. As an onsite engineer, Bill regularly walked around the property to ensure that safety codes and measures were observed. Over time Bill began to expand his rounding to include talking with staff—and not only about engineering concerns but any and all concerns they might have.

"This did not go over well at first." Bill told me. "At first nurses in particular got angry with me. They got angry because when I asked them what their concerns were and they told me, I then asked them what solutions they were willing to offer. What solutions they were willing to bring about. They did not like my approach at all. So much so, that they complained to the CEO. He invited me to his office. Once I told him how I was trying to encourage employees to take more ownership for solving their concerns, the CEO encouraged me to continue what I was doing. I have been doing this for three years now. Now the staff, especially the nurses, present concerns and possible solutions as I round from ward to ward."

That is what the leader-leader does; they confirm us in our potential by providing opportunities for us to prove ourselves. They do this by providing more leader-moments for us to learn how we are equipped and called upon to provide solutions. In effect, leader-leader encounters help us fine-tune our leadership acumen.

The leader-leader confirms the unique leadership capacity within each of us.

When was your last leader-leader encounter? Who was the leader-leader? Never had one? Is it possible you missed it? It is possible you may have missed it. Within the formal and hierarchical structures of organizations most people are not leaders. As a result most people do not see themselves as ever leading. However, everybody leads. Given the right situation, everybody leads from time to time. This is where the leader-leader comes in; the leader-leader helps us recognize our leader-moments. To do this, the leader-leader exposes us to situations which increase our awareness of how and when we are best equipped to lead. This is what John the CEO and Bill the engineer do so very well. This is also what my Daddy, Vernon, and other leader-leaders did for me.

Let us review: The leader-leader develops others by giving us important tasks to perform. They do this not to be magnanimous, but out of necessity. The most successful leaders, those who are true leader-leaders, know that their success, and the success of the enterprise, depends upon how well all employees are able and willing to optimize their leader-moments. The leader-leader wants us to be heroes. They want us to learn and grow through each leader-moment we experience. The leader-leader points us to the leader within.

Chapter 8.

The Leader-Leader and Your Success

I t was my third trip in four days, and as I sat in the anonymous waiting area of Washington's Dulles International Airport, I found myself questioning everything I was doing. "What is all this about? Why am I sitting here?" To the outside observer, I was just another business professional: Armani suit, custom-made shoes, and power tie. But despite the trappings of success, I was feeling stuck. "Why am I here at 6 in the morning, enduring the ramblings of an overly nervous, over-caffeinated, cell-phone-babbling fellow traveler, waiting to get on yet another flight to go see yet another client?"

I was suffering from stinking thinking, sabotaging myself before the day had barely begun. But there was more than peevishness at work. And so I forced myself to tune out my nervous colleague's noisy banter, and focused instead on the core of my questions. Why do I subject myself to the hardships, the annoyances, and dangers of contemporary travel? Is it the money and prestige that accompany a successful career? Is it the lifestyle my labors support, for myself and my family? Or is there a more noble, a more altruistic motivation?

In short, what is it that has me—most of the time—fascinated? The myriad rewards—or the work itself? These are weighty questions at anytime. At 6:15 a.m. they are gargantuan. Settling into my question, I asked myself, one more time: "Why do I do this job? "

At that moment my flight was announced and my fellow road warriors and I boarded our plane. As the plane leveled out at cruising altitude, the flight attendants began the in-flight service. As I sat there, some time later, still in somewhat of a foul mood, it dawned on me that somehow everyone seated around me had received their drink orders and I had not. I stopped a passing attendant and brought my dire craving for coffee to her attention. She assured me that I would be taken care of immediately. I returned to my musings about why I work and became lost again in thought. Several minutes later I realized that I had not yet, as promised, been served. I became disturbed and concerned about the reasons for this double neglect and since I was already in a "poor me" state of mind, it was easy for me to slip into the next level. I decided that the flight attendants had schemed to mistreat me. That made me angry. I accosted the next passing attendant and demanded to speak with the person in charge. When the bursar came to me, I informed her in firm words that I would be filing a complaint about the poor service I had received from her and her colleagues. She listened quietly until I took a break from my ranting. She waited until I had said my piece. Then, she informed me that the flight attendant who was assigned to serve my area, a long-time professional named Wendy, had been particularly impressed with my demeanor and greeting as I boarded the plane.

I thought back: I had done my usual, "Good-morning-how-are-you-today?" routine while having a somewhat miserable morning myself. But this flight attendant, the bursar continued, had requested to be the one to serve me, because the flight attendant had said, "He is a Jesse Jackson-type. I know he is a preacher or something like that, and I just want to sit and chat with him during my break."

"She asked us to let her serve you," the bursar said. "She is preparing to bring your coffee and one of our special treats. You will enjoy her. She has an album of pictures spanning her multi-decade career as a flight attendant, including pictures with Queen Elizabeth that she thought you would find interesting.

This is normal for her. She usually finds someone to chat with on long flights during her break."

I was laid out, emotionally. As close as I come to speechless. With stammering words, I apologized to the bursar for my behavior. I begged her to ask the flight attendant—who I now saw as a person, as Wendy—to please come, sit and share her story with me.

I got my second chance. Wendy, an attractive elegant and humble lady, accepted my invitation and apology. As she sat and shared her very interesting and eventful 40-year career with me, I realized how close I came to missing the fourth person we need to succeed. I almost missed the leader-leader in Wendy. Even when we fail to recognize the leader-leader, the leader-leader recognizes us and our leadership-capacity. And thank goodness, even when we are being a jerk, the worst kind of passenger, fatigued and nearing burnout, or whatever state we are in the leader-leader provides the appropriate leader-moment. Wendy, through her bursar, had recognized my better self—my leader self—and given me the chance to redeem myself. To step up to the plate and be the polite, self-contained leader she saw I could be. Just as I was questioning my own role, my own fascination, she gave me that chance. Once again, I was fascinated.

Heather Wern, director of food services in a busy cafeteria, had such a leader-leader-moment. In her case, it saved the life of one of her staff.

"A few months after I took over as the director of food services," Heather told me, "one of my top performing kitchen workers stopped me." Early on I had recognized that this particular employee appeared to have the potential to take on more responsibility than she had been given up to that point by her previous directors. So, I gradually started giving her various opportunities in order to assess where was the best fit for her. I was pleased when in each instance she shone. In fact, it seemed that with each new task I assigned her she did the new task better than the one before. I was very pleased with her. So when she stopped me and said, 'Thank you, Miss Heather, for helping me.' I immediately replied, 'No, thank you. Thank *you* for being so very good at your job.'

It wasn't what the staff worker had expected—nor was her reaction what Heather thought it would be. Instead of a pleased smile, the woman broke down in tears. Sobbing, body-shaking tears. "I pulled her quickly into the office there at the back of the kitchen," Heather recalls. "Then she told me her story, and tears flowed freely from my eyes, too. This kitchen worker of many years, told me how just prior to my coming to work in the cafeteria she had concluded that life was not worth living anymore. She had made up her mind to end her life. She had been busy putting things in order and making plans for her suicide. However, once I started calling upon her at work, she began to reconsider. She began to wonder if maybe there was some reason to live after all."

"'I just want to thank you for saving my life,' she said to me. 'Miss Heather, you just don't know how much you mean to me.'" The leader-leader helps us discover or, sometimes as in Heather's case, rediscover our mission and meaning in life.

Sometimes within that leader-moment, the leader-leader shows us who we are being in the present. And in doing this, they put us back on track to live and lead the way we are meant to lead. The leader-leader does four essential things for us:

1. They hold up a mirror for us: Van Brown a preacher friend of mine, and an effective leader-leader, sat with a group of men in his church and asked them, "What would you do differently if you had a chance to start all over again?"

Each of them without hesitation identified specific and concrete examples of how they had failed to be the leader in some way, whether in their homes, in the church, or in life. "I was surprised," Van said, "and a little disappointed, to hear the sense of loss and resignation in their voice. I was several weeks into my series teaching on the subject *Walking in Your Greatness*. My disappointment was driven by the sense of loss and I was moved to take action.

"'What prevents you from accomplishing those goals

now?' I asked them. Together, we discussed their answers—and together we saw how those obstacles did not have to be permanent. They did not even have to stand in their way right now. For each member of that group, we were able to brainstorm about how at least some version of each man's dreams was realizable still, in the present day. We did this together, as a group. All I did was reflect what they were saying back to them."

2. They provide leadership-defining moments: When Vernon assigned me the task of pulling up that anchor, the successful accomplishment of that important task made an indelible impression upon me. More importantly, by providing that opportunity he allowed me to access my personal leadership zone. This is what leader-leaders do when they trust others with important tasks. They allow us to rehearse making our unique leadership contribution.

3. They help us clarify the mission attached to our leadership: "Ken, you feel it, you feel it in your bones." Don Clifton, mentor, friend, dream-maker, and leader-leader said to me. "You feel it in your bones; that's when you know what you are meant to do." Don stressed, taught and lived the concept of personal mission and purpose. In his book, *Soar With Your Strengths*, he writes: "Mission gives purpose to life. It adds meaning to what one does. In its purest form, it is so deeply felt that it explains why one does what one does." Don was a dream-making partner and a leader-leader to me during the three years when he and I worked on my first book together. He helped me to identify and optimize my leader-moments, he taught me to "feel it in my bones."

4. They teach us to become solution-providers: The leader-leader directs us to focus on the solution rather than become fixated upon the problem. The biggest gift the leader-leader gives us is the gift of solution-ownership. They induce our craving for solutions by calling us to recognize the leader-ship capacity within us.

Let's review: The leader-leader confirms us. He or she con-firms us by allowing and, many times, arranging leader-moments for us. These leader-moments provide the opportunity for us to rehearse making our unique leadership contribution, for us to practice our true leader skills. The leader-leader helps us dis-cover our leadership zone. They help us enter into that "sweet-spot" where we lead best.

How can I get the most benefit from the leader-leader in my life?

Leader-leaders are coaches in our life and career. They confirm us. They help us clarify our leadership contribution. They help us recognize the "sweet-spot" where our leadership-capacity is best suited for the situation. In doing this the leader-leader enhances the value we add as we serve others and our organizations. However, in order to exercise your leadership capacity, in order to be all that you can be as a leader, here are some strategies for optimizing your leader-moments:

1. **Do I lead or follow?** Right now, in this situation, am I supposed to lead or follow? If you have to ask, the answer is "follow." There are several very important reasons why this is so. First, you will know when you have what is required to lead based upon the specific elements and people present in the situation. When the situation suits your leadership acumen, you will automatically lead or want to lead. Second, except in a hostile or low-trust work environment, those working along with you, will quickly recognize and allow your leadership-capacity and expertise to be utilized. Here is a quick mental check list to use:

   a. In the present situation, what value can I add by taking a leadership role?
   b. If I choose not to lead in the present instance, is any injury done to me, to others, or to the organization?
   c. In the present instance, is it required by law or cultural norm that I get permission to lead?

2. **Where is my leadership territory?** Claim your territory. Get it clearly in your mind what activity and in what situations you tend to be at your leader best. You may use these three strengths-identifying questions to help you pinpoint where you lead best:

a.   In which activities or situations do others ask me to
      take charge?
b.   When I do lead, in which instances have I gotten my
      best results?
c.   Are there instances or activities where I would gladly
      lead more often?

3. What do I see in the mirror? If we examine our history closely we are likely to discover a pattern to our leader-moments. For me, the pattern involves adventure and daring. For others it may involve some sort of rescue or service to others. These three questions can help you see your patterns more clearly:

a.   What leader-moment is clearest in my mind?
b.   In which situations do I consistently have a strong
      urge to lead?
c.   Do I have a sense of regret or relief when I have
      resisted the urge to lead? If so, why? In which situa-
      tions?

4. Do I leader-lead? The leader-leader helps people discover their leadership capacity. They are driven to help others learn to step up and lead at the appropriate time. Leader-leader urges come upon them and they act. Here are some ways you can know for sure if you are a natural leader-leader:

a.   Is there a person within the last six months whom you
      have helped to discover her or his leadership opportu-
      nities?
b.   In your work, does your role require you to partner
      directly with someone? Who leads most of the time?
c.   If you or another person were given only one oppor-
      tunity to lead, would you take charge or would you
      rather let them lead?

Celebrating the Leader-leader

Who are the leader-leaders in your life at the present?

1. _____

2. _____

3. _____

Name some of the leader-moments they have brought about for you?

1. _____

2. _____

3. _____

Out of all the leader-leaders in your life, who made the most indelible impression upon you?

_____

Why? _____

Note of appreciation to the leader-leader in your life: Dear _____, thank you for helping me to step out and take the lead as is appropriate. Knowing that I can and should lead at times has helped me contribute in ways I would not have other wise. I promise to continue to learn where and when I am to lead.

Chapter 9

Are You Fascinated?

Brad Brodigan, a fellow consultant and I walked into a McDonalds restaurant in Chicago, expecting just to eat breakfast and prepare for an upcoming business meeting. What we got was an invaluable lesson about human performance and success.

We had just entered when a man approached us. "Good morning gentlemen," he said, a cloth and spray bottle in hand, "My name is Jim. Please come in, make yourselves comfortable, I know it is cold out there. There are some nice warm seats over here, close to the fireplace" he said, pulling out chairs, gesturing for us to sit.

I bet right now you're wondering if you read correctly. A fireplace in a fast-food restaurant? Yes, this McDonalds has a sunken dining area with a fireplace. Then Jim continued, "Sir," he said, turning to me, "I could not help but notice you as you came in: that is a very sharp outfit you are wearing. That tie and that shirt with that suit is a really, really perfect combination. You are going to have a very successful day."

With that, he left to go clean another table. Brad and I sat there a minute looking at each other. We both shared the same sense of surprise over what had just happened. We both agreed how refreshing and inspiring and, yes, unusual his early morning salutation was. We were so captured by his approach that we talked for some time about what kind of wiring, what kind of strengths, he possessed in order to be so welcoming, to put such an emphasis on hospitality in what was, let's face it, a quickie food stop for most people.

To learn a little bit more about such a person, we decided to watch him. Sure enough, as we watched and listened, he was at it again in a gentle and unobtrusive way chatting with other customers as they sat down, inspiring them as he had us. He was clearly fascinated by his calling—and we were intrigued! So, after we finished eating, we went over to him in pursuit of some answers. We discovered that, Jim, had worked at that same McDonalds, cleaning tables for 25 years. We learned that he loved the owners and really enjoyed his work. And, we discovered that Jim had a word to describe his behavior. "Fascinated!"

"I am fascinated! People fascinate me," said Jim, when we asked him what drove him to be so inviting and inspiring to customers. "Take you gentlemen, for example, I could see that you are going to an important meeting. So, I want to do what I can to help you have a good experience while here in our restaurant so that your meeting will be successful."

What a wonderful start to our day! Jim fascinated us—and both Brad and I went to our meeting fascinated!

The wonder of our day didn't stop there. Fascination is like an energy source, lighting up everything it touches. Our fascinated state had direct positive impact upon the results we got from our meeting. He was fascinated. We became fascinated—and that fascination lent its power to everything we did. Jim's response, and the subsequent result upon our psyche, validates the distinct and reliable way fascination works. People who are fascinated are *fascinating*; the fascinated manager inspires employees with fascination for the task at hand, resulting in higher performance outcomes. The fascinated nurse fascinates her patients by anticipating their needs even before they can push the call button—and as a result, the patient feels cared for and can rest and heal. The fascinated grocery store clerk fascinates the customer by advising him or her about which melon to choose and why, and that customer leaves not only with better produce—but with a sense of value, of being appreciated, and of appreciation for the fascinated store clerk who took the extra time to care and to advise.

Research confirms this common sense conclusion. Study after study shows that employees who are enthralled—who are fascinated at work—go beyond the bare minimum of what is required. They are more productive and thus positively impact customers and clients. They miss fewer days at work and remain employed longer with the same employer than their colleagues who are apathetic or emotionally distracted. In short, fascinated people serve their organizations, customers, and others at a higher level than those who are not fascinated.

Are you fascinated?

We asked this question around the world. We queried people in multiple industries, people doing all kinds of different jobs and job functions, and included a wide range of adults, that is, people over the age of 18, in a large number of different groupings. The sad truth was, among this huge sampling of adults, the answers were overwhelmingly negative. A full 70 percent of people in our research, when asked "Are you fascinated," replied, "No," or some variation of a negative response. Only 30 percent were able to respond "absolutely! I am fascinated."

How sad this sounds when we realize that we can all be fascinated—with what we do, with who we are. But if we look at the survey numbers closer, we find some very interesting statistics. For example, age seemed to play a role in the answer, and youth does not necessarily equate with happiness. Respondents 18 to 24 years old were *less* likely than any other age group to be fascinated. When they did report fascination, that fascination was more likely to occur outside of work. On the other hand, 50 percent of the respondents in age groups 25-30 years old and 31-36 years old responded "Absolutely!" Both these groups cited a job-related incident, within the last six months, as their most recent occasion when they were fascinated. 24 percent of the group 37-44 years old responded "absolutely." While 45 percent of those 45 years old and above responded "absolutely." These groups were just as likely to cite a job-related incident, as they were to cite activity outside of work, as their most recent occasion, within the last six months, when they were fascinated. Maybe fascination—or the ability to find fascination in our lives—is something we can learn.

Gender, too, is a factor in whether we are fascinated. Overall, 60 percent of males responded absolutely compared to 19 percent of females responded "absolutely." When we think about how the world still views women—and traditional women's roles and women's jobs—we begin to get a clue as to why these numbers are so far apart. Could it be that being appreciated helps us become fascinated?

And lest you begin to think that fascination is the same as responsibility or pay grade, here are some other numbers. Managers were *less* fascinated than employees; 23 percent of managers responded absolutely compared to 39 percent of employees responded "absolutely." Which proves that it is in us, in our dreams and our goals, to find fascination—not in a fancy title or big salary. The fact, as stated above, that as many as seven out of every 10 persons on the survey were unable to respond positively—were unable to say "absolutely!"—reveals the sad truth. Most people are *not* fascinated at work, in their relationships or in life generally.

Are *you* fascinated?

You can be. There are four people you interact with on a regular basis who are uniquely equipped to help you live a fascinated life. For some of you, as you read the previous chapters, you were introduced to these four people for the first time. Now that you have the tools to recognize these four people, you will find yourself meeting them again and again—and reaping the benefits that they are looking to share with you.

For others of you, you were reminded that you are one of them; they are, you are; the people-picker, possibility-vendor, dream-maker and leader-leader. Over the years I have worked for and with many of these wonderful people who have helped me become who I am meant to be. In small ways, I trust that I have helped them, too, to become more of who they are meant to be as well. These days, this mutual exchange continues to take place as I lead my own company, Ken Tucker and Associates, which allows me to serve organizations and people around the world. Many times, just when I needed them, I have met the four people I needed to succeed, and today I see these people everywhere. Watching them help people become what they can become, and sometimes being a part of making it happen myself, fascinates me. I want to help others just like you, find the four people you need to succeed, and along the way find your fascination as well.

You have the opportunity to share this gift, and to prosper yourself as a result. You can be fascinated, and can share that fascination with your friends, your colleagues, your employer or employees, and your clients. You can be that special person who changes someone's life.

For many of us, the opportunities exist to both meet these people—and receive the gifts they will bring us—and to *be* these people in the lives of others. We need these four people to succeed, and we can be the necessary person who helps others succeed. Now, *that* is fascinating!

Those who fascinate us, help us succeed.

Frequently Asked Questions

1.   *Is it possible that I have never had an expert people-picker in my life?*

Not likely, although, you may have overlooked their presence in the past. Expert people-pickers can be inconspicuous at times, working behind the scenes without being obvious. For example, Duncan Wallace served as the expert people-picker in the life of Sunder, the delivery boy in Chapter 2. It was not until sometime later that Sunder (pizza boy) became aware of Duncan's influence on his behalf. However, now that you are aware of the role of the expert people-picker, you can keep your eyes open for this first important person.

2.   *How are possibility-vendors different from expert people-pickers?*

The expert people-picker helps us develop our unique talents; they guide us towards identifying and owning our strengths. The possibility-vendor, on the other hand, plants the sticky idea, the dream or goal, in our minds, but leaves it up to us to exert the effort and commitment to bring that idea into being. Ideally, we use the strengths the people-picker helped us to identify to work on the sticky idea from the possibility-vendor

3.   *Should I approach someone and invite him or her to become a dream-making partner with me?*

Usually, the dream-maker initiates the partnership in some way. That is one of the specific characteristics of the dream-maker; dream-makers are on the prowl looking for dream-making candidates. But you *can* put yourself in the path of the dream-maker! Get out there and start working. Be working toward your goal, toward the sticky idea that your possibility vendors have given you. Be on the lookout for opportunities, for the people who *want* to help you by being your dream-makers. Be available. Your dream-maker will find you. Then, once that invitation has been given, make it clear to them that you want to sign on to a partnership with them to help you make your dreams come true. Here are a few things to help you get off to a good start:

a. Know your immediate goals: It is not unusual to not have a clear and detailed picture of your ultimate dream. However, you should be able to articulate clearly the immediate goal(s) that your dream-making partner can help you achieve right now.

b. Be flexible: Dreams evolve, and they take on a life and a direction that mere mortals cannot control. The genuine dream-maker is a partner in your evolution. Sometimes the opportunities or the direction your dream-maker opens up for you may not fit in with what you initially had in mind, or even be something you would normally pursue. Trust the process. Trust the calling on your life. Go with the flow.

4. Can I be a leader-leader without having a leadership position?

Yes! The leader-leader can be anyone who has influence in your life. Family members, friends, co-workers are all likely candidates to be leader-leaders in your life. The essential requirement for the leader-leader role is the capacity to help someone else recognize and optimize their unique leader-moments as they occur.

5. Is it possible that one person can be all four of the people I need to succeed all in one?

Yes, someone can have the characteristics of all four of the people you need to succeed. However, the four are distinct in the roles they play in our lives, and we tend to need each of the four at different stages of our development. So, the expert people-picker, the possibility-vendor, the dream-maker, and the leader-leader, are more likely to be separate individuals. These individuals are usually more involved with our life for a season than on a permanent basis. However, there are times when an important and influential individual comes back into our life, helping us take the next step. What is vital for you is that you recognize these four people and how you need them to succeed. What they will all share is that they are fascinated by life, by their work— and by you. Working with them, partnering with them for the next step in your success will help you move forward until you, too, can finally say: "*I am fascinated!*"

Become a fascinated manager, employee, parent and person, attend one of our seminars:
Are You Fascinated? Leadership Impact Seminar
Building a Center of Fascination Seminar

For upcoming events, dates, locations or further discussion and ideas go to
www.Areyoufascinated.com
www.Areyoufascinated.blogspot.com

For more about Ken Tucker and Associates visit:
www.Ktawebsite.com